Low Fat

Practical Cookery

Low Fat

This is a Parragon Publishing Book
First printed in 2000

Parragon Publishing
Queen Street House
4 Queen Street
Bath BA1 1HE, UK

ISBN: 0-75253-965-5

Printed in Indonesia

NOTE

Unless otherwise stated,
milk is assumed to be whole, eggs are large,
and pepper is freshly ground black pepper.

Recipes using uncooked eggs should be
avoided by infants, the elderly, pregnant women, and anyone
suffering from an illness

Contents

Introduction 8

Soups

Mixed Bean Soup .20
Red Pepper Soup .21
Tomato and Pepper Soup 22
Cucumber and Tomato Soup 23
Chilled Cucumber Soup 24
Beet and Potato Soup 25
Spiced Fruit Soup 26
Yogurt and Spinach Soup 27
Minted Pea and Yogurt Soup 28
Red Lentil Soup with Yogurt 29
Spicy Lentil Soup 30
Sweet Potato and Onion Soup 31
Fish and Crab Chowder 32
Mushroom and Ginger Soup 33
Carrot and Cumin Soup 34

Spicy Dal and Carrot Soup 35
Indian Potato and Pea Soup 36
Consommé 37
Beef and Vegetable Soup 38
Chunky Potato and Beef Soup 39
Split Pea and Ham Soup 40
Lentil and Ham Soup 41
Bacon, Bean, and Garlic Soup 42
Lamb and Barley Broth 43
Chicken and Leek Soup 44
Chicken and Coconut Soup 45
Mediterranean Fish Soup 46
Coconut and Crab Soup 47
Partan Bree 48
Smoked Haddock Soup 49

Starters & Snacks

Minted Onion Bhajis 52
Vegetables with Tahini Dip 53
Spinach Cheese Molds 54
Lentil Pâté 55
Potato and Bean Pâté 56
Potato Skins with Guacomole 57
Potato and Mushroom Hash 58
Spicy Jacket Potatoes 59
Bruschetta 60
Cheese, Herb, and Onion Rolls 61
Cheese and Chive Scones 62
Savory Pepper Bread 63
Pasta Provençale .64
Spicy Garbanzo Bean Snack 65
Baked Stuffed Onions 66
Stuffed Mushrooms 67
Soufflé Omelet 68

Smoked Fish and Potato Pâté 69
Crêpes with Curried Crab 70
Thai Potato Crab Cakes 71
Rice and Tuna Peppers 72
Red Mullet and Coconut Loaf 73
Turkey and Vegetable Loaf 74
Cranberry Turkey Burgers 75
Parsley, Chicken, and Ham Pâté 76
Sweet and Sour Drumsticks 77
Oat-Crusted Chicken Pieces 78
Chicken and Cheese Jackets 79
Spicy Chicken Tortillas 80
Chicken and Almond Rissoles 81
Minty Lamb Burgers 82
Lamb and Tomato Koftas 83
Italian Platter 84
Cheesy Ham Savory 85

Chilli con Carne 88
Beef and Orange Curry 89
Rogan Josh 90
Tamarind Beef Balti 91
Beef Goulash 92
Boiled Beef and Carrots 93
Shepherd's Pie 94
Steak in a Wine Marinade 95
Beef Daube 96
Beef Teriyaki 97
Ginger Beef with Chili 98
Pork with Fennel and Aniseed 99
Fish-Flavored Pork 100
Red Roast Pork in Soy Sauce 101
Pork Stroganoff .102
Pork with Ratatouille Sauce 103
Fruity Pork Skewers 104
Pork and Apple Skewers 105

Pork with Plums .106
Pan-Cooked Pork Medallions 107
Tangy Pork Fillet 108
Pork Chops and Spicy Beans 109
Lamb with Rosemary 110
Turkish Lamb Stew 111
Lamb Hotch Potch 112
Sweet Lamb Fillets 113
Stir-Fried Lamb with Orange 114
Savory Hotch Potch 115
Kibbeh 116
Minty Lamb Kabobs 117
Lamb Kabobs with Herbs 118
Lamb and Potato Moussaka 119
Masala Kabobs .120
Lamb Couscous .121
Lamb Dopiaza 122
Venison and Garlic Mash 123

Poultry
& Game

Chicken with a Yoghurt Crust 126
Chicken in Spicy Yoghurt 127
Spicy Tomato Chicken 128
Karahi Chicken .129
Chicken Tikka 130
Chicken Tikka Kabobs 131
Spiced Apricot Chicken 132
Thai Red Chicken 133
Thai-Style Chicken Skewers 134
Ginger Chicken and Corn 135
Steamed Chicken Packets 136
Crispy Stuffed Chicken 137
Teppanyaki 138
Sweet and Sour Chicken 139
Chicken and Ginger Stir-Fry 140
Filipino Chicken 141

Poussin with Dried Fruits 142
Pot-Roast Orange Chicken 143
Harlequin Chicken 144
Mediterranean Chicken 145
Chicken with Two Sauces 146
Chicken with Whisy Sauce 147
Two-in-One Chicken 148
Sticky Chicken Wings 149
Jerk Chicken 150
Lime Fricassée of Chicken 151
Mexican Chicken 152
Grilled Chicken .153
Festive Apple Chicken 154
Roast Duck with Apple 155
Citrus Duckling Skewers 156
Turkey with Redcurrant 157

Fish &
Seafood

Oriental Shellfish Kabobs 160
Scallop Skewers 161
Salmon Yakitori .162
Butterfly Shrimp 163
Monkfish with Coconut 164
Caribbean Shrimp 165
Lemony Angler Fish Skewers 166
Balti Scallops 167
Seafood Stir-Fry 168
Provençale-Style Mussels 169
Yucatan Fish 170
Shrimp Bhuna 171
Charred Tuna Steaks 172
Poached Salmon 173
Salmon with Caper Sauce 174
Mackerel with Lime 175

Delicately Spiced Trout 176
Baked Sea Bass 177
Indonesian-Style Spicy Cod 178
Japanese Plaice 179
Herrings with Tarragon 180
Steamed Stuffed Snapper 181
Crab-Stuffed Red Snapper 182
Pan-Seared Halibut 183
Sole Paupiettes 184
Smoky Fish Pie .185
Seafood Pizza 186
Green Fish Curry 187

Vegetables & Salads

Stuffed Tomatoes 190
Risotto Verde 191
Fragrant Asparagus Risotto 192
Mexican-Style Pizzas 193
Potato and Tomato Calzone 194
Potato Hash 195
Chinese Vegetable Pancakes 196
Oriental Vegetable Noodles 197
Biryani with Onions 198
Balti Dal 199
Vegetable Curry 200
Eggplant Cake 201
Spicy Mexican Beans 202
Mixed Bean Stir-Fry 203
Lemony Spaghetti 204

Basil and Tomato Pasta 205
Pesto Pasta 206
Mushroom Cannelloni 207
Beet and Orange Salad 208
Mexican Potato Salad 209
Grapefruit and Coconut Salad 210
Hot and Spicy Rice Salad 211
Melon and Mango Salad 212
Cool Cucumber Salad 213
Moroccan Couscous Salad 214
Coleslaw 215
Green Bean and Carrot Salad 216
Spinach and Orange Salad 217
Minted Fennel Salad 218
Pear and Roquefort Salad 219

Summer Pudding 222
Summer Fruit Clafoutis 223
Autumn Fruit Bread Pudding 224
Winter Puddings 225
Crispy-Topped Fruit Bake 226
Fruit and Nut Loaf 227
Fruit Loaf with Apple Spread 228
New Age Spotted Dick 229
Rich Fruit Cake 230
Chocolate and Pineapple Cake 231
Carrot and Ginger Cake 232
Banana and Lime Cake 233
Strawberry Roulade 234
Fruity Potato Cake 235
Fruity Muffins 236
Paper-Thin Fruit Pies 237

Baked Pears with Cinnamon 238
Apricot and Orange Jellies 239
Strawberry Meringues 240
Pears with Maple Cream 241
Sticky Sesame Bananas 242
Summer Fruit Salad 243
Chocolate Cheese Pots 244
Almond Trifles 245
Spun Sugar Pears 246
Tropical Fruit Fool 247
Cottage Cheese Hearts 248
Orange Syllabub 249
Mixed Fruit Brûlées 250
Pavlova 251
Almond Cheesecakes 252
Mocha Swirl Mousse 253

Index   254

Introduction

Whether you are on a low-fat diet or simply want to introduce healthier eating habits to your lifestyle, this is the book for you. Although the majority of recipes are low in fat, some have been included because they are highly nutritious and add important variety of ingredients.

Nutritionists agree that typical modern diets usually contain too much fat and that this can be detrimental to health. Scarcely a day passes without a television programme or a magazine article giving advice on cutting down our intake of fat. In fact, so much attention is given to the subject that people could be forgiven for believing that all their health problems would be solved if they never ate another gram of fat in their lives. Nothing could be further from the truth. A moderate intake of

fat is essential for good health. For example, the body requires fat-soluble vitamins. Fish oils are one of the richest sources of vitamins A and D, and vitamin E is found in vegetable oils. Fats are also a concentrated source of energy, providing over twice as much as carbohydrates or proteins. The aim should be to reduce fat in the diet, but not to cut it out altogether.

How much is too much?

The body's nutrient requirements, including how much fat is needed, vary with age, sex, general state of health, level of physical activity, and even genetic inheritance. However, the proportions in which the different

nutrients are required are much the same from one person to another. The World Health Organization recommends that fats should not exceed 30 per cent of the daily intake of energy. (Energy is measured in calories, kilocalories, or kilojoules.) It has conducted studies in countries with an exceptionally high rate of heart disease and the research has revealed that this almost invariably coincides with a high-fat diet, where fats comprise as much as 40 per cent of the body's daily energy intake.

If 2,000 calories a day is taken as the average, then, for good health, only 600 of them should be supplied by fats. 0.04 ounce of pure fat yields nine calories, whereas 0.04 of pure carbohydrate or pure protein yields only one calorie. Simple arithmetic, therefore, indicates that the maximum daily intake of fats should be 600 divided by nine, or 66.6 grams of fat.

Fats are broken down and digested in a rather different way from proteins and carbohydrates and the human body is designed to store them for times of need. In the Western world, food no longer becomes scarce every winter and we do not need to rely on stored fat to provide the energy for day-to-day life. So if a lot of fat is stored, the body becomes overweight, even obese. Worse still, a mechanism that is not yet properly understood can suddenly trigger fat deposits in the arteries, resulting in their becoming narrower and eventually leading to heart disease. Anyone who is already overweight and keen to return to a healthier size can reduce their fat intake to well below the 30 per cent maximum. However, it is probably better and the long-term effects will be more permanent if the overall intake of calories is reduced, but the proportions of nutrients remains within the normal range. Everyone, overweight or not, should observe the no-more-than-30 per-cent rule to ensure long-term health and vitality.

Types of Fat

When you are thinking about reducing your intake of fat, it is important to know that fats can broadly be divided into two categories: saturated and unsaturated fat. Although they are still fats, unsaturated fats are healthier than the saturated variety and it is important to consider this when buying food.

Fats are made up of a combination of fatty acids and glycerol. Fatty acids consist of a chain of carbon atoms linked to hydrogen atoms. The way these are linked determines the type of fat – saturated or unsaturated. The type of fat you eat is just as important as the amount.

Saturated fats

Saturated fatty acids contain as many hydrogen atoms as possible – there are no empty links on the chain. They are mainly found in animal products, such as meat and dairy foods, although some vegetable oils, including palm and coconut oil, also contain them. Foods labeled as containing hydrogenated vegetable oils, such as some types of margarine, also contain saturated fats as a by-product of their processing. They are easy to recognize as they are usually solid at room temperature.

These are the fats that the body has difficulty processing and which it tends to store. They also increase cholesterol levels in the bloodstream, which can increase the risk of heart disease. It is, therefore, sensible to reduce the level of saturated fats in the diet. They should comprise no more than 30 per cent of the total fat intake or no more than nine per cent of the total energy intake.

Unsaturated fats

These fatty acids have spare links in the carbon chain and some hydrogen atoms are missing. There are two types: monounsaturated fats which have one pair of hydrogen atoms missing and polyunsaturated fats which have more than one pair missing. They are normally liquid or soft at room temperature. They are both thought to reduce the level of cholesterol in the bloodstream.

Monounsaturated fats are mainly of vegetable origin, but are also found in oily fish, such as mackerel. Other rich sources include olive oil, many kinds of nuts, and avocados.

Cooking Techniques

One of the easiest and least disruptive ways to reduce your fat intake is to change the way you cook. Trying new recipes, even with familiar ingredients, is fun and will result in the pleasure of eating delicious meals that are also healthier.

Frying

This is undoubtedly the technique that most dramatically raises the level of fats in the diet. You do not have to abandon fries or sausages completely, but it is sensible to make sure that they are only occasional treats rather than the staple diet. Fried-food fans might find it helpful to know that ingredients absorb much more fat when shallow-fried than they do during deep-frying, but even deep-frying should be used only occasionally. If you do enjoy a shallow-fried dish once in a while, invest in a good quality, heavy-bottomed, non-stick skillet and you will then require much less oil. Use a vegetable oil, high in polyunsaturates, for frying rather than a solid fat and measure the quantity you add to the pan, rather than just tipping it in. A spray oil is a useful way of controlling how much you use.

Try the Chinese cooking technique of stir-frying. The ingredients are cooked very rapidly over an extremely high heat, using a small amount of oil. Consequently, they absorb little fat and, as an additional advantage, largely retain their color, flavor, texture, and nutritional content.

Broiling

This is a good alternative to frying, producing a similar crisp and golden coating while remaining moist and tender inside. Ingredients with a delicate texture and which can easily dry out, such as white fish or chicken breasts, will require brushing with oil, but more robust foods, such as red meat or oily fish, can usually be broiled without additional fat, providing the heat is not too fierce. Consider marinating meat and fish in wine, soy sauce, cider, sherry, beer, and herbs or spices. Not only will this tenderize meat and provide additional flavor, the marinade can be brushed on during broiling, so that additional fat will not be required. When broiling, always place the food on a rack, so that the fat drains away.

Poaching

This is an ideal technique for ingredients with a delicate texture or subtle flavor, such as chicken and fish, and is fat-free. Poached food does not have to be bland and uninteresting. You can use all kinds of liquids, including stock, wine and acidulated water, flavored with vegetables and herbs. The cooking liquid can be used as the basis for a sauce to provide additional flavor, as well as preserving any dissolved nutrients.

Steaming

Another fat-free technique, this is becoming an increasingly popular way of cooking meat, fish, chicken, and vegetables. Ingredients retain the color, flavor, and texture, fewer nutrients are leached out and it is very economical because steamers can be stacked on top of one another. The addition of herbs and other flavorings to the cooking liquid or the ingredients being cooked, results in a wonderfully aromatic dish. An additional advantage is that when meat is steamed, the fat melts and

drips into the cooking liquid. In that case, do not use the cooking liquid for making gravy or sauces.

Braising and stewing

Slow cooking techniques produce succulent dishes that are especially welcome in winter. Trim all visible fat from meat and always remove the skin from chicken. If red meat is to be browned first, consider dry-frying it in a heavy-bottomed pan and drain off any fat before continuing with the recipe. Straining the cooking liquid, reducing it and then skimming off the fat before serving is a classic way of preparing braised food and concentrates the flavor as well as reducing the fat content.

Roasting

Fat is an integral part of this cooking technique. Without it, meat or fish would dry out and become too brown. If you are planning a roast dish, stand

meat on a rack over a tray or roasting pan so that the fat drains off. When making gravy, use stock or vegetable cooking water rather than the meat juices.

Baking

Many baked dishes are virtually fat free. Foil-wrapped packets of meat or fish are always delicious. Add a little fruit juice or wine, rather than oil or butter, for a moist texture and delicious flavor.

Microwave

Food cooked in this way rarely requires additional fat.

Basic Recipes

Chinese Stock

This basic stock is used in Chinese cooking not only as the basis for soup-making, but also whenever liquid is required instead of plain water.

MAKES 2½ QUARTS

1 lb 10 oz chicken pieces

1 lb 10 oz pork spareribs

3½ quarts cold water

3-4 pieces gingerroot, crushed

3-4 scallions, each tied into a knot

3-4 tbsp Chinese rice wine or dry sherry

1 Trim off any excess fat from the chicken and spareribs; chop them into large pieces.

2 Place the chicken and pork in a large pan with the water; add the ginger and scallion knots.

3 Bring to the boil and skim off the scum. Reduce the heat and simmer uncovered for at least 2-3 hours.

4 Strain the stock, discarding the chicken, pork, ginger, and scallions; add the wine and return to a boil, simmer for 2-3 minutes.

5 Refrigerate the stock when cool; it will keep for up to 4-5 days. Alternatively, it can be frozen in small containers and be defrosted as required.

Fresh Chicken Stock

MAKES 1¾ QUARTS

2 lb 4 oz chicken, skinned

2 celery stalks

1 onion

2 carrots

1 garlic clove

few sprigs of fresh parsley

2¼ quarts water

salt and pepper

1 Put all the ingredients together into a large saucepan.

2 Bring to a boil. Skim away surface scum using a large flat spoon. Reduce the heat to a gentle simmer, partially cover, and cook for 2 hours. Allow to cool.

3 Line a strainer with clean cheesecloth and place over a large jug or bowl. Pour the stock through the strainer. The cooked chicken can be used in another recipe. Discard the other solids. Cover the stock and chill.

4 Skim away any fat that forms before using. Store in the refrigerator for up to 3-4 days, until required, or freeze in small batches.

Fresh Vegetable Stock

This can be kept chilled for up to three days or frozen for up to three months. Salt is not added when cooking the stock: it is better to season it according to the dish in which it its to be used.

MAKES 1½ QUARTS

9 oz shallots

1 large carrot, diced

1 celery stalk, chopped

½ fennel bulb

1 garlic clove

1 bay leaf

a few fresh parsley and tarragon sprigs

2 quarts water

pepper

1 Put all the ingredients in a large saucepan and bring to a boil.

2 Skim off the surface scum with a flat spoon and reduce to a gentle simmer. Partially cover and cook for 45 minutes. Leave to cool.

3 Line a strainer with clean cheesecloth and put over a large jug or bowl. Pour the stock through the strainer and then discard the herbs and vegetables.

4 Cover and store in small quantities in the refrigerator for up to three days.

Fresh Lamb Stock

MAKES 1¾ QUARTS

2 lb 4 oz bones from a cooked joint or
   raw chopped lamb bones

2 onions, studded with 6 cloves, or sliced
   or chopped coarsely

2 carrots, sliced

1 leek, sliced

1-2 celery stalks, sliced

1 Bouquet Garni

2 quarts water

1 Chop or break up the bones and place in a large saucepan together with the other ingredients.

2 Bring to a boil and remove any scum from the surface with a draining spoon. Cover and simmer gently for 3-4 hours. Strain the stock and leave to cool.

3 Remove any fat from the surface and chill. If stored for more than 24 hours the stock must be boiled every day, cooled quickly, and chilled again. The stock may be frozen for up to 2 months; place in a large plastic bag and seal, leaving at least 1 inch of headspace to allow for some expansion.

Fresh Fish Stock

MAKES 1¾ QUARTS

1 head of a cod or salmon, plus the
   trimmings, skin, and bones or just
   the trimmings, skin, and bones

1-2 onions, sliced

1 carrot, sliced

1-2 celery stalks, sliced

good squeeze of lemon juice

1 Bouquet Garni or 2 fresh or dried bay
   leaves

1 Wash the fish head and trimmings and place in a saucepan. Cover with water and bring to a boil.

2 Remove any scum with a draining spoon, then add the remaining ingredients. Cover and simmer for about 30 minutes.

3 Strain and cool. Store in the refrigerator and use within 2 days.

Cornstarch Paste

Cornstarch paste is made by mixing 1 part cornstarch with about 1½ parts of cold water. Stir until smooth. The paste is used to thicken sauces.

Plain rice

Use long-grain rice or patna rice, or better still, try fragrant Thai rice

SERVES 4

9 oz long-grain rice

1 cup cold water

pinch of salt

½ tsp oil (optional)

1 Wash and rinse the rice just once. Place the rice in a saucepan and add enough water so that there is no more than $^3/_4$ inch of water above the surface of the rice.

2 Bring to a boil, add salt and oil (if using), and stir to prevent the rice sticking to the bottom of the pan.

3 Reduce the heat to very, very low, cover and cook for 15-20 minutes.

4 Remove from the heat and let the pan stand, covered, for 10 minutes or so. Fluff up the rice with a fork or spoon before serving.

How to Use This Book

Each recipe contains a wealth of useful information, including a breakdown of nutritional quantities, preparation, and cooking times, and level of difficulty. All of this information is explained in detail below.

This amount of time represents the actual cooking time.

The nutritional information provided for each recipe is per serving or per portion. Optional ingredients, variations, or serving suggestions have not been included in the calculations.

The number of chef's hats represents the difficulty of each recipe, ranging from easy (1 chef's hat) to difficult (5 chef's hats).

This amount of time represents the preparation of ingredients, including cooling, chilling, and soaking times.

The ingredients for each recipe are listed in the order that they are used.

The method is illustrated with step-by-step photographs, making the recipe easy to follow.

A full-color photograph of the finished dish.

Variations and cook's tips provide useful information regarding ingredients or cooking techniques.

The method is clearly explained with step-by-step instructions that are easy to follow.

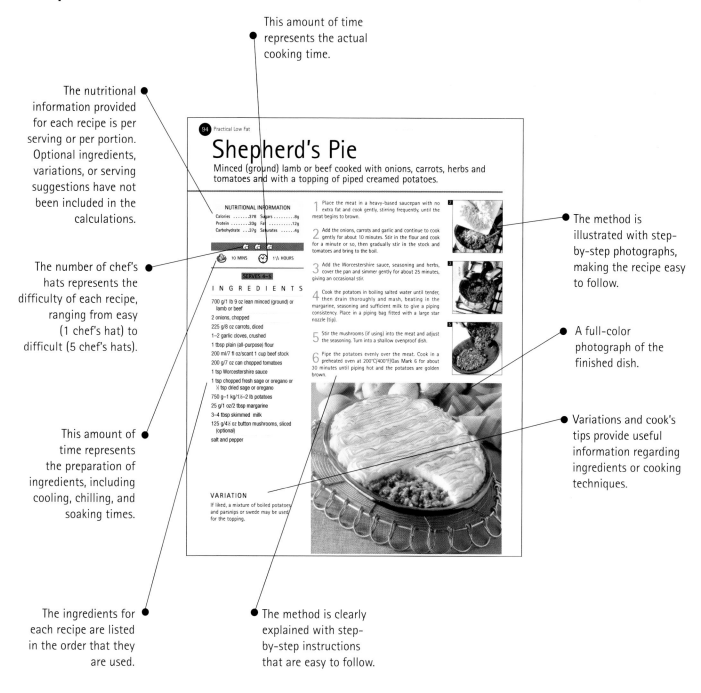

94 Practical Low Fat

Shepherd's Pie

Minced (ground) lamb or beef cooked with onions, carrots, herbs and tomatoes and with a topping of piped creamed potatoes.

NUTRITIONAL INFORMATION

Calories . . . . . . .378 Sugars 8g
Protein . . . . . . .33g Fat 12g
Carbohydrate . . .37g Saturates 4g

10 MINS   1¹/₂ HOURS

SERVES 4–5

INGREDIENTS

700 g/1 lb 9 oz lean minced (ground) or lamb or beef
2 onions, chopped
225 g/8 oz carrots, diced
1–2 garlic cloves, crushed
1 tbsp plain (all-purpose) flour
200 ml/7 fl oz/scant 1 cup beef stock
200 g/7 oz can chopped tomatoes
1 tsp Worcestershire sauce
1 tsp chopped fresh sage or oregano or ½ tsp dried sage or oregano
750 g–1 kg/1½–2 lb potatoes
25 g/1 oz/2 tbsp margarine
3–4 tbsp skimmed milk
125 g/4½ oz button mushrooms, sliced (optional)
salt and pepper

1 Place the meat in a heavy-based saucepan with no extra fat and cook gently, stirring frequently, until the meat begins to brown.

2 Add the onions, carrots and garlic and continue to cook gently for about 10 minutes. Stir in the flour and cook for a minute or so, then gradually stir in the stock and tomatoes and bring to the boil.

3 Add the Worcestershire sauce, seasoning and herbs, cover the pan and simmer gently for about 25 minutes, giving an occasional stir.

4 Cook the potatoes in boiling salted water until tender, then drain thoroughly and mash, beating in the margarine, seasoning and sufficient milk to give a piping consistency. Place in a piping bag fitted with a large star nozzle (tip).

5 Stir the mushrooms (if using) into the meat and adjust the seasoning. Turn into a shallow ovenproof dish.

6 Pipe the potatoes evenly over the meat. Cook in a preheated oven at 200°C/400°F/Gas Mark 6 for about 30 minutes until piping hot and the potatoes are golden brown.

VARIATION

If liked, a mixture of boiled potatoes and parsnips or swede may be used for the topping.

Soups

The traditional way to start a meal is with a soup, but they can also be a satisfying meal in themselves, depending on their ingredients or if they are served with crusty bread. For best results use homemade stock—use the liquor left after cooking vegetables and the juices from fish and meat that have been used as the base of casseroles. Ready-made

stocks in the form of cubes or granules tend to contain large amounts of salt and flavorings which can overpower the delicate flavors. Although making fresh stock takes a little longer, it is well worth it for the superior taste. It is a good idea to make a large batch and freeze the remainder, in smaller quantities, for later use. Potato can be added to thicken soups rather than stirring in the traditional thickener of flour and water—or, worse, flour and fat.

Mixed Bean Soup

This is a really hearty soup, filled with color, flavor, and goodness, which may be adapted to any vegetables that you have at hand.

NUTRITIONAL INFORMATION

Calories	190	Sugars 9g
Protein	........10g	Fat 4g
Carbohydrate	...30g	Saturates 0.5g

 5 MINS   40 MINS

SERVES 4

INGREDIENTS

1 tbsp vegetable oil

1 red onion, halved and sliced

⅔ cup potato, diced

1 carrot, diced

1 leek, sliced

1 green chili, sliced

3 garlic cloves, minced

1 tsp ground coriander

1 tsp chili powder

4 cups vegetable stock

1 lb mixed canned beans, such as red kidney, black eye or smal navy, drained

salt and pepper

2 tbsp chopped cilantro, to garnish

COOK'S TIP

Serve this soup with slices of warm corn bread or a cheese loaf.

1 Heat the vegetable oil in a large saucepan and add the prepared onion, potato, carrot, and leek. Sauté for about 2 minutes, stirring, until the vegetables are slightly softened.

2 Add the sliced chili and crushed garlic and cook for 1 minute.

3 Stir in the ground coriander, chili powder, and the vegetable stock.

4 Bring the soup to a boil, reduce the heat and cook for 20 minutes or until the vegetables are tender.

5 Stir in the beans, season well with salt and pepper, and cook for a further 10 minutes, stirring occasionally.

6 Transfer the soup to a warm tureen or individual bowls, garnish with chopped cilantro and serve.

Red Bell Pepper Soup

This soup has a real Mediterranean flavor, using sweet red bell peppers, tomato, chili, and basil. It is great served with a warm olive bread.

NUTRITIONAL INFORMATION

Calories 55   Sugar 10g
Protein ....2g   Fats 0.5g
Carbohydrates ...11g   Saturates 0.1g

 5 MINS   25 MINS

SERVES 4

INGREDIENTS

8 oz red bell peppers, seeded and sliced

1 onion, sliced

2 garlic cloves, minced

1 green chili, chopped

1½ cups sieved tomatoes

2½ cups vegetable stock

2 tbsp chopped basil

fresh basil sprigs, to garnish

1 Put the bell peppers in a large saucepan with the onion, garlic, and chili. Add the sieved tomatoes and vegetable stock and bring to a boil, stirring well.

2 Reduce the heat to a simmer and cook for 20 minutes or until the bell peppers have softened. Drain, reserving the liquid and vegetables separately.

3 Sieve the vegetables by pressing through a strainer with the back of a spoon. Alternatively, blend in a food processor until smooth.

4 Return the vegetable purée to a clean saucepan with the reserved cooking liquid. Add the basil and heat through until hot. Garnish the soup with fresh basil sprigs and serve.

VARIATION

This soup is also delicious served cold with ¼ cup of unsweetened yogurt swirled into it.

Tomato & Bell Pepper Soup

Sweet red bell peppers and tangy tomatoes are blended together in a smooth vegetable soup that makes a perfect starter or light lunch.

NUTRITIONAL INFORMATION

Calories	52	Sugar	........9g
Protein	........3g	Fats	........0.4g
Carbohydrates	...10g	Saturates	......0g

1¼ HOURS   35 MINS

SERVES 4

INGREDIENTS

2 large red bell peppers

1 large onion, chopped

2 stalks celery, trimmed and chopped

1 garlic clove, minced

2½ cups Fresh Vegetable Stock (see page 14)

2 bay leaves

2 x 14 oz cans plum tomatoes

salt and pepper

2 spring scallions, finely shredded, to garnish

crusty bread, to serve

1 Preheat the broiler to hot. Halve and seed the bell peppers, arrange them on the broiler rack and cook, turning occasionally, for 8–10 minutes until softened and charred.

2 Leave to cool, then carefully peel off the charred skin. Reserving a small piece for garnish, chop the bell pepper flesh and place in a large saucepan.

3 Mix in the onion, celery, and garlic. Add the stock and the bay leaves. Bring to a boil, cover, and simmer for 15 minutes. Remove from the heat.

4 Stir in the tomatoes and transfer to a blender. Process for a few seconds until smooth. Return to the saucepan.

5 Season to taste and heat for 3–4 minutes until very hot. Ladle into warm bowls and garnish with the reserved bell pepper cut into strips and the scallion. Serve with crusty bread.

COOK'S TIP

If you prefer a coarser, more robust soup, lightly mash the tomatoes with a wooden spoon and omit the blending process in step 4.

Cucumber & Tomato Soup

Although this chilled soup is not an authentic Indian dish, it is wonderful served as a 'cooler' between hot, spicy courses.

NUTRITIONAL INFORMATION

Calories 73   Sugar 16g
Protein ....2g   Fats 1g
Carbohydrates ...16g   Saturates 0.2g

 12 HOURS   0 MINS

SERVES 6

I N G R E D I E N T S

4 tomatoes, peeled and seeded

3 lb 5 oz watermelon, seedless if available

4 inch piece cucumber, peeled and deseeded

2 scallions, green part only, chopped

1 tbsp chopped fresh mint

salt and pepper

fresh mint sprigs, to garnish

1 Using a sharp knife, cut 1 tomato into ½ inch dice.

2 Remove the rind from the melon, and remove the seeds if it is not seedless.

3 Put the 3 remaining tomatoes into a blender or food processor and, with the motor running, add the seeded cucumber, chopped scallions, and watermelon. Blend until smooth.

4 If not using a food processor, push the seeded watermelon through a strainer. Stir the diced tomatoes and mint into the melon mixture. Adjust the seasoning to taste. Chop the cucumber, scallions, and the 3 remaining tomatoes finely and add to the melon.

5 Chill the cucumber and tomato soup overnight in the refrigerator. Check the seasoning and transfer to a serving dish. Garnish with mint sprigs.

COOK'S TIP

Although this soup does improve if chilled overnight, it is also delicious as a quick appetizer if whipped up just before a meal, and served immediately.

Chilled Cucumber Soup

Serve this soup over ice on a warm summer day as a refreshing starter. It has the fresh tang of yogurt and a dash of spice from the Tabasco sauce.

NUTRITIONAL INFORMATION

Calories 83   Sugars 7g
Protein ....12g   Fat 1g
Carbohydrate ....7g   Saturates 0.3g

 3½ HOURS   0 MINS

SERVES 4

INGREDIENTS

1 cucumber, peeled and diced

1⅔ cups Fresh Fish Stock, chilled (see page 15)

⅔ cup tomato juice

⅔ cup low-fat unsweetened yogurt

⅔ cup low-fat fromage blanc (or double the quantity of yogurt)

4½ oz peeled shrimp, thawed if frozen, roughly chopped

few drops Tabasco sauce

1 tbsp fresh mint, chopped

salt and white pepper

ice cubes, to serve

TO GARNISH

sprigs of mint

cucumber slices

whole peeled shrimp

1 Place the diced cucumber in a blender or food processor and work for a few seconds until smooth. Alternatively, chop the cucumber finely and push through a strainer.

2 Transfer the cucumber to a bowl. Stir in the stock, tomato juice, yogurt, fromage blanc (if using), and shrimp, and mix well.

3 Add the Tabasco sauce and season to taste.

4 Stir in the chopped mint, cover, and chill for at least 2 hours.

5 Ladle the soup into glass bowls and add a few ice cubes. Serve garnished with mint, cucumber slices and whole shrimp.

VARIATION

Instead of shrimp, add white crabmeat or minced chicken. For a vegetarian version of this soup, omit the shrimp and add an extra 4½ oz finely diced cucumber. Use fresh vegetable stock instead of fish stock.

Beet & Potato Soup

A deep red soup makes a stunning first course. Adding a swirl of soured cream and a few sprigs of dill gives a very pretty effect.

NUTRITIONAL INFORMATION

Calories 120   Sugars 11g
Protein . . . . .4g   Fat 2g
Carbohydrate . . .22g   Saturates 1g

 20 MINS   🕐 30 MINS

SERVES 6

I N G R E D I E N T S

| 1 onion, chopped |
| 12 oz potatoes, diced |
| 1 small cooking apple, peeled, cored, and grated |
| 3 tbsp water |
| 1 tsp cumin seeds |
| 1 lb cooked beet, peeled and diced |
| 1 dried bay leaf |
| pinch of dried thyme |
| 1 tsp lemon juice |
| 2½ cups hot vegetable stock |
| 4 tbsp soured cream |
| salt and pepper |
| few sprigs of fresh dill, to garnish |

1 Place the onion, potatoes, apple, and water in a large bowl. Cover and cook on HIGH power for 10 minutes.

2 Stir in the cumin seeds and cook on HIGH power for 1 minute.

3 Stir in the beet, bay leaf, thyme, lemon juice, and stock. Cover and cook on HIGH power for 12 minutes, stirring halfway through. Leave to stand, uncovered, for 5 minutes.

4 Remove and discard the bay leaf. Strain the vegetables and reserve the liquid in a jug.

5 Purée the vegetables with a little of the reserved liquid in a food processor or blender, until they are smooth and creamy. Alternatively, either mash the soup or press it through a strainer.

6 Pour the vegetable purée into a clean bowl with the reserved liquid and mix well. Season with salt and pepper to taste. Cover and cook on HIGH power for 4–5 minutes until very hot.

7 Serve the soup in warmed bowls. Swirl 1 tablespoon of soured cream into each serving and garnish with a few sprigs of fresh dill.

Spiced Fruit Soup

This delicately flavored apple and apricot soup is gently spiced with ginger and allspice, and finished with a swirl of soured cream.

NUTRITIONAL INFORMATION

Calories	147	Sugar	........28g
Protein	.........3g	Fats	.........0.4g
Carbohydrates	...29g	Saturates	......0g

 7³/₄ HOURS 🕐 25 MINS

SERVES 4–6

INGREDIENTS

⅔ cup dried apricots, soaked overnight or no-need-to-soak dried apricots

1 lb dessert apples, peeled, cored, and chopped

1 small onion, chopped

1 tbsp lemon or lime juice

3 cups Fresh Chicken Stock (see page 14)

⅔ cup dry white wine

¼ tsp ground ginger

good pinch of ground allspice

salt and pepper

TO GARNISH

4–6 tbsp soured cream or natural fromage blanc

little ground ginger or ground allspice

1 Drain the apricot if necessary and chop.

2 Put in a saucepan and add the apples, onion, lemon or lime juice, and stock. Bring to a boil, cover and simmer gently for about 20 minutes.

3 Leave the soup to cool a little, then press through a strainer or blend in a food processor or blender until smooth.

Next pour the fruit soup into a clean pan.

4 Add the wine and spices and season to taste. Bring back to a boil, then leave to cool. If too thick, add a little more stock or water and then chill thoroughly.

5 Put a spoonful of soured cream or fromage blanc on top of each portion and lightly dust with ginger or allspice.

VARIATION

Other fruits can be combined with apples to make fruit soups–try raspberries, blackberries, blackcurrants, or cherries. If the fruits have a lot of pips or pits, the soup should be strained after puréeing.

Yogurt & Spinach Soup

Whole young spinach leaves add vibrant color to this unusual soup. Serve with hot, crusty bread for a nutritious light meal.

NUTRITIONAL INFORMATION

Calories 227	Sugars 13g
Protein 14g	Fat 7g
Carbohydrate ...29g	Saturates 2g

 15 MINS   30 MINS

SERVES 4

INGREDIENTS

2½ cups chicken stock

4 tbsp long-grain rice, rinsed and drained

4 tbsp water

1 tbsp cornstarch

2½ cups low-fat unsweetened yogurt

juice of 1 lemon

3 egg yolks, lightly beaten

12 oz young spinach leaves, washed and drained

salt and pepper

1 Pour the stock into a large pan, season and bring to a boil. Add the rice and simmer for 10 minutes, until barely cooked. Remove from the heat.

2 Combine the water and cornstarch to make a smooth paste.

3 Pour the yogurt into a second pan and stir in the cornstarch mixture. Set the pan over a low heat and bring the yogurt slowly to a boil, stirring with a wooden spoon in one direction only. This will stabilize the yogurt and prevent it from separating or curdling on contact with the hot stock. When the yogurt has reached boiling point, stand the pan on a heat diffuser and leave to simmer slowly for 10 minutes. Remove the pan from the heat and allow the mixture to cool slightly before stirring in the beaten egg yolks.

4 Pour the yogurt mixture into the stock, stir in the lemon juice, and stir to blend thoroughly. Keep the soup warm, but do not allow it to boil.

5 Blanch the washed and drained spinach leaves in a large pan of boiling, salted water for 2-3 minutes until they begin to soften but have not wilted. Tip the spinach into a colander, drain well and stir it into the soup. Let the spinach warm through. Taste the soup and adjust the seasoning if necessary. Serve in wide shallow soup plates, with hot, fresh crusty bread.

Minted Pea & Yogurt Soup

A deliciously refreshing soup that is full of goodness. It is also extremely tasty served chilled.

NUTRITIONAL INFORMATION

Calories 208	Sugars 9g
Protein 10g	Fat 7g
Carbohydrate ...26g	Saturates 2g

 10 MINS ⏱ 25 MINS

SERVES 4

INGREDIENTS

2 tbsp vegetable ghee or oil

2 onions, peeled and coarsely chopped

8 oz potato, peeled and coarsely chopped

2 garlic cloves, peeled

1 inch gingerroot, peeled and chopped

1 tsp ground coriander

1 tsp ground cumin

1 tbsp all-purpose flour

3½ cups vegetable stock

1 lb frozen English peas

2-3 tbsp chopped fresh mint, to taste

salt and freshly ground black pepper

⅔ cup low-fat unsweetened yogurt

½ tsp cornstarch

¼ cups skimmed milk

a little extra yogurt, for serving (optional)

mint sprigs, to garnish

1 Heat the ghee or oil in a saucepan, add the onions and potato and cook gently for 3 minutes. Stir in the garlic, ginger, coriander, cumin, and flour and cook for 1 minute, stirring. Add the stock, peas, and half the mint and bring to a boil, stirring. Reduce the heat, cover, and simmer gently for 15 minutes.

2 Purée the soup in a blender or food processor. Return the mixture to the pan and season with salt and pepper to taste. Blend the yogurt with the cornstarch and stir into the soup.

3 Add the milk and bring almost to a boil, stirring all the time. Cook very gently for 2 minutes. Serve hot, sprinkled with the remaining mint and a swirl of extra yogurt, if wished.

COOK'S TIP

The yogurt is mixed with a little cornstarch before being added to the hot soup–this helps to stabilize the yogurt and prevents it separating when heated.

Red Lentil Soup with Yogurt

Tasty red lentil soup flavored with chopped cilantro. The yogurt adds a light piquancy to the soup.

NUTRITIONAL INFORMATION

Calories ....280 Sugars 6g
Protein ....17g Fat 7g
Carbohydrate ...40g Saturates 4g

5 MINS   30 MINS

SERVES 4

INGREDIENTS

2 tbsp butter

1 onion, chopped finely

1 celery stalk, chopped finely

1 large carrot, grated

1 dried bay leaf

1 cup red lentils

5 cups hot vegetable or chicken stock

2 tbsp chopped fresh cilantro

4 tbsp low-fat unsweetened yogurt

salt and pepper

fresh cilantro sprigs, to garnish

1 Place the butter, onion, and celery in a large bowl. Cover and cook on HIGH power for 3 minutes.

2 Add the carrot, bay leaf, and lentils. Pour over the stock. Cover and cook on HIGH power for 15 minutes, stirring halfway through.

3 Remove from the microwave oven and stand, covered, for 5 minutes.

4 Remove the bay leaf, then blend in batches in a food processor, until smooth. Alternatively, press the soup through a strainer.

5 Pour into a clean bowl. Season with salt and pepper to taste and stir in the cilantro. Cover and cook on HIGH power for 4–5 minutes until very hot.

6 Serve in warmed bowls. Stir 1 tablespoon of yogurt into each serving and garnish with sprigs of fresh cilantro.

COOK'S TIP

For an extra creamy soup try adding low-fat crème fraîche or soured cream instead of yogurt.

Spicy Lentil Soup

For a warm, satisfying meal on a cold day, this lentil dish is packed full of taste and goodness.

NUTRITIONAL INFORMATION

Calories 155   Sugars 4g
Protein ....11g   Fat 3g
Carbohydrate ...22g   Saturates 0.4g

🍲 1 HOUR   🕐 1¼ HOURS

SERVES 4

INGREDIENTS

½ cup red lentils

2 tsp vegetable oil

1 large onion, chopped finely

2 garlic cloves, crushed

1 tsp ground cumin

1 tsp ground coriander

1 tsp garam masala

2 tbsp tomato paste

4½ cups Fresh Vegetable Stock (see page 14)

about 12 oz can corn, drained

salt and pepper

TO SERVE

low-fat unsweetened yogurt

chopped fresh parsley

warmed pocket bread

1 Rinse the red lentils in cold water. Drain the lentils well and put to one side for a while.

2 Heat the oil in a large non-stick saucepan and fry the onion and garlic gently until soft but not browned.

3 Stir in the cumin, coriander, garam masala, tomato paste, and 4 tablespoons of the stock. Mix well and simmer gently for 2 minutes.

4 Add the lentils and pour in the remaining stock. Bring to a boil, reduce the heat and simmer, covered, for 1 hour until the lentils are tender and the soup thickened. Stir in the corn and heat through for 5 minutes. Season well.

5 Ladle into warmed soup bowls and top each with a spoonful of yogurt and a sprinkling of parsley. Serve with warmed pocket bread.

COOK'S TIP

Many of the ready-prepared ethnic breads available today either contain fat or are brushed with oil before baking. Always check the ingredients list for fat content.

Sweet Potato & Onion Soup

This simple recipe uses the sweet potato with its distinctive flavor and color, combined with a hint of orange and cilantro.

NUTRITIONAL INFORMATION

Calories 320   Sugars 26g
Protein ....7g   Fat 7g
Carbohydrate ...62g   Saturates 1g

15 MINS   30 MINS

SERVES 4

INGREDIENTS

2 tbsp vegetable oil

2 lb sweet potatoes, diced

1 carrot, diced

2 onions, sliced

2 garlic cloves, crushed

2½ cups vegetable stock

1¼ cups unsweetened orange juice

1 cup low-fat unsweetened yogurt

2 tbsp chopped fresh cilantro

salt and pepper

TO GARNISH

cilantro sprigs

orange rind

1 Heat the vegetable oil in a large saucepan and add the diced sweet potatoes and carrot, sliced onions and garlic. Sauté the vegetables together gently for 5 minutes, stirring constantly.

2 Pour in the vegetable stock and orange juice and bring them to a boil.

3 Reduce the heat to a simmer, cover the saucepan and cook the vegetables for 20 minutes or until the sweet potato and carrot cubes are tender.

4 Transfer the mixture to a food processor or blender in batches and process for 1 minute until puréed. Return the purée to the rinsed-out saucepan.

5 Stir in the yogurt and chopped cilantro and season to taste.

6 Serve the soup in warm bowls and garnish with cilantro sprigs and orange rind.

VARIATION

This soup can be chilled before serving, if preferred. If chilling, stir the yogurt into the dish just before serving. Serve in chilled bowls.

Fish & Crab Chowder

Packed full of flavor, this delicious fish dish is a meal in itself, but it is ideal accompanied with a crisp side salad.

NUTRITIONAL INFORMATION

Calories . . . . . . .440 Sugars 10g
Protein . . . . .49g Fat 7g
Carbohydrate . . .43g Saturates 1g

1¼ HOURS   25 MINS

SERVES 4

INGREDIENTS

1 large onion, chopped finely

2 celery stalks, chopped finely

⅔ cup dry white wine

2½ cups Fresh Fish Stock (see page 15)

2½ cups skimmed milk

1 dried bay leaf

1½ cups smoked cod fillets, skinned and cut into 1 inch cubes

8 oz undyed smoked haddock fillets, skinned and cut into 1 inch cubes

2 x 6 oz cans crabmeat, drained

8 oz blanched green beans, sliced into 1 inch pieces

1½ cups cooked brown rice

4 tsp cornstarch mixed with 4 tablespoons cold water

salt and pepper

chopped fresh parsley to garnish

mixed green salad, to serve

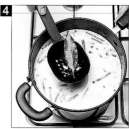

1 Place the onion, celery, and wine in a large non-stick saucepan. Bring to a boil, cover and cook for 5 minutes.

2 Uncover and cook for 5 minutes until the liquid has evaporated.

3 Pour in the stock and milk and add the bay leaf. Bring to a simmer and stir in the cod and haddock. Simmer gently, uncovered, for 5 minutes.

4 Add the crabmeat, green beans, and rice and cook gently for 2–3 minutes until heated through. Remove the bay leaf with a draining spoon.

5 Stir in the cornstarch mixture until thickened slightly. Season to taste and ladle into 4 warmed soup bowls. Garnish with chopped parsley and serve with a mixed salad.

Mushroom & Ginger Soup

Thai soups are very quickly and easily put together, and are cooked so that each ingredient can still be tasted in the finished dish.

NUTRITIONAL INFORMATION

Calories 74   Sugars 1g
Protein . . . . .3g   Fat 3g
Carbohydrate . . . .9g   Saturates 0.4g

🍲 1½ HOURS   🕐 15 MINS

SERVES 4

INGREDIENTS

¼ cup dried Chinese mushrooms or 1⅓
   cups field or crimini mushrooms

4 cups hot Fresh
   Vegetable Stock (see page 14)

4½ oz thread egg noodles

2 tsp sunflower oil

3 garlic cloves, minced

1 inch piece ginger,
   shredded finely

½ tsp mushroom catsup

1 tsp light soy sauce

2 cups mung bean sprouts

cilantro leaves, to garnish

1 Soak the dried Chinese mushrooms (if using) for at least 30 minutes in 1¼ cups of the hot vegetable stock. Remove the stalks and discard, then slice the mushrooms. Reserve the stock.

2 Cook the noodles for 2–3 minutes in boiling water. Drain and rinse. Set them aside.

3 Heat the oil over a high heat in a wok or large, heavy skillet. Add the garlic and ginger, stir, and add the mushrooms. Stir over a high heat for 2 minutes.

4 Add the remaining vegetable stock with the reserved stock and bring to a boil. Add the mushroom catsup and soy sauce.

5 Stir in the bean sprouts and cook until tender. Put some noodles in each bowl and ladle the soup on top. Garnish with cilantro leaves and serve.

COOK'S TIP

Rice noodles contain no fat and are ideal for for anyone on a low-fat diet.

Carrot & Cumin Soup

Carrot soups are very popular and and here cumin, tomato, potato, and celery give the soup both richness and depth.

NUTRITIONAL INFORMATION

Calories 114   Sugars 8g
Protein . . . . .3g   Fat 6g
Carbohydrate . . .12g   Saturates 4g

2¹/₂ HOURS   45 MINS

SERVES 4–6

INGREDIENTS

3 tbsp butter or margarine

1 large onion, chopped

1–2 garlic cloves, minced

12 oz carrots, sliced

3½ cups Chicken or Vegetable Stock
(see page 14)

¾ tsp ground cumin

2 celery stalks, sliced thinly

4 oz potato, diced

2 tsp tomato paste

2 tsp lemon juice

2 fresh or dried bay leaves

about 1¼ cups skimmed milk

salt and pepper

celery leaves to garnish

1 Melt the butter or margarine in a large saucepan. Add the onion and garlic and fry very gently until the onion begins to soften.

2 Add the carrots and continue to fry gently for a further 5 minutes, stirring frequently and taking care they do not brown.

3 Add the stock, cumin, seasoning, celery, potato, tomato paste, lemon juice, and bay leaves and bring to a boil. Cover and simmer gently for about 30 minutes until all the vegetables are very tender.

4 Discard the bay leaves, cool the soup a little, and then press it through a strainer or blend in a food processor or blender until smooth.

5 Pour the soup into a clean pan, add the milk, and bring slowly to a boil. Taste and adjust the seasoning.

6 Garnish each serving with a small celery leaf and serve.

COOK'S TIP

This soup can be frozen for up to 3 months. Add the milk when reheating.

Spicy Dal & Carrot Soup

This delicious, warming, and nutritious soup includes a selection of spices to give it a 'kick'. It is simple to make and extremely good to eat.

NUTRITIONAL INFORMATION

Calories . . . . . . .173 Sugars 11g
Protein . . . . .9g Fat 5g
Carbohydrate . . .24g Saturates 1g

10 MINS   50 MINS

SERVES 6

INGREDIENTS

4½ oz split red lentils

5 cups vegetable stock

12 oz carrots, peeled and sliced

2 onions, peeled and chopped

9 oz can chopped tomatoes

2 garlic cloves, peeled and chopped

2 tbsp vegetable ghee or oil

1 tsp ground cumin

1 tsp ground coriander

1 fresh green chlli, seeded and chopped, or use 1 tsp minced chili (from a jar)

½ tsp ground turmeric

1 tbsp lemon juice

salt

1¼ cups skimmed milk

2 tbsp chopped fresh cilantro

yogurt, to serve

1 Place the lentils in a strainer and wash well under cold running water. Drain and place in a large saucepan with 3½ cups of the vegetable stock, the carrots, onions, tomatoes, and garlic. Bring the mixture to a boil, reduce the heat, cover, and simmer for 30 minutes.

2 Meanwhile, heat the ghee or oil in a small pan, add the cumin, coriander, chili and turmeric and fry gently for 1 minute.

3 Remove from the heat and stir in the lemon juice and salt to taste.

4 Purée the soup in batches in a blender or food processor. Return the soup to the saucepan, add the spice mixture and the remaining 1¼ cups stock or water and simmer for 10 minutes.

5 Add the milk to the soup and adjust the seasoning according to taste.

6 Stir in the chopped cilantro and reheat gently. Serve hot, with a swirl of yogurt.

Indian Potato & Pea Soup

A slightly hot and spicy Indian flavor is given to this soup with the use of garam masala, chili, cumin, and ground coriander.

NUTRITIONAL INFORMATION

Calories 153	Sugars 6g	
Protein 6g	Fat 6g	
Carbohydrate ...18g	Saturates 1g	

5 MINS   35 MINS

SERVES 4

INGREDIENTS

2 tbsp vegetable oil

8 oz mealy potatoes, diced

1 large onion, chopped

2 garlic cloves, minced

1 tsp garam masala

1 tsp ground coriander

1 tsp ground cumin

3¾ cups vegetable stock

1 red chili, chopped

3½ oz frozen English peas

4 tbsp low-fat unsweetened yogurt

salt and pepper

chopped fresh cilantro, to garnish

1 Heat the vegetable oil in a large saucepan and add the diced potatoes, onion, and garlic. Sauté gently for about 5 minutes, stirring constantly. Add the ground spices and cook for 1 minute, stirring all the time.

2 Stir in the vegetable stock and chopped red chili and bring the mixture to a boil. Reduce the heat, cover the pan, and simmer for 20 minutes.

3 Add the peas and cook for a further 5 minutes. Stir in the yogurt and season to taste.

4 Pour the soup into warmed bowls, garnish with the chopped fresh cilantro and serve hot with warm bread.

COOK'S TIP

For slightly less heat, seed the chili before adding it to the soup. Always wash your hands after handling chilies as they contain volatile oils that can irritate the skin and make your eyes burn if you touch your face.

Consommé

A traditional clear soup made from beef bones and lean ground beef. Thin strips of vegetables provide a colorful garnish.

NUTRITIONAL INFORMATION

Calories . . . . 109 Sugars 6g

Protein . . . . .13g Fat 3g

Carbohydrate . . . .7g Saturates 1g

6¼ HOURS   1¼ HOURS

SERVES 4–6

I N G R E D I E N T S

5 cups strong beef stock

1 cup extra lean ground beef

2 tomatoes, skinned, seeded and chopped

2 large carrots, chopped

1 large onion, chopped

2 celery stalks, chopped

1 turnip, chopped (optional)

1 Bouquet Garni (see page 31)

2–3 egg whites

shells of 2–4 eggs, minced

1–2 tbsp sherry (optional)

salt and pepper

Melba Toast, to serve

T O   G A R N I S H

julienne strips of raw carrot, turnip, celery or celeriac or a one-egg omelet, cut into julienne strips

1 Put the stock and ground beef in a saucepan. Leave for 1 hour. Add the tomatoes, carrots, onion, celery, turnip (if using), bouquet garni, 2 of the egg whites, the crushed shells of 2 of the eggs, and plenty of seasoning. Bring to almost boiling point, whisking hard all the time with a flat whisk.

2 Cover and simmer for 1 hour, taking care not to allow the layer of froth on top of the soup to break.

3 Pour the soup through a jelly bag or scalded fine cloth, keeping the froth back until the last, then pour the ingredients through the cloth again into a clean pan. The resulting liquid should be completely clear.

4 If the soup is not quite clear, return it to the pan with another egg white and the crushed shells of 2 more eggs. Repeat the whisking process as before and then boil for 10 minutes; strain again.

5 Add the sherry (if using) to the soup and reheat gently. Place the garnish in the warmed soup bowls and carefully pour in the soup. Serve with melba toast.

Beef & Vegetable Soup

This comforting broth is perfect for a cold day and is just as delicious made with lean lamb or pork fillet.

NUTRITIONAL INFORMATION

Calories 138   Sugars 2g
Protein ....13g   Fat 3g
Carbohydrate ...15g   Saturates 1g

12 HOURS   1 ¼ HOURS

SERVES 4

INGREDIENTS

⅓ cup pearl barley, soaked overnight

5 cups fresh beef stock

1 tsp dried mixed herbs

8 oz lean rump or sirloin beef

1 large carrot, diced

1 leek, shredded

1 medium onion, chopped

2 stalks celery, sliced

salt and pepper

2 tbsp fresh parsley, chopped, to garnish

crusty bread, to serve

1 Place the pearl barley in a large saucepan. Pour over the stock and add the mixed herbs. Bring to a boil, cover and simmer gently over a low heat for 10 minutes.

VARIATION

A vegetarian version can be made by omitting the beef and beef stock and using vegetable stock instead. Just before serving, stir in 6 oz fresh bean curd, drained and diced.

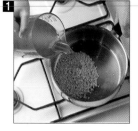

2 Meanwhile, trim any fat from the beef and cut the meat into thin strips.

3 Skim away any scum that has risen to the top of the stock with a flat ladle.

4 Add the beef, carrot, leek, onion, and celery to the pan. Bring back to a boil, cover and simmer for about 1 hour or until the barley, meat, and vegetables are just tender.

5 Skim away any remaining scum that has risen to the top of the soup with a flat ladle. Blot the surface with absorbent paper towels to remove any fat. Adjust the seasoning according to your taste.

6 Ladle the soup into warm bowls and sprinkle with freshly chopped parsley. Serve very hot, and accompanied with crusty bread.

Chunky Potato & Beef Soup

This is a real winter warmer–pieces of tender beef and chunky mixed vegetables are cooked in a liquor flavored with sherry.

NUTRITIONAL INFORMATION

Calories 187	Sugars 3g
Protein 14g	Fat 9g
Carbohydrate ...12g	Saturates 2g

 5 MINS   35 MINS

SERVES 4

INGREDIENTS

2 tbsp vegetable oil

8 oz lean braising or frying steak, cut into strips

8 oz new potatoes, halved

1 carrot, diced

2 celery stalks, sliced

2 leeks, sliced

3¾ cups beef stock

8 baby-corn-on-the-cobs, sliced

1 bouquet garni

2 tbsp dry sherry

salt and pepper

chopped fresh parsley, to garnish

1 Heat the vegetable oil in a large saucepan.

2 Add the strips of meat to the saucepan and cook for 3 minutes, turning constantly.

3 Add the halved potatoes, diced carrot, sliced celery, and leeks. Cook for a further 5 minutes, stirring.

4 Pour the beef stock into the saucepan and bring to a boil. Reduce the heat until the liquid is simmering, then add the sliced baby-corn-on-the-cobs and the bouquet garni.

5 Cook the soup for a further 20 minutes or until cooked through.

6 Remove the bouquet garni from the saucepan and discard. Stir the dry sherry into the soup and then season to taste with salt and pepper.

7 Pour the soup into warmed bowls and garnish with the chopped fresh parsley. Serve at once with crusty bread.

COOK'S TIP

Make double the quantity of soup and freeze the remainder in a rigid container for later use. When ready to use, leave in the refrigerator to defrost thoroughly, then heat until very hot.

Split Pea & Ham Soup

You can use either yellow or green split peas in this recipe, but both types must be well washed and soaked overnight before use.

NUTRITIONAL INFORMATION

Calories 323	Sugars 9g	
Protein 17g	Fat 9g	
Carbohydrate ...45g	Saturates 4g	

  12¼ HOURS   2¾ HOURS

SERVES 6

INGREDIENTS

1¼ cups dried yellow split peas

7½ cups water

2 onions, chopped finely

1 small turnip, chopped finely

2 carrots, chopped finely

2–4 celery stalks, chopped finely

1 lean ham knuckle

1 Bouquet Garni

½ tsp dried thyme

½ tsp ground ginger

1 tbsp white wine vinegar

salt and pepper

1 Wash the dried peas thoroughly, then place in a bowl with half of the water and leave to soak overnight.

2 Put the soaked peas and their liquor, the remaining water, the onions, turnip, carrots, and celery into a large saucepan, then add the ham knuckle, bouquet garni, dried thyme, and ginger. Bring slowly to a boil.

3 Remove any scum from the surface of the soup, cover the pan and simmer gently for 2–2½ hours until the peas are very tender.

4 Remove the ham knuckle and bouquet garni. Strip about ³/₄–1 cup of the meat from the knuckle and chop it finely.

5 Add the chopped ham and vinegar to the soup and season to taste.

6 Bring back to a boil and simmer for 3–4 minutes. Serve.

VARIATION

If preferred, this soup can be strained or blended in a food processor or blender until smooth. You can vary the vegetables, depending on what is available. Leeks, celeriac, or chopped or canned tomatoes are particularly good.

Lentil & Ham Soup

This is a good hearty soup, based on a stock made from a ham knuckle, with plenty of vegetables and red lentils to thicken it and add flavor.

NUTRITIONAL INFORMATION

Calories . . . . .219 Sugars 4g
Protein . . . . .17g Fat 3g
Carbohydrate . . .33g Saturates 1g

 2¼ HOURS 1¾ HOURS

SERVES 4–6

INGREDIENTS

1 cup red lentils

6¼ cups stock or water

2 onions, chopped

1 garlic clove, minced

2 large carrots, chopped

1 lean ham knuckle or 6 oz lean bacon, chopped

4 large tomatoes, skinned and chopped

2 fresh or dried bay leaves

9 oz potatoes, chopped

1 tbsp white wine vinegar

¼ tsp ground allspice

salt and pepper

chopped scallions or chopped fresh parsley, to garnish

1 Put the lentils and stock or water in a saucepan and leave to soak for 1–2 hours.

2 Add the onions, garlic, carrots, ham knuckle or bacon, tomatoes, bay leaves, and seasoning.

3 Bring the mixture in the saucepan to a boil, cover and simmer for about 1 hour until the lentils are tender, stirring occasionally to prevent the lentils from sticking to the bottom of the pan.

4 Add the potatoes and continue to simmer for about 20 minutes until the potatoes and ham knuckle are tender.

5 Discard the bay leaves. Remove the knuckle and chop ¾ cup of the meat and reserve. If liked, press half the soup through a strainer or blend in a food processor or blender until smooth. Return to the pan with the rest of the soup.

6 Adjust the seasoning, add the vinegar and allspice and the reserved chopped ham. Simmer gently for a further 5–10 minutes. Serve sprinkled liberally with scallions or chopped parsley.

Bacon, Bean, & Garlic Soup

A mouth-wateringly healthy vegetable, bean, and bacon soup with a garlic flavor. Serve with granary or whole wheat bread.

NUTRITIONAL INFORMATION

Calories 261   Sugars 5g
Protein . . . . .23g   Fat 8g
Carbohydrate . . .25g   Saturates 2g

 5 MINS   20 MINS

SERVES 4

I N G R E D I E N T S

8 oz lean smoked back bacon slices

1 carrot, sliced thinly

1 celery stalk, sliced thinly

1 onion, chopped

1 tbsp oil

3 garlic cloves, sliced

3 cups hot vegetable stock

7 oz can chopped tomatoes

1 tbsp chopped fresh thyme

about 14 oz can cannellini beans, drained

1 tbsp tomato paste

salt and pepper

grated Cheddar cheese, to garnish

COOK'S TIP

For a more substantial soup add 2 oz cup small pasta shapes or short lengths of spaghetti when you add the stock and tomatoes. You will also need to add an extra ²/₃ cup vegetable stock.

1 Chop 2 slices of the bacon and place in a bowl. Cook on HIGH power for 3–4 minutes until the fat runs out and the bacon is well cooked. Stir the bacon halfway through cooking to separate the pieces. Transfer to a plate lined with paper towels and leave to cool. When cool, the bacon pieces should be crisp and dry. Place the carrot, celery, onion, and oil in a large bowl. Cover and cook on HIGH power for 4 minutes.

2 Chop the remaining bacon and add to the bowl with the garlic. Cover and cook on HIGH power for 2 minutes.

3 Add the stock, the contents of the can of tomatoes, the thyme, beans, and tomato paste. Cover and cook on HIGH power for 8 minutes, stirring halfway through. Season to taste. Ladle the soup into warmed bowls and sprinkle with the crisp bacon and grated cheese.

Lamb & Barley Broth

Warming and nutritious, this broth is perfect for a cold winter's day. The slow cooking allows you to use one of the cheaper cuts of meat.

NUTRITIONAL INFORMATION

Calories 304	Sugars 4g	
Protein 29g	Fat 14g	
Carbohydrate ...16g	Saturates 6g	

🎩 15 MINS   🕑 2¼ HOURS

SERVES 4

I N G R E D I E N T S

1 tbsp vegetable oil

1 lb lean neck of lamb

1 large onion, sliced

2 carrots, sliced

2 leeks, sliced

4 cups vegetable stock

1 bay leaf

few sprigs of fresh parsley

⅓ cup pearl barley

1 Heat the vegetable oil in a large, heavy-bottomed saucepan and add the pieces of lamb, turning them to seal and brown on both sides.

2 Lift the lamb out of the pan and set aside until required.

3 Add the onion, carrots, and leeks to the saucepan and cook gently for about 3 minutes.

4 Return the lamb to the saucepan and add the vegetable stock, bay leaf, parsley, and pearl barley to the saucepan.

5 Bring the mixture in the pan to a boil, then reduce the heat. Cover and simmer for 1½–2 hours.

6 Discard the parsley sprigs. Lift the pieces of lamb from the broth and allow them to cool slightly.

7 Remove the bones and any fat and chop the meat. Return the lamb to the broth and reheat gently.

8 Ladle the lamb and parsley broth into warmed bowls and serve immediately.

COOK'S TIP

This broth will taste even better if made the day before, as this allows the flavors to fully develop. It also means that any fat will solidify on the surface so you can then lift it off. Keep the broth in the refrigerator until required.

Chicken & Leek Soup

This satisfying soup can be served as a main course. You can add rice and bell peppers to make it even more hearty, as well as colorful.

NUTRITIONAL INFORMATION

Calories	183	Sugar 4g
Protein	........21g	Fats 9g
Carbohydrates	....4g	Saturates 5g

 5 MINS   1¼ HOURS

SERVES 4–6

I N G R E D I E N T S

2 tbsp butter

12 oz boneless chicken

12 oz leeks, cut into 1-inch pieces

5 cups Fresh Chicken Stock (see page 14)

1 bouquet garni sachet

8 pitted prunes, halved

salt and white pepper

cooked rice and diced bell peppers
  (optional)

1 Melt the butter in a large saucepan.

2 Add the chicken and leeks to the saucepan and fry for 8 minutes.

3 Add the chicken stock and bouquet garni sachet and stir well.

4 Season well with salt and pepper to taste.

5 Bring the soup to a boil and simmer for 45 minutes.

6 Add the prunes to the saucepan with some cooked rice and diced bell peppers (if using) and simmer for about 20 minutes.

7 Remove the bouquet garni sachet from the soup and discard. Serve the chicken and leek soup immediately.

VARIATION

Instead of the bouquet garni sachet, you can use a bunch of fresh mixed herbs, tied together with string. Choose herbs such as parsley, thyme, and rosemary.

Chicken & Coconut Soup

This fragrant, Thai-style soup combines citrus flavors with coconut and a hint of piquancy from chilies.

NUTRITIONAL INFORMATION

Calories 345	Sugar 2g	
Protein 28g	Fats 24g	
Carbohydrates 5g	Saturates 18g	

2³/₄ HOURS   15 MINS

SERVES 4

INGREDIENTS

1¾ cups cooked, skinned chicken breast

1⅓ cups unsweetened crushed coconut

2 cups boiling water

2 cups Fresh Chicken Stock (see page 14)

4 spring scallions, white and green parts, sliced thinly

2 stalks lemon grass

1 lime

1 tsp grated gingerroot

1 tbsp light soy sauce

2 tsp ground coriander

2 large fresh red chilies

1 tbsp chopped fresh cilantro

1 tbsp cornstarch mixed with 2 tbsp cold water

salt and white pepper

chopped red chili, to garnish

1 Slice the chicken into thin strips. Place the coconut in a heatproof bowl and pour the boiling water over.

2 Place a fine strainer over another bowl and pour in the coconut water. Work the coconut through the strainer.

3 Add the coconut water, the stock and the scallions to a large saucepan. Slice the base of each lemon grass and discard the damaged leaves. Bruise the stalks and add to the saucepan.

4 Peel the rind from the lime, keeping it in large strips. Slice the lime in half and extract the juice. Add the lime strips, juice, ginger, soy sauce, and ground coriander to the saucepan.

5 Bruise the chilies with a fork then add to the pan. Heat the pan to just below boiling point. Add the chicken and fresh cilantro to the pan, bring to a boil, then simmer for 10 minutes.

6 Discard the lemon grass, lime rind, and chilies. Pour the blended cornstarch mixture into the saucepan and stir until slightly thickened. Season, then garnish with the red chili.

Mediterranean Fish Soup

Juicy chunks of fish and sumptuous shellfish are cooked in a flavorsome stock. Serve with toasted bread rubbed with garlic.

NUTRITIONAL INFORMATION

Calories 316	Sugar 4g
Protein 53g	Fats 7g
Carbohydrates 5g	Saturates 1g

🍞 1 HOUR   🕐 15 MINS

SERVES 4

I N G R E D I E N T S

1 tbsp olive oil

1 large onion, chopped

2 garlic cloves, finely chopped

1¾ cups Fresh Fish Stock (see page 15)

⅔ cup dry white wine

1 bay leaf

1 sprig each fresh thyme, rosemary, and oregano

1 lb firm white fish fillets (such as cod or halibut), skinned and cut into 1 inch cubes

1 lb fresh mussels, prepared

14 oz can chopped tomatoes

8 oz peeled shrimp, thawed if frozen

salt and pepper

sprigs of thyme, to garnish

TO SERVE

lemon wedges

4 slices toasted French bread, rubbed with cut garlic clove

1 Heat the olive oil in a large saucepan and gently fry the onion and garlic for 2–3 minutes until just softened.

2 Pour in the stock and wine and bring to a boil.

3 Tie the bay leaf and herbs together with clean string and add to the saucepan together with the fish and mussels. Stir well, cover and simmer for 5 minutes.

4 Stir in the tomatoes and shrimp and continue to cook for a further 3–4 minutes until very hot and the fish is cooked through.

5 Discard the herbs and any mussels that have not opened. Season to taste, then ladle into warm bowls.

6 Garnish with sprigs of fresh thyme and serve with lemon wedges and toasted bread.

Coconut & Crab Soup

Thai red curry paste is quite fiery, but adds a superb flavor to this dish. It is available in jars or packets from supermarkets.

NUTRITIONAL INFORMATION

Calories ....122 Sugar 9g
Protein ....11g Fats 4g
Carbohydrates ...11g Saturates 1g

🥗 5 MINS   🕐 10 MINS

SERVES 4

I N G R E D I E N T S

1 tbsp groundnut oil

2 tbsp Thai red curry paste

1 red bell pepper, seeded and sliced

2½ cups coconut milk

2½ cups fish stock

2 tbsp fish sauce

8 oz canned or fresh white crabmeat

8 oz fresh or frozen crab claws

2 tbsp chopped fresh cilantro

3 spring scallions, trimmed and sliced

1 Heat the oil in a large preheated wok.

2 Add the red curry paste and red bell pepper to the wok and stir-fry for 1 minute.

3 Add the coconut milk, fish stock, and fish sauce and bring to a boil.

4 Add the crabmeat, crab claws, cilantro and scallions to the wok.

5 Stir the mixture well and heat thoroughly for 2–3 minutes or until everything is warmed through.

6 Transfer the soup to warm bowls and serve hot.

COOK'S TIP

Clean the wok after use by washing it with water, using a mild detergent if necessary, and a soft cloth or brush. Do not scrub or use any abrasive cleaner as this will scratch the surface. Dry thoroughly then wipe the surface all over with a little oil to protect the surface.

Partan Bree

This traditional Scottish soup is thickened with a purée of rice and crab meat cooked in milk. Add soured cream, if liked, at the end of cooking.

NUTRITIONAL INFORMATION

Calories 112   Sugars 5g
Protein . . . . .7g   Fat 2g
Carbohydrate . . .18g   Saturates 0.3g

1 HOUR   35 MINS

SERVES 6

INGREDIENTS

1 medium-sized boiled crab

scant ½ cup long-grain rice

2½ cups skimmed milk

2½ cups Fish Stock (see page 15)

1 tbsp anchovy paste

2 tsp lime or lemon juice

1 tbsp chopped fresh parsley or I tsp chopped fresh thyme

3–4 tbsp soured cream (optional)

salt and pepper

snipped chives, to garnish

1 Remove and reserve all the brown and white meat from the crab, then crack the claws and remove and chop that meat; reserve the claw meat.

COOK'S TIP

If you are unable to buy a whole crab, use about 6 oz frozen crabmeat and thaw thoroughly before use; or a 6 oz can of crabmeat which just needs thorough draining.

2 Put the rice and milk into a saucepan and bring slowly to a boil. Cover and simmer gently for about 20 minutes.

3 Add the reserved white and brown crabmeat and seasoning and simmer for a further 5 minutes.

4 Cool a little, then press through a strainer, or blend in a food processor or blender until smooth.

5 Pour the soup into a clean saucepan and add the fish stock and the reserved claw meat. Bring slowly to a boil, then add the anchovy paste and lime or lemon juice and adjust the seasoning to taste.

6 Simmer for a further 2–3 minutes. Stir in the parsley or thyme and then swirl soured cream (if using) through each serving. Garnish with snipped chives.

Smoked Haddock Soup

Smoked haddock gives this soup a wonderfully rich flavor, while the mashed potatoes and cream thicken and enrich the stock.

NUTRITIONAL INFORMATION

Calories 169   Sugars 8g
Protein ....16g   Fat 5g
Carbohydrate ...16g   Saturates 3g

  25 MINS   40 MINS

SERVES 4–6

I N G R E D I E N T S

8 oz smoked haddock fillet

1 onion, chopped finely

1 garlic clove, minced

2½ cups skimmed milk

1–1½ cups hot mashed potatoes

2 tbsp butter

about 1 tbsp lemon juice

6 tbsp low-fat unsweetened fromage blanc

4 tbsp fresh parsley, chopped

salt and pepper

1 Put the fish, onion, garlic, and water into a saucepan. Bring to a boil, cover and simmer for 15–20 minutes.

2 Remove the fish from the pan, strip off the skin and remove all the bones. Flake the flesh finely.

3 Return the skin and bones to the cooking liquor and simmer for 10 minutes. Strain, discarding the skin and bone. Pour the liquor into a clean pan.

4 Add the milk, flaked fish, and seasoning to the pan, bring to the boil and simmer for about 3 minutes.

5 Gradually whisk in sufficient mashed potato to give a fairly thick soup, then stir in the butter and sharpen to taste with lemon juice.

6 Add the fromage blanc and 3 tablespoons of the chopped parsley. Reheat gently and adjust the seasoning. Sprinkle with the remaining parsley and serve immediately.

COOK'S TIP

Undyed smoked haddock may be used in place of the bright yellow fish; it will give a paler color but just as much flavor. Alternatively, use smoked cod or smoked whiting.

Appetizers & Snacks

If you prefer not to start your meal with soup, this chapter contains a range of appetizers from all around the world to whet your appetite. This is a truly international

selection of low-fat dishes from as far afield as India, Mexico, and Italy. Some of them are extremely easy to make, such as some of the pâté and pasta recipes, while others take a little longer to make; all, however, are delicious. Whether cooking a cosy family supper or hoping to impress your friends around the dinner table, you will find many innovative new starter ideas here alonside some old favorites.

Minted Onion Bhajis

Besan flour is a fine yellow flour made from garbanzo beans and is available from supermarkets and Asian food shops.

NUTRITIONAL INFORMATION

Calories 251   Sugars 7g
Protein . . . . .7g   Fat 8g
Carbohydrate . . .39g   Saturates 1g

 5 MINS   15 MINS

MAKES 12

INGREDIENTS

1 cup besan flour

¼ tsp cayenne pepper

¼–½ tsp ground coriander

¼–½ tsp ground cumin

1 tbsp chopped fresh mint

4 tbsp strained thick low-fat yogurt

¼ cup cold water

1 large onion, quartered and thinly sliced

vegetable oil, for frying

salt and pepper

sprigs of mint, to garnish

1 Put the besan flour into a bowl, add the cayenne pepper, coriander, cumin, and mint and season with salt and pepper to taste. Stir in the yogurt, water, and sliced onion and mix well together.

2 One-third fill a large, deep skillet with oil and heat until very hot. Drop heaped spoonfuls of the mixture, a few at a time, into the hot oil and use two forks to shape the mixture into rough ball-shapes.

3 Fry the bhajis until golden brown and cooked through, turning frequently.

4 Drain the bhajis on absorbent paper towels and keep warm while cooking the remainder in the same way.

5 Arrange the bhajis on a platter and garnish with sprigs of fresh mint. Serve hot or warm.

COOK'S TIP

Besan flour is excellent for making batter and is used in India in place of flour. It can be made from ground split peas as well as garbanzo beans.

Vegetables with Tahini Dip

This tasty dip is great for livening-up simply-cooked vegetables.
You can vary the vegetables according to the season.

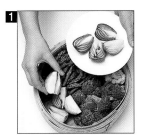

NUTRITIONAL INFORMATION

Calories 126	Sugars 7g	
Protein 11g	Fat 6g	
Carbohydrate 8g	Saturates 1g	

5 MINS   20 MINS

SERVES 4

I N G R E D I E N T S

8 oz small broccoli florets

8 oz small cauliflower florets

8 oz asparagus, sliced into 2 inch lengths

2 small red onions, quartered

1 tbsp lime juice

2 tsp toasted sesame seeds

1 tbsp chopped fresh chives, to garnish

HOT TAHINI & GARLIC DIP

1 tsp sunflower oil

2 garlic cloves, minced

½–1 tsp chili powder

2 tsp tahini

⅔ cup low-fat unsweetened fromage blanc

2 tbsp chopped fresh chives

salt and pepper

1 Line the base of a steamer with baking parchment and arrange the vegetables on top.

2 Bring a wok or large saucepan of water to a boil, and place the steamer on top. Sprinkle with lime juice and steam for 10 minutes.

3 To make the hot tahini & garlic dip, heat the sunflower oil in a small non-stick saucepan, add the garlic, chili powder, and seasoning to taste and fry gently for 2–3 minutes until the garlic is softened.

4 Remove the saucepan from the heat and stir in the tahini and fromage blanc. Return to the heat and cook gently for 1–2 minutes without boiling. Stir in the chives.

5 Remove the vegetables from the steamer and place on a warmed serving platter. Sprinkle with the sesame seeds and garnish with chopped chives. Serve with the hot dip.

Spinach Cheese Molds

These flavor-packed little molds are a perfect starter or a tasty light lunch. Serve them with warm pocket bread.

NUTRITIONAL INFORMATION

Calories	119	Sugars	. . . . .2g
Protein	. . . . .6g	Fat	. . . . .9g
Carbohydrate	. . . .2g	Saturates	. . . . . .6g

1¼ HOURS   50 MINS

SERVES 4

I N G R E D I E N T S

3½ oz fresh spinach leaves

10½ oz skimmed milk soft cheese

2 garlic cloves, minced

sprigs of fresh parsley, tarragon, and chives, finely chopped

salt and pepper

T O   S E R V E

salad leaves and fresh herbs

pocket bread

1 Trim the stalks from the spinach leaves and rinse the leaves under running water. Pack the leaves into a saucepan while still wet, cover and cook for 3–4 minutes until wilted–they will cook in the steam from the wet leaves (do not overcook). Drain well and pat dry with absorbent paper towels.

2 Base-line 4 small pudding bowls or individual ramekin dishes with baking parchment. Line the bowls or ramekins with spinach leaves so that the leaves overhang the edges if they are large enough to do so.

3 Place the cheese in a bowl and add the garlic and herbs. Mix together thoroughly and season to taste.

4 Spoon the cheese and herb mixture into the bowls or ramekins and pull over the overlapping spinach to cover the cheese, or lay extra leaves to cover the top. Place a waxed paper circle on top of each dish and weigh down with a 3½ oz weight. Leave to chill in the refrigerator for 1 hour.

5 Remove the weights and peel off the paper. Loosen the molds gently by running a small spatula around the edges of each dish and turn them out on to individual serving plates. Serve the molds with a mixture of salad leaves and fresh herbs, and warm pocket bread.

Lentil Pâté

Red lentils are used in this spicy recipe for speed as they do not require pre-soaking. If you use other lentils, soak and pre-cook them first.

NUTRITIONAL INFORMATION

Calories	267	Sugars	........12g
Protein	........14g	Fat	..........8g
Carbohydrate	...37g	Saturates	......1g

  25 MINS   1¼ HOURS

SERVES 4

I N G R E D I E N T S

1 tbsp vegetable oil, plus extra for greasing

1 onion, chopped

2 garlic cloves, minced

1 tsp garam masala

½ tsp ground coriander

1¼ cups vegetable stock

¾ cup red lentils

1 small egg

2 tbsp milk

2 tbsp mango chutney

2 tbsp chopped parsley

chopped parsley, to garnish

salad leaves and warm toast, to serve

1 Heat the vegetable oil in a large saucepan and sauté the onion and garlic for 2–3 minutes, stirring. Add the spices and cook for a further 30 seconds. Stir in the stock and lentils and bring the mixture to a boil. Reduce the heat and simmer for 20 minutes until the lentils are cooked and softened. Remove the pan from the heat and drain off any excess moisture.

2 Put the mixture in a food processor and add the egg, milk, mango chutney, and parsley. Blend until smooth.

3 Grease and line the base of a 1 lb loaf pan and spoon the mixture into the pan. Cover and cook in a preheated oven at 400°F for 40–45 minutes or until firm.

4 Allow the pâté to cool in the pan for 20 minutes, then transfer to the refrigerator to cool completely. Slice the pâté and garnish with chopped parsley. Serve with salad leaves and warm toast.

VARIATION

Use other spices, such as chili powder or Chinese five-spice powder, to flavor the pâté and add tomato relish or chili relish instead of the mango chutney, if you prefer.

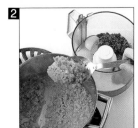

Potato & Bean Pâté

This pâté is easy to prepare and may be stored in the refrigerator for up to two days. Serve with small toasts, Melba toast, or crudités.

NUTRITIONAL INFORMATION

Calories 94	Sugars 5g	
Protein 6g	Fat 1g	
Carbohydrate ...17g	Saturates 0.2g	

 5 MINS   10 MINS

SERVES 4

INGREDIENTS

3½ oz mealy potatoes, diced

8 oz mixed canned beans, such as borlotti, small navy, and kidney beans, drained

1 garlic clove, minced

2 tsp lime juice

1 tbsp chopped fresh cilantro

2 tbsp low-fat unsweetened yogurt

salt and pepper

chopped fresh cilantro, to garnish

1 Cook the potatoes in a saucepan of boiling water for 10 minutes until tender. Drain well and mash.

2 Transfer the potato to a food processor or blender and add the beans, garlic, lime juice, and the fresh cilantro.

3 Season the mixture with salt and pepper and process for 1 minute to make a smooth purée. Alternatively, mix the beans with the potato, garlic, lime juice, and cilantro and mash.

4 Turn the purée into a bowl and add the yogurt. Mix well and season with salt and pepper to taste.

5 Spoon the pâté into a serving dish and garnish with the chopped cilantro. Serve at once or leave to chill.

COOK'S TIP

If you do not have a food processor or you would prefer to make a chunkier pâté, simply mash the ingredients with a fork.

Potato Skins with Guacamole

Although avocados do contain fat, if they are used in small quantities you can still enjoy their creamy texture.

NUTRITIONAL INFORMATION

Calories	399	Sugars	.........4g
Protein	........10g	Fat	..........15g
Carbohydrate	...59g	Saturates	......4g

🥔 45 MINS   🕐 1³/₄ HOURS

SERVES 4

I N G R E D I E N T S

4 x 8 oz baking potatoes

2 tsp olive oil

coarse sea salt and pepper

chopped fresh chives, to garnish

G U A C A M O L E   D I P

6 oz ripe avocado

1 tbsp lemon juice

2 ripe, firm tomatoes, chopped finely

1 tsp grated lemon rind

½ cup low-fat soft cheese
with herbs and garlic

4 scallions, chopped
finely

a few drops of Tabasco sauce

salt and pepper

1 Bake the potatoes in a preheated oven at 400°F for 1¼ hours. Remove from the oven and allow to cool for 30 minutes. Reset the oven to 425°.

2 Halve the potatoes lengthwise and scoop out 2 tablespoons of the flesh. Slice in half again. Place on a baking tray sheet and brush the flesh side lightly with oil. Sprinkle with salt and pepper. Bake for a further 25 minutes until golden and crisp.

3 To make the guacamole dip, mash the avocado with the lemon juice. Add the remaining ingredients and mix.

4 Drain the potato skins on paper towels and transfer to a warmed serving platter. Garnish with chives. Pile the avocado mixture into a serving bowl.

COOK'S TIP

Mash the leftover potato flesh with unsweetened yogurt and seasoning, and serve as an accompaniment to meat, fish, and vegetarian dishes.

Potato & Mushroom Hash

This is a quick one-pan dish which is ideal for a quick snack. Packed with color and flavor, you can add any other vegetable you have at hand.

NUTRITIONAL INFORMATION

Calories . . . . . . .378 Sugars 14g
Protein . . . . .18g Fat 26g
Carbohydrate . . .20g Saturates 7g

10 MINS   35 MINS

SERVES 4

I N G R E D I E N T S

1½ lb potatoes, cubed

1 tbsp olive oil

2 garlic cloves, crushed

1 green bell pepper, cubed

1 yellow bell pepper, cubed

3 tomatoes, diced

1 cup button mushrooms, halved

1 tbsp Worcester sauce

2 tbsp chopped basil

salt and pepper

fresh basil sprigs, to garnish

warm, crusty bread, to serve

1 Cook the potatoes in a saucepan of boiling salted water for 7–8 minutes. Drain well and reserve.

2 Heat the oil in a large, heavy-bottomed skillet and cook the potatoes for 8–10 minutes, stirring until browned.

3 Add the garlic and bell peppers to the skillet and cook for 2–3 minutes.

4 Stir in the tomatoes and mushrooms and cook, stirring, for 5–6 minutes.

5 Stir in the Worcester sauce and basil and season well. Garnish with the fresh basil and serve with crusty bread.

COOK'S TIP

Most brands of Worcester sauce contain anchovies. If cooking for vegetarians, make sure you choose a vegetarian variety.

Spicy Jacket Potatoes

These twice-baked potatoes have an unusual filling of the Middle Eastern flavours of garbanzo beans, cumin, and cilantro.

NUTRITIONAL INFORMATION

Calories 451   Sugars 6g
Protein . . . . .18g   Fat 4g
Carbohydrate . . .91g   Saturates 0.5g

  20 MINS   1½ HOURS

SERVES 4

I N G R E D I E N T S

4 baking potatoes, each about 10½ oz

1 tbsp vegetable oil (optional)

15½ oz can garbanzo beans, drained

1 tsp ground coriander

1 tsp ground cumin

4 tbsp fres cilantro, chopped

⅔ cup low-fat unsweetened yogurt

salt and pepper

S A L A D

2 tomatoes

4 tbsp fresh cilantro

½ cucumber

½ red onion

4 Meanwhile, place the garbanzo beans in a large mixing bowl and mash with a fork or potato masher.

5 Stir in the ground coriander, cumin, and half the chopped fresh cilantro. Cover the bowl with plastic wrap and set aside.

6 Halve the cooked potatoes and scoop the flesh into a bowl, keeping the shells intact. Mash the flesh until smooth and gently mix into the garbanzo bean mixture with the unsweetened yogurt. Season well with salt and pepper to taste.

7 Place the potato shells on a baking sheet, and fill with the potato and garbanzo bean mixture. Return the potatoes to the oven and bake for 10–15 minutes until heated through.

8 Meanwhile, make the salad. Using a sharp knife, chop the tomatoes and fresh cilantro. Slice the cucumber and cut the red onion into thin slices. Toss all the ingredients together in a serving dish.

9 Serve the potatoes sprinkled with the remaining chopped cilantro and the prepared salad.

1 Preheat the oven to 400°F.

2 Scrub the potatoes and pat them dry with absorbent paper towels. Prick the potatoes all over with a fork, brush with oil (if using) and season with salt and pepper.

3 Place the potatoes on a baking sheet and bake for 1–1¼ hours or until cooked through. Cool for 10 minutes.

Bruschetta

Traditionally, this Italian savory is enriched with olive oil. Here, sun-dried tomatoes are a good substitute and only a little oil is used.

NUTRITIONAL INFORMATION

Calories	178	Sugars	.........2g
Protein	.........8g	Fat	...........6g
Carbohydrate	...24g	Saturates	......2g

45 MINS 5 MINS

SERVES 4

I N G R E D I E N T S

¼ cup dry-pack sun-dried tomatoes

1¼ cups boiling water

14 inch long Granary or whole wheat stick of French bread

1 large garlic clove, halved

¼ cup pitted black olives in brine, drained and quartered

2 tsp olive oil

2 tbsp chopped fresh basil

⅓ cup grated low-fat Mozzarella cheese

salt and pepper

fresh basil leaves, to garnish

1 Place the sun-dried tomatoes in a heatproof bowl and pour over the boiling water.

2 Set aside for 30 minutes to soften. Drain well and pat dry with paper towels. Slice into thin strips and set aside.

3 Trim and discard the ends from the bread and cut into 12 slices. Arrange on a broiler rack and place under a preheated hot broiler and cook for 1–2 minutes on each side until lightly golden.

4 Rub both sides of each piece of bread with the cut sides of the garlic. Top with strips of sun-dried tomato and olives.

5 Brush lightly with olive oil and season well. Sprinkle with the basil and Mozzarella cheese and return to the broiler for 1–2 minutes until the cheese is melted and bubbling.

6 Transfer to a warmed serving platter and garnish with fresh basil leaves.

COOK'S TIP

If you use sun-dried tomatoes packed in oil, drain them, rinse well in warm water and drain again on paper towels to remove as much oil as possible.
Sun-dried tomatoes give a rich, full flavor to this dish, but thinly-sliced fresh tomatoes can be used instead.

Cheese, Herb, & Onion Rolls

A great texture and flavor are achieved by mixing white and granary flours together with minced onion, grated cheese, and fresh herbs.

NUTRITIONAL INFORMATION

Calories 529   Sugars 2g
Protein . . . . .24g   Fat 7g
Carbohydrate . . .98g   Saturates 4g

 2 HOURS   🕐 15 MINS

SERVES 4

I N G R E D I E N T S

2 cups strong white flour

1½ tsp salt

1 tsp dried mustard powder

good pinch of pepper

2 cups granary or malted
    wheat flour

2 tbsp chopped fresh mixed herbs

2 tbsp finely chopped scallions

1–1½ cups sharp low-fat Cheddar cheese,
    grated

½ oz compressedyeast; or 1½ tsp dried
    yeast plus 1 tsp superfine sugar;
    or 1 envelope easy-blend yeast
    plus 1 tbsp oil

300 ml/½ pint/1¼ cups warm water

1 Sift the white flour with the salt, mustard, and pepper into a bowl. Mix in the granary flour, herbs, scallions and most of the cheese.

2 Blend the fresh yeast with the warm water or, if using dried yeast, dissolve the sugar in the water, sprinkle the yeast on top and leave in a warm place for about 10 minutes until frothy. Add the yeast mixture of your choice to the dry ingredients and mix to form a firm dough, adding more flour if necessary.

3 Knead until smooth and elastic. Cover with an oiled plastic bag and leave in a warm place to rise for 1 hour or until doubled in size. punch down and knead the dough until smooth. Divide into 10–12 pieces and shape into round or long rolls, coils, or knots.

4 Alternatively, make one large plaited loaf. Divide the dough into 3 even pieces and roll each into a long thin sausage and join at one end. Beginning at

the joined end, plait to the end and secure. Place on greased baking sheets, cover with an oiled plastic wrap and leave to rise until doubled in size. Remove the polythene.

5 Sprinkle with the rest of the cheese. Bake in a preheated oven at 400°F for 15–20 minutes for the rolls, or 30–40 minutes for the loaf.

Cheese & Chive Scones

These tea-time classics have been given a healthy twist by the use of low-fat soft cheese and reduced-fat Cheddar cheese.

NUTRITIONAL INFORMATION

Calories ......297 Sugars 3g
Protein ....13g Fat 7g
Carbohydrate ...49g Saturates 4g

10 MINS   20 MINS

MAKES 10

INGREDIENTS

8 oz self-raising flour

1 tsp powdered mustard

½ tsp cayenne pepper

½ tsp salt

3½ oz low-fat soft cheese with
  added herbs

2 tbsp fresh snipped chives, plus extra to
  garnish

2 tbsp skimmed milk

2 oz reduced-fat sharp Cheddar cheese,
  grated

low-fat soft cheese, to serve

1 Preheat the oven to 400°F. Sift the flour, mustard, cayenne pepper, and salt into a mixing bowl.

2 Add the soft cheese to the mixture and mix together until well incorporated. Stir in the snipped chives.

3 Make a well in the center of the ingredients and gradually pour in 3½ fl oz milk, stirring as you pour, until the mixture forms a soft dough.

4 Turn the dough on to a floured surface and knead lightly. Roll out until ¾ inch thick and use a 2 inch plain pastry cutter to stamp out as many rounds as you can. Transfer the rounds to a baking sheet.

5 Re-knead the dough trimmings together and roll out again. Stamp out more rounds–you should be able to make 10 scones in total.

6 Brush the scones with the remaining milk and sprinkle with the grated cheese. Bake in the oven for 15–20 minutes until risen and golden. Transfer to a wire rack to cool. Serve warm with low-fat soft cheese, garnished with chives.

VARIATION

For sweet scones, omit the mustard, cayenne pepper, chives, and grated cheese. Replace the flavored soft cheese with plain low-fat soft cheese. Add 2³/₄ oz currants and 1 oz superfine sugar. Serve with low-fat soft cheese and fruit spread.

Savory Bell Pepper Bread

This flavorsome bread contains only the minimum amount of fat.
Serve with a bowl of hot soup for a filling and nutritious light meal.

NUTRITIONAL INFORMATION

Calories	468	Sugars	........11g
Protein	........16g	Fat	...........5g
Carbohydrate	...97g	Saturates	......1g

2 HOURS   50 MINS

SERVES 4

I N G R E D I E N T S

1 small red bell pepper

1 small green bell pepper

1 small yellow bell pepper

2 oz dry-pack sun-dried tomatoes

¼ cup boiling water

2 tsp dried yeast

1 tsp superfine sugar

⅔ cup tepid water

1 lb strong white bread flour

2 tsp dried rosemary

2 tbsp tomato paste

⅔ cup low-fat unsweetened yogurt

1 tbsp coarse salt

1 tbsp olive oil

1 Preheat the oven to 425°F and the broiler to hot. Halve and seed the bell peppers, arrange on the broiler rack and cook until the skin is charred. Leave to cool for 10 minutes, peel off the skin and chop the flesh. Slice the tomatoes into strips, place in a bowl, and pour over the boiling water. Leave to soak.

2 Place the yeast and sugar in a small jug, pour over the tepid water and leave for 10–15 minutes until frothy. Sift the flour into a bowl and add 1 tsp dried rosemary. Make a well in the center and pour in the yeast mixture.

3 Add the tomato paste, tomatoes, and soaking liquid, bell peppers, yogurt and half the salt. Mix to form a soft dough. Turn out on to a lightly floured surface and knead for 3–4 minutes until smooth and elastic. Place in a lightly floured bowl, cover and leave in a warm room for 40 minutes until doubled in size.

4 Knead the dough again and place in a lightly greased 9 inch round springform pan. Using a wooden spoon, form 'dimples' in the surface. Cover and leave for 30 minutes. Brush with oil and sprinkle with rosemary and salt. Bake for 35–40 minutes, cool for 10 minutes and release from the tin. Leave to cool on a rack and serve.

COOK'S TIP

For a quick, filling snack serve the bread with a bowl of hot soup in winter, or a crisp leaf salad in summer.

Pasta Provençale

A combination of Italian vegetables tossed in a tomato dressing, served on a bed of assorted salad leaves, makes an appetizing meal.

NUTRITIONAL INFORMATION

Calories 197	Sugars 5g
Protein 10g	Fat 5g
Carbohydrate ...30g	Saturates 1g

  10 MINS 15 MINS

SERVES 4

INGREDIENTS

8 oz penne

1 tbsp olive oil

1 oz pitted black olives, drained and chopped

1 oz dry-pack sun-dried tomatoes, soaked, drained, and chopped

14 oz can artichoke hearts, drained and halved

4 oz baby zucchini, trimmed and sliced

4 oz baby plum tomatoes, halved

3½ oz assorted baby salad leaves

salt and pepper

shredded basil leaves, to garnish

DRESSING

4 tbsp sieved tomatoes

2 tbsp low-fat (unsweetened yogurt)

1 tbsp unsweetened orange juice

1 small bunch fresh basil, shredded

1 Cook the penne according to the directions on the packet. Do not overcook the pasta–it should still have 'bite'. Drain well and return to the pan.

2 Stir in the olive oil, salt and pepper, olives, and sun-dried tomatoes. Leave to cool.

3 Gently mix the artichokes, zucchini and plum tomatoes into the cooked pasta. Arrange the salad leaves in a serving bowl.

4 To make the dressing, mix all the ingredients together and toss into the vegetables and pasta.

5 Spoon the mixture on top of the salad leaves and garnish with shredded basil leaves.

Spicy Garbanzo Bean Snack

You can use fresh garbanzo beans, soaked overnight, for this popular Indian snack, but the canned variety is just as flavorsome.

NUTRITIONAL INFORMATION

Calories 190   Sugars 4g
Protein . . . . .9g   Fat 3g
Carbohydrate . . .34g   Saturates 0.3g

5 MINS   10 MINS

SERVES 4

INGREDIENTS

14 oz can garbanzo beans, drained

2 medium potatoes

1 medium onion

2 tbsp tamarind paste

6 tbsp water

1 tsp chili powder

2 tsp sugar

1 tsp salt

TO GARNISH

1 tomato, sliced

2 fresh green chilies, chopped

fresh cilantro leaves

1 Place the garbanzo beans in a bowl.

COOK'S TIP

Garbanzo beans have a nutty flavor and slightly crunchy texture. Indian cooks also grind these to make a flour called besan, which is used to make breads, thicken sauces, and to make batters for deep-fried dishes.

2 Using a sharp knife, cut the potatoes into dice.

3 Place the potatoes in a saucepan of water and boil until cooked through. Test by inserting the tip of a knife into the potatoes–they should feel soft and tender. Set the potatoes aside.

4 Using a sharp knife, finely chop the onion. Set aside until required.

5 Mix together the tamarind paste and water. Add the chili powder, sugar, and salt and mix again. Pour the mixture over the garbanzo beans.

6 Add the onion and the diced potatoes, and stir to mix. Season to taste.

7 Transfer to a serving bowl and garnish with tomatoes, chilies and cilantro leaves.

Baked Stuffed Onions

Spanish onions are ideal for this recipe, as they have a milder, sweeter flavor that is not too overpowering.

NUTRITIONAL INFORMATION

Calories ....182 Sugars 6g
Protein ....10g Fat 9g
Carbohydrate ...18g Saturates 5g

15 MINS   2¼ HOURS

SERVES 4

INGREDIENTS

4 large Spanish onions

2 slices streaky bacon, diced

½ red bell pepper, seeded and diced

4½ oz lean ground beef

1 tbsp chopped mixed fresh herbs
  such as parsley, thyme, and rosemary
  or 1 tsp dried mixed herbs

1 oz/½ cup fresh white bread crumbs

1¼ cups beef stock

salt and pepper

chopped fresh parsley to garnish

long grain rice to serve

GRAVY

2 tbsp butter

4½ oz mushrooms, chopped finely

1¼ cups beef stock

2 tbsp cornstarch

2 tbsp water

1 Put the onions in a saucepan of lightly salted water. Bring to a boil, then simmer for 15 minutes until tender.

2 Remove the onions from the pan, drain and cool slightly, then hollow out the centers and finely chop.

3 Heat a skillet and cook the bacon until the fat runs. Add the chopped onion and bell pepper and cook for 5–7 minutes, stirring frequently.

4 Add the beef to the skillet and cook, stirring, for 3 minutes, until browned. Remove from the heat and stir in the herbs, bread crumbs, and seasoning.

5 Grease an ovenproof dish and stand the whole onions in it. Pack the beef mixture into the centers and pour the stock around them.

6 Bake the stuffed onions in a preheated oven at 350°F for 1–1½ hours or until tender.

7 To make the gravy, heat the butter in a small saucepan and fry the mushrooms for 3–4 minutes. Strain the liquid from the onions and add to the pan with the stock. Cook for 2–3 minutes.

8 Mix the cornstarch with the water then stir into the gravy and heat, stirring, until thickened and smooth. Season with salt and pepper to taste. Serve the onions with the gravy and rice, garnished with chopped fresh parsley.

Stuffed Mushrooms

Large mushrooms have more flavor than the smaller button mushrooms.
Serve these mushrooms as a side vegetable or appetizer.

NUTRITIONAL INFORMATION

Calories	148	Sugars	.........1g
Protein	........11g	Fat	..........7g
Carbohydrate	....11g	Saturates	......3g

10 MINS   15 MINS

SERVES 4

INGREDIENTS

12 open-cap mushrooms

4 spring scallions, chopped

4 tsp olive oil

3½ oz fresh brown breadcrumbs

1 tsp fresh oregano, chopped

3½ oz low-fat sharp Cheddar cheese

1 Wash the mushrooms and pat dry with paper towels. Remove the stalks and chop the stalks finely.

2 Sauté the mushroom stalks and scallions in half of the oil.

3 In a large bowl, mix together the mushroom stalks and scallions.

4 Add the bread crumbs and oregano to the mushrooms and scallions, mix, and set aside.

5 Crumble the cheese into small pieces in a small bowl. Add the cheese to the breadcrumb mixture and mix well. Spoon the stuffing mixture into the mushroom caps.

6 Drizzle the remaining oil over the mushrooms. grill on an oiled rack over medium hot coals for 10 minutes or until cooked through.

7 Transfer the mushrooms to serving plates and serve hot.

VARIATION

For a change replace the cheese with finely-chopped chorizo sausage (remove the skin first), chopped hard-cooked eggs, chopped olives, or chopped anchovy fillets. Mop up the juices with some crusty bread.

Soufflé Omelet

The sweet cherry tomatoes, mushrooms, and peppery arugula leaves make a mouthwatering filling for these light, fluffy omelets.

NUTRITIONAL INFORMATION

Calories	146	Sugars	.........2g
Protein	........10g	Fat	...........11g
Carbohydrate	....2g	Saturates	......2g

1¼ HOURS   45 MINS

SERVES 4

INGREDIENTS

6 oz cherry tomatoes

8 oz mixed mushrooms (such as button, chestnut, shiitake, oyster, and wild mushrooms)

4 tbsp Fresh Vegetable Stock (see page 14)

small bunch fresh thyme

4 medium eggs, separated

4 medium egg whites

4 tsp olive oil

1 oz arugula leaves

salt and pepper

fresh thyme sprigs, to garnish

1 Halve the tomatoes and place them in a saucepan. Wipe the mushrooms with paper towels, trim if necessary and slice if large. Place the tomatoes and mushrooms in the saucepan.

2 Add the stock and thyme to the pan. Bring to the boil, cover and simmer for 5–6 minutes until tender. Drain, remove the thyme and discard, and keep the mixture warm.

3 Meanwhile, separate the eggs and whisk the egg yolks with 8 tbsp water until frothy. In a clean, grease-free bowl, mix the 8 egg whites until stiff and dry.

4 Spoon the egg yolk mixture into the egg whites and, using a metal spoon, fold together until well mixed. Take care not to knock out too much of the air.

5 For each omelet, brush a small omelet pan with 1 tsp oil and heat until hot. Pour in a quarter of the egg mixture and cook for 4–5 minutes until the mixture has set.

6 Preheat the broiler to medium and finish cooking the omelet for 2–3 minutes.

7 Transfer the omelet to a warm serving plate. Fill the omelet with a few arugula leaves, and a quarter of the mushroom and tomato mixture. Flip over the top of the omelet, garnish with sprigs of thyme and serve.

Smoked Fish & Potato Pâté

This smoked fish pâté is given a tart fruity flavor by the gooseberries, which complement the fish perfectly.

NUTRITIONAL INFORMATION

Calories 418	Sugars 4g
Protein 18g	Fat 25g
Carbohydrate . . .32g	Saturates 6g

20 MINS   10 MINS

SERVES 4

I N G R E D I E N T S

1 lb 7 oz mealy potatoes, diced

10½ oz smoked mackerel, skinned and flaked

2¾ oz cooked gooseberries

2 tsp lemon juice

2 tbsp low-fat crème fraîche

1 tbsp capers

1 gherkin, chopped

1 tbsp chopped dill pickle

1 tbsp chopped fresh dill

salt and pepper

lemon wedges, to garnish

toast or warm crusty bread, to serve

1 Cook the diced potatoes in a saucepan of boiling water for 10 minutes until tender, then drain well.

2 Place the cooked potatoes in a food processor or blender.

3 Add the skinned and flaked smoked mackerel and process for 30 seconds until fairly smooth. Alternatively, place the ingredients in a bowl and mash with a fork.

4 Add the cooked gooseberries, lemon juice, and crème fraîche to the fish and potato mixture. Blend for a further 10 seconds or mash well.

5 Stir in the capers, chopped gherkin, and dill pickle, and chopped fresh dill. Season well with salt and pepper.

6 Turn the fish pâté into a serving dish, garnish with lemon wedges and serve with slices of toast or warm crusty bread cut into chunks or slices.

COOK'S TIP

Use stewed, canned, or bottled cooked gooseberries for convenience and to save time, or when fresh gooseberries are out of season.

Crêpes with Curried Crab

Home-made crêpes are delicious–here, white crabmeat is lightly flavored with curry spices and tossed in a low-fat dressing.

NUTRITIONAL INFORMATION

Calories ....279 Sugars 9g
Protein ....25g Fat 7g
Carbohydrate ...31g Saturates 1g

 40 MINS   25 MINS

SERVES 4

I N G R E D I E N T S

4 oz buckwheat flour

1 large egg, beaten

1¼ cups skimmed milk

4½ oz frozen spinach, thawed, well-drained, and chopped

2 tsp vegetable oil

FILLING

12 oz white crabmeat

1 tsp mild curry powder

1 tbsp mango chutney

1 tbsp reduced-calorie mayonnaise

2 tbsp low-fat unsweetened yogurt

2 tbsp fresh cilantro, chopped

TO SERVE

green salad

lemon wedges

1 Sift the flour into a bowl and remove any husks that remain in the strainer. Make a well in the center of the flour and add the egg. Whisk in the milk, then blend in the spinach. Transfer to a pitcher and leave for 30 minutes.

2 To make the filling, mix together all the ingredients, except the cilantro, in a bowl, cover and chill until required. Whisk the batter. Brush a small crêpe pan with a little oil, heat until hot and pour in enough batter to cover the base thinly. Cook for 1–2 minutes, turn over and cook for 1 minute until golden. Repeat to make 8 pancakes, layering them on a plate with baking parchment.

3 Stir the cilantro into the crab mixture. Fold each pancake into quarters. Open one fold and fill with the crab mixture. Serve warm, with a green salad and lemon wedges.

VARIATION

Try lean diced chicken in a light white sauce or peeled shrimp instead of the crab.

Thai Potato Crab Cakes

These small crab cakes are based on a traditional Thai recipe. They make a delicious snack when served with this sweet and sour cucumber sauce.

NUTRITIONAL INFORMATION

Calories 254	Sugars 9g	
Protein 12g	Fat 6g	
Carbohydrate ...40g	Saturates 1g	

10 MINS   30 MINS

SERVES 4

I N G R E D I E N T S

1 lb mealy potatoes, diced

6 oz white crabmeat, drained if canned

4 scallions, chopped

1 tsp light soy sauce

½ tsp sesame oil

1 tsp chopped lemon grass

1 tsp lime juice

3 tbsp all-purpose flour

2 tbsp vegetable oil

salt and pepper

S A U C E

4 tbsp finely chopped cucumber

2 tbsp clear honey

1 tbsp garlic wine vinegar

½ tsp light soy sauce

1 chopped red chili

T O   G A R N I S H

1 red chili, sliced

cucumber slices

1 Cook the diced potatoes in a saucepan of boiling water for 10 minutes until cooked through. Drain well and mash.

2 Mix the crabmeat into the potato with the scallions, soy sauce, sesame oil, lemon grass, lime juice, and flour. Season with salt and pepper.

3 Divide the potato mixture into 8 portions of equal size and shape them into small rounds, using floured hands.

4 Heat the oil in a wok or skillet and cook the cakes, 4 at a time, for 5-7 minutes, turning once. Keep warm and repeat with the remaining crab cakes.

5 Meanwhile, make the sauce. In a small serving bowl, mix the cucumber, honey, vinegar, soy sauce, and chopped red chili.

6 Garnish the cakes with the sliced red chili and cucumber slices and serve with the sauce.

Rice & Tuna bell Peppers

Broiled mixed sweet bell peppers are filled with tender tuna, corn, nutty brown and wild rice, and grated, reduced-fat cheese.

NUTRITIONAL INFORMATION

Calories 332   Sugars 13g
Protein . . . . .27g   Fat 8g
Carbohydrate . . .42g   Saturates 4g

 10 MINS   35 MINS

SERVES 4

I N G R E D I E N T S

⅓ cup wild rice

⅓ cup brown rice

4 assorted medium bell peppers

7 oz can tuna fish in brine,
   drained and flaked

11½ oz can corn kernels (with no added
   sugar or salt), drained

3½ oz reduced-fat sharp Cheddar cheese,
   grated

1 bunch fresh basil leaves, shredded

2 tbsp dry white breadcrumbs

1 tbsp Parmesan cheese, freshly
   grated

salt and pepper

fresh basil leaves, to garnish

crisp salad leaves, to serve

1 Place the wild rice and brown rice in different saucepans, cover with water and cook for about 15 minutes or according to the directions on the packet. Drain the rice well.

2 Meanwhile, preheat the broiler to medium. Halve the bell peppers, remove the seeds and stalks, and arrange the peppers on the broiler rack, cut side down. Cook for 5 minutes, turn over and cook for a further 4–5 minutes.

3 Transfer the cooked rice to a mixing bowl and add the flaked tuna and drained corn. Gently fold in the grated cheese. Stir the basil leaves into the rice mixture and season with salt and pepper to taste.

4 Divide the tuna and rice mixture into 8 equal portions. Pile each portion into each cooked bell pepper half. Mix together the breadcrumbs and Parmesan cheese and sprinkle over each bell pepper.

5 Place the bell peppers back under the broiler for 4–5 minutes until hot and golden-brown.

6 Serve the bell peppers immediately, garnished with basil and accompanied with fresh, crisp salad leaves.

Red Mullet & Coconut Loaf

This fish and coconut loaf is ideal to take along on picnics, as it can be served cold as well as hot.

NUTRITIONAL INFORMATION

Calories	138	Sugars	........12g
Protein	........11g	Fat	...........1g
Carbohydrate	...23g	Saturates	......0g

15 MINS   1¼ HOURS

SERVES 4–6

I N G R E D I E N T S

8 oz red mullet fillets, skinned

2 small tomatoes, seeded and chopped finely

2 green bell peppers, chopped finely

1 onion, chopped finely

1 fresh red chilli, chopped finely

2½ cups bread crumbs

2½ cups coconut liquid

salt and pepper

H O T   P E P P E R   S A U C E

½ cup tomato catsup

1 tsp West Indian hot pepper sauce

¼ tsp hot mustard

T O   G A R N I S H

lemon twists

sprigs of fresh chervil

COOK'S TIP

Be careful when preparing chilies because the juices can irritate the skin, especially the face. Wash your hands after handling them or wear clean rubber gloves to prepare them if preferred.

1 Finely chop the fish and mix with the tomatoes, bell peppers, onion, and chili.

2 Stir in the breadcrumbs, coconut liquid, and seasoning. If using fresh coconut, use a hammer and screwdriver or the tip of a sturdy knife to poke out the three 'eyes' in the top of the coconut and pour out the liquid.

3 Grease and base-line a 1 lb loaf pan and add the fish.

4 Bake in a preheated oven at 400°F for 1–1¼ hours until set.

5 To make the hot pepper sauce, mix together the tomato catsup, hot pepper sauce, and mustard until smooth and creamy.

6 To serve, cut the loaf into slices, garnish with lemon twists and chervil, and serve hot or cold with the hot pepper sauce.

Turkey & Vegetable Loaf

This impressive-looking turkey loaf is flavored with herbs and a layer of juicy tomatoes, and covered with zucchini ribbons.

NUTRITIONAL INFORMATION

Calories 165   Sugars 1g
Protein ....36g   Fat 2g
Carbohydrate ....1g   Saturates 0.5g

10 MINS   1¼ HOURS

SERVES 6

INGREDIENTS

1 medium onion, finely chopped

1 garlic clove, minced

2 lb lean turkey, ground

1 tbsp fresh parsley, chopped

1 tbsp fresh chives, chopped

1 tbsp fresh tarragon, chopped

1 medium egg white, lightly beaten

2 zucchini, 1 medium, 1 large

2 medium tomatoes

salt and pepper

tomato and herb sauce, to serve

  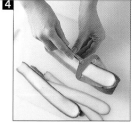

1 Preheat the oven to 375°F and line a non-stick loaf pan with baking parchment. Place the onion, garlic, and turkey in a bowl, add the herbs and season well. Mix together with your hands, then add the egg white to bind.

2 Press half of the turkey mixture into the base of the pan. Thinly slice the medium zucchini and the tomatoes and arrange the slices over the meat. Top with the rest of the turkey and press down firmly.

3 Cover with a layer of kitchen foil and place in a roasting pan. Pour in enough boiling water to come half-way up the sides of the loaf pan. Bake in the oven

for 1–1¼ hours, removing the foil for the last 20 minutes of cooking. Test the loaf is cooked by inserting a skewer into the centre–the juices should run clear. The loaf will also shrink away from the sides of the pan.

4 Meanwhile, trim the large zucchini. Using a vegetable peeler or hand-held metal cheese slicer, cut the zucchini into thin slices. Bring a saucepan of water

to a boil and blanch the zucchini ribbons for 1–2 minutes until just tender. Drain and keep warm.

5 Remove the turkey loaf from the pan and transfer to a warm serving plate. Drape the zucchini ribbons over the turkey loaf and serve with a tomato and herb sauce.

Cranberry Turkey Burgers

This recipe is bound to be popular with children and it is easy to prepare for their supper or tea.

NUTRITIONAL INFORMATION

Calories 209	Sugars 15g	
Protein 22g	Fat 5g	
Carbohydrate ...21g	Saturates 1g	

   45 MINS 🕐 25 MINS

SERVES 4

INGREDIENTS

1½ cups lean ground turkey

1 onion, chopped finely

1 tbsp chopped fresh sage

6 tbsp dry white bread crumbs

4 tbsp cranberry sauce

1 egg white, size 2, lightly beaten

2 tsp sunflower oil

salt and pepper

TO SERVE

4 toasted granary or whole wheat
   burger buns

½ lettuce, shredded

4 tomatoes, sliced

4 tsp cranberry sauce

1 Mix together the turkey, onion, sage, seasoning, bread crumbs, and cranberry sauce, then bind with egg white.

2 Press into 4 x 4 inch rounds, about ¾ inch thick. Chill the burgers for 30 minutes.

3 Line a broiler rack with baking parchment, making sure the ends are secured underneath the rack to ensure they don't catch fire. Place the burgers on top and brush lightly with oil. Put under a preheated medium broiler and cook for 10 minutes. Turn the burgers over, brush again with oil. Cook for a further 12–15 minutes until cooked through.

4 Fill the burger rolls with lettuce, tomato, and a burger, and top with cranberry sauce.

COOK'S TIP

Look out for a variety of ready ground meats at your butchers or supermarket. If unavailable, you can grind your own by choosing lean cuts and processing them in a blender or food processor.

Parsley, Chicken, & Ham Pâté

Pâté is easy to make at home, and this combination of lean chicken and ham mixed with herbs is especially straightforward.

NUTRITIONAL INFORMATION

Calories	119	Sugars	.........2g
Protein	........20g	Fat	...........3g
Carbohydrate	....2g	Saturates	......1g

 55 MINS   🕐 0 MINS

SERVES 4

INGREDIENTS

8 oz lean, skinless chicken, cooked

3½ oz lean ham, trimmed

small bunch fresh parsley

1 tsp lime rind, grated

2 tbsp lime juice

1 garlic clove, peeled

½ cup low-fat unsweetened yogurt

salt and pepper

1 tsp lime zest, to garnish

TO SERVE

wedges of lime

crisp bread

green salad

VARIATION

This pâté can be made successfully with other kinds of ground, lean, cooked meat such as turkey, beef, and pork. Alternatively, replace the meat with peeled shrimp and/or white crabmeat, or with canned tuna in brine, drained.

1 Dice the chicken and ham and place in a blender or food processor.

2 Add the parsley, lime rind, and juice, and garlic to the chicken and ham, and process well until finely minced. Alternatively, finely chop the chicken, ham, parsley, and garlic and place in a bowl. Mix gently with the lime rind and juice.

3 Transfer the mixture to a bowl and mix in the yogurt. Season with salt and pepper to taste, cover and leave to chill in the refrigerator for about 30 minutes.

4 Pile the pâté into individual serving dishes and garnish with lime zest. Serve the pâtés with lime wedges, crisp bread, and a fresh green salad.

Sweet & Sour Drumsticks

Chicken drumsticks are marinated to impart a tangy, sweet and sour flavor and a shiny glaze before being cooked on a grill.

NUTRITIONAL INFORMATION

Calories . . . . .171 Sugars 9g
Protein . . . . .23g Fat 5g
Carbohydrate . . .10g Saturates 1g

 1¼ HOURS 🕐 20 MINS

SERVES 4

I N G R E D I E N T S

8 chicken drumsticks

4 tbsp red wine vinegar

2 tbsp tomato paste

2 tbsp soy sauce

2tbsp clear honey

1tbsp Worcestershire sauce

1 garlic clove

good pinch cayenne pepper

salt and pepper

crisp salad leaves, to serve

1 Skin the chicken if desired and slash 2–3 times with a sharp knife.

2 Put the chicken drumsticks into a non-metallic container.

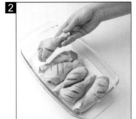

3 Mix all the remaining ingredients and pour over the chicken.

4 Leave to marinate in the refrigerator for 1 hour. Cook the drumsticks on a preheated grill for about 20 minutes, brushing with the glaze several times during cooking until the chicken is well browned and the juices run clear when pierced with a skewer. Serve with crisp salad greens.

COOK'S TIP

For a tangy flavor, add the juice of 1 lime to the marinade. While the drumsticks are broiling, check regularly to ensure that they are not burning.

Oat-Crusted Chicken Pieces

A very low-fat chicken recipe with a refreshingly light, mustard-spiced sauce, which is ideal for a healthy lunchbox or a light meal with salad.

NUTRITIONAL INFORMATION

Calories 120	Sugars 3g
Protein 15g	Fat 3g
Carbohydrate 8g	Saturates 1g

 5 MINS   40 MINS

SERVES 4

INGREDIENTS

⅓ cup rolled oats

1 tbsp chopped fresh rosemary

4 skinless chicken quarters

1 egg white

½ cup unsweetened low-fat yogurt

2 tsp wholegrain mustard

salt and pepper

grated carrot salad, to serve

1 Mix together the rolled oats, chopped fresh rosemary, and salt and pepper.

2 Brush each piece of chicken evenly with egg white, then coat in the oat mixture.

3 Place the chicken pieces on a baking sheet and bake in a preheated oven, 400°F, for about 40 minutes. Test to see if the chicken is cooked by inserted a skewer into the thickest part of the chicken–the juices should run clear without a trace of pink.

4 Mix together the yogurt and mustard, season with salt and pepper to taste.

5 Serve the chicken, hot or cold, with the sauce and a grated carrot salad.

Chicken & Cheese Jackets

Use the breasts from a roasted chicken to make these delicious potatoes and serve as a light lunch or supper dish.

NUTRITIONAL INFORMATION

Calories 417   Sugars 4g
Protein . . . . .28g   Fat 10g
Carbohydrate . . .57g   Saturates 5g

 10 MINS   50 MINS

SERVES 4

INGREDIENTS

4 large baking potatoes 8 oz cooked, boneless chicken breasts

4 scallions

1 cup low-fat soft cheese or Quark

pepper

1 Scrub the potatoes and pat dry with absorbent paper towels.

2 Prick the potatoes all over with a fork. Bake in a preheated oven, 400°F, for about 50 minutes until tender, or cook in a microwave on HIGH power for 12–15 minutes.

3 Using a sharp knife, dice the chicken and trim and thickly slice the scallions. Place the chicken and scallions in a bowl.

4 Add the low-fat soft cheese or Quark to the chicken and spring scallions and stir well to combine.

5 Cut a cross through the top of each potato and pull slightly apart. Spoon the chicken filling into the potatoes and sprinkle with pepper.

6 Serve the chicken and cheese jackets immediately with coleslaw, green salad or a mixed salad.

COOK'S TIP

Look for Quark in the chilled section. It is a low-fat, white, fresh curd cheese made from cow's milk with a delicate, slightly sour flavor.

Spicy Chicken Tortillas

The chicken filling for these easy-to-prepare tortillas has a mild, mellow spicy heat and a fresh salad makes a perfect accompaniment.

NUTRITIONAL INFORMATION

Calories . . . . . . .650 Sugars 15g
Protein . . . . .48g Fat 31g
Carbohydrate . . .47g Saturates 10g

10 MINS   35 MINS

SERVES 4

I N G R E D I E N T S

2 tbsp oil

8 skinless, boneless chicken thighs, sliced

1 onion, chopped

2 garlic cloves, chopped

1 tsp cumin seeds, roughly crushed

2 large dried chilies, sliced

14 oz can tomatoes

14 oz can red kidney beans, drained

⅔ cup chicken stock

2 tsp sugar

salt and pepper

lime wedges, to garnish

TO SERVE

1 large ripe avocado

1 lime

8 soft tortillas

1 cup thick yogurt

1 Heat the oil in a large skillet or wok, add the chicken and fry for 3 minutes.

2 Add the chopped onion and fry for 5 minutes, stirring until browned.

3 Add the chopped garlic, cumin, and chilies, with their seeds, and cook for about 1 minute.

4 Add the tomatoes, kidney beans, stock, sugar, and salt and pepper.

Bring to a boil, breaking up the tomatoes. Cover and simmer for 15 minutes. Remove the lid and cook for 5 minutes, stirring occasionally until the sauce has thickened.

5 Halve the avocado, discard the stone and scoop out the flesh onto a plate. Mash the avocado with a fork.

6 Cut half of the lime into 8 thin wedges. Now squeeze the juice from the remaining lime over the mashed avocado.

7 Warm the tortillas according to the directions on the pack. Put two tortillas on each serving plate, fill with the chicken mixture and top with spoonfuls of avocado and yogurt. Garnish the tortillas with lime wedges.

Chicken & Almond Rissoles

Cooked potatoes and cooked chicken are combined to make tasty rissoles rolled in chopped almonds then served with stir-fried vegetables.

NUTRITIONAL INFORMATION

Calories	161	Sugars	.........3g
Protein	........12g	Fat	...........9g
Carbohydrate	....8g	Saturates	......1g

35 MINS   20 MINS

SERVES 4

I N G R E D I E N T S

4½ oz par-boiled potatoes

½ cup carrots

1 cup cooked chicken meat

1 garlic clove, minced

½ tsp dried tarragon or thyme

generous pinch of ground allspice or ground coriander seeds

1 egg yolk, or ½ egg, beaten

about ¼ cup slivered almonds

salt and pepper

STIR-FRIED VEGETABLES

1 celery stalk

2 scallions, trimmed

1 tbsp oil

8 baby-corn-on-the-cobs

about 10–12 snow peas or sugar snap peas, trimmed

2 tsp balsamic vinegar

salt and pepper

1 Grate the boiled potatoes and raw carrots coarsely into a bowl. Chop finely or grind the chicken. Add to the vegetables with the garlic, herbs and spices, and plenty of salt and pepper.

2 Add the egg and bind the ingredients together. Divide in half and shape into sausages. Chop the almonds and then evenly coat each rissole in the nuts. Place the rissoles in a greased ovenproof dish and cook in a preheated oven, 400°F, for about 20 minutes until browned.

3 To prepare the stir-fried vegetables, cut the celery and scallions on the diagonal into narrow slices. Heat the oil in a skillet and toss in the vegetables. Cook over a high heat for 1–2 minutes, then add the corn-on-the-cobs and peas, and cook for 2–3 minutes. Finally, add the balsamic vinegar and season well with salt and pepper.

4 Place the rissoles on to a serving plate and add the stir-fried vegetables.

Minty Lamb Burgers

A tasty alternative to traditional hamburgers, these lamb burgers are flavored with mint and are accompanied with a smooth minty dressing.

NUTRITIONAL INFORMATION

Calories	320	Sugars	........11g
Protein	........28g	Fat	..........10g
Carbohydrate	...33g	Saturates	......4g

 40 MINS   20 MINS

SERVES 4

I N G R E D I E N T S

12 oz lean lamb, ground

1 medium onion, finely chopped

4 tbsp dry whole-wheat bread crumbs

2 tbsp mint jelly

salt and pepper

TO SERVE

4 whole-wheat baps, split

2 large tomatoes, sliced

small piece of cucumber, sliced

lettuce leaves

RELISH

4 tbsp low-fat unsweetened yogurt

1 tbsp mint jelly, softened

2 inch piece cucumber, finely diced

1 tbsp chopped fresh mint

1 Place the lamb in a large bowl and mix in the onion, breadcrumbs and mint jelly. Season well, then mold the ingredients together with your hands to form a firm mixture.

2 Divide the mixture into 4 and shape each portion into a round measuring 4 inches across. Place the rounds on a plate lined with baking parchment and leave to chill for 30 minutes.

3 Preheat the broiler to medium. Line a broiler rack with baking parchment, securing the ends under the rack, and place the burgers on top. Cook for 8 minutes, then turn over the burgers and cook for a further 7 minutes or until cooked through.

4 Meanwhile, make the relish. In a small bowl, mix together the unsweetened yogurt, mint jelly, cucumber, and freshly chopped mint. Cover the relish with plastic wrap and leave to chill in the refrigerator for an hour or until required.

5 Drain the burgers on absorbent paper towels. Serve the burgers inside the baps with sliced tomatoes, cucumber, lettuce, and relish.

Lamb & Tomato Koftas

These little meatballs, served with a minty yogurt dressing, can be prepared well in advance, ready to cook when required.

NUTRITIONAL INFORMATION

Calories	183	Sugars	.........5g
Protein	........15g	Fat	...........11g
Carbohydrate	....5g	Saturates	......4g

 15 MINS   🕐 10 MINS

SERVES 4

I N G R E D I E N T S

8 oz finely ground lean lamb

1½ onions, peeled

1-2 garlic cloves, peeled and minced

1 dried red chili, finely chopped (optional)

2-3 tsp garam masala

2 tbsp chopped fresh mint

2 tsp lemon juice

salt

2 tbsp vegetable oil

4 small tomatoes, quartered

mint sprigs, to garnish

Y O G U R T   D R E S S I N G

⅔ cup low-fat yogurt

2 inch piece cucumber, grated

2 tbsp chopped fresh mint

½ tsp toasted cumin seeds (optional)

1 Place the ground lamb in a bowl. Finely chop 1 onion and add to the bowl with the garlic and chili (if using). Stir in the garam masala, mint, and lemon juice and season well with salt. Mix well.

2 Divide the mixture in half, then divide each half into 10 equal portions and form each into a small ball. Roll the balls in the oil to coat. Quarter the remaining onion half and separate into layers.

3 Thread 5 of the spicy meatballs, 4 tomato quarters and some of the onion layers on to each of 4 pre-soaked bamboo or metal skewers.

4 Brush the vegetables with the remaining oil and cook the koftas under a hot grill for about 10 minutes, turning frequently until they are browned all over and cooked through.

5 Meanwhile, prepare the yogurt dressing for the koftas. In a small bowl mix together the yogurt, grated cucumber, mint, and toasted cumin seeds (if using).

6 Garnish the lamb and tomato koftas with mint sprigs and place on a large serving plate. Serve the koftas hot with the yogurt dressing.

Italian Platter

This popular hors d'oeuvre usually consists of vegetables soaked in olive oil and rich, creamy cheeses. Try this great low-fat version.

NUTRITIONAL INFORMATION

Calories 198	Sugars 12g
Protein 12g	Fat 6g
Carbohydrate ...25g	Saturates 3g

 10 MINS   0 MINS

SERVES 4

I N G R E D I E N T S

4½ oz reduced-fat Mozzarella cheese, drained

2 oz lean prosciutto

14 oz can artichoke hearts, drained

4 ripe figs

1 small mango

few plain Grissini (bread sticks), to serve

D R E S S I N G

1 small orange

1 tbsp sieved tomatoes

1 tsp wholegrain mustard

4 tbsp low-fat unsweetened yogurt

fresh basil leaves

salt and pepper

1 Cut the cheese into 12 sticks, 2½ inches long. Remove the fat from the ham and slice the meat into 12 strips. Carefully wrap a strip of ham around each stick of cheese and arrange neatly on a serving platter.

2 Halve the artichoke hearts and cut the figs into quarters. Arrange them on the serving platter in groups.

3 Peel the mango, then slice it down each side of the large, flat central stone. Slice the flesh into strips and arrange them so that they form a fan shape on the serving platter.

4 To make the dressing, pare the rind from half of the orange using a vegetable peeler. Cut the rind into small strips and place them in a bowl. Extract the juice from the orange and add it to the bowl containing the rind.

5 Add the sieved tomatoes, mustard, yogurt, and seasoning to the bowl and mix together. Shred the basil leaves and mix them into the dressing.

6 Spoon the dressing into a small dish and serve with the Italian Platter, accompanied with bread sticks.

VARIATION

For a change, serve with a French stick or an Italian bread, widely available from supermarkets, and use to mop up the delicious dressing.

Cheesy Ham Savory

Lean ham wrapped around crisp celery, topped with a light crust of cheese and scallions, makes a delicious light lunch.

NUTRITIONAL INFORMATION

Calories 188	Sugars 5g
Protein 15g	Fat 12g
Carbohydrate 5g	Saturates 7g

 10 MINS    10 MINS

SERVES 4

I N G R E D I E N T S

4 stalks celery, with leaves

12 thin slices of lean ham

1 bunch scallions

6 oz low-fat soft cheese with garlic and herbs

6 tbsp low-fat unsweetened yogurt

4 tbsp Parmesan cheese, freshly grated

celery salt and pepper

T O   S E R V E

tomato salad

crusty bread

1 Wash the celery, remove the leaves and reserve (if wished). Slice each celery stalk into 3 equal portions.

2 Cut any visible fat off the ham and lay the slices on a chopping board. Place a piece of celery on each piece of ham and roll up. Place 3 ham and celery rolls in each of 4 small, heatproof dishes.

3 Trim the scallions, then finely shred both the white and green parts. Sprinkle the scallions over the ham and celery rolls and season with celery salt and pepper.

4 Mix the soft cheese and yogurt and spoon over the ham and celery rolls.

5 Preheat the broiler to medium. Sprinkle each portion with 1 tbsp grated Parmesan cheese and grill for 6–7 minutes until hot and the cheese has formed a crust. If the cheese starts to brown too quickly, lower the broiler setting slightly.

6 Garnish with celery leaves (if using) and serve with a tomato salad and crusty bread.

COOK'S TIP

Parmesan is useful in low-fat recipes because its intense flavor means you only need to use a small amount.

Meat Dishes

The growing awareness of the importance of healthy eating means that supermarkets and butchers now offer leaner, lower-fat cuts of meat. Although these are slightly

more expensive than standard cuts, you do not need to buy as much if you combine them with lots of tasty vegetables and low-fat sauces. It is also worth spending a little extra time cooking the meat carefully to enhance its flavor. Always remember to cut any visible fat from beef and pork before you cook it. Liver, kidney, and venison are relatively low in fat. Look out for extra lean ground meats which can be dry-fried without the addition of oil or fat.

Chili con Carne

Probably the best-known Mexican dish and one that is a great favorite with all. The chili content can be increased to suit your taste.

NUTRITIONAL INFORMATION

Calories 443	Sugars 11g
Protein 48g	Fat 15g
Carbohydrate ...30g	Saturates 4g

 5 MINS   2¹/₂ HOURS

SERVES 4

INGREDIENTS

1 lb 10 oz lean braising or stewing steak

2 tbsp oil

1 large onion, sliced

2–4 garlic cloves, minced

1 tbsp all-purpose flour

¾ pint tomato juice

14 oz can tomatoes

1–2 tbsp sweet chili sauce

1 tsp ground cumin

salt and pepper

15 oz can red kidney beans, drained

½ teaspoon dried oregano

1–2 tbsp chopped fresh parsley

chopped fresh herbs, to garnish

boiled rice and tortillas, to serve

1 Cut the beef into cubes of about ¾ inch. Heat the oil in a flameproof casserole and fry the beef until well sealed. Remove from the casserole.

2 Add the onion and garlic to the casserole and fry until lightly browned; then stir in the flour and cook for 1–2 minutes.

3 Stir in the tomato juice and tomatoes and bring to a boil. Replace the beef and add the chili sauce, cumin, and seasoning. Cover and place in a preheated oven at 325°F for 1¹/₂ hours, or until almost tender.

4 Stir in the kidney beans, oregano, and parsley, and adjust the seasoning to taste. Cover the casserole and return to the oven for 45 minutes. Serve sprinkled with chopped fresh herbs and with boiled rice and tortillas.

COOK'S TIP

Because chili con carne requires quite a lengthy cooking time, it saves time and fuel to prepare double the quantity you need and freeze half of it to serve on another occasion. Defrost and use within 3–4 weeks.

Beef & Orange Curry

A citrusy, spicy blend of tender chunks of tender beef with the tang of orange and the warmth of Indian spices.

NUTRITIONAL INFORMATION

Calories 345	Sugars 24g
Protein 28g	Fat 13g
Carbohydrate . . .31g	Saturates 3g

 5¹/₄ HOURS   1¹/₄ HOURS

SERVES 4

I N G R E D I E N T S

1 tbsp vegetable oil

8 oz shallots, halved

2 garlic cloves, minced

1 lb lean rump or sirloin beef, trimmed and cut into ¾ inch cubes

3 tbsp curry paste

2 cups fresh beef stock

4 medium oranges

2 tsp cornstarch

salt and pepper

2 tbsp fresh cilantro, chopped, to garnish

basmati rice, freshly boiled, to serve

R A I T A

½ cucumber, finely diced

3 tbsp chopped fresh mint

⅔ cup low-fat unsweetened yogurt

1 Heat the oil in a large saucepan. Gently fry the shallots, garlic, and the cubes of beef for 5 minutes, stirring occasionally, until the beef is evenly browned all over.

2 Blend together the curry paste and stock. Add the mixture to the beef and stir to mix thoroughly. Bring to a boil, cover and simmer for about 1 hour.

3 Grate the rind of one orange. Extract the juice from the orange and from one other. Peel the other two oranges, removing the pith. Slice between each segment and remove the flesh.

4 Blend the cornstarch with the orange juice. At the end of the cooking time, stir the orange rind into the beef along with the orange and cornstarch mixture. Bring to a boil and simmer, stirring, for

3–4 minutes until the sauce thickens. Season to taste and stir in the orange segments.

5 To make the raita, mix the cucumber with the mint and stir in the yogurt. Season with salt and pepper to taste.

6 Serve the curry with rice and the cucumber raita, garnished with the chopped cilantro.

Rogan Josh

This is one of the best-known curries. Rogan Josh means 'red curry', and is so-called because of the red chilies in the recipe.

NUTRITIONAL INFORMATION

Calories . . . . . . .248 Sugars 2g
Protein . . . . .35g Fat 11g
Carbohydrate . . . .2g Saturates 5g

 10 MINS   1¾ HOURS

SERVES 6

INGREDIENTS

2 tbsp ghee

2 lb lean braising steak, cut into
    1 inch cubes

1 onion, chopped finely

3 garlic cloves

1 inch piece gingerroot, grated

4 fresh red chilies, chopped

4 green cardamom pods

4 cloves

2 tsp coriander seeds

2 tsp cumin seeds

1 tsp paprika

1 tsp salt

1 bay leaf

¼ cup low-fat yogurt

1 inch piece cinnamon stick

⅔ cup hot water

¼ tsp garam masala

pepper

1 Heat the ghee in a large flameproof casserole and brown the meat in batches. Remove the meat from the casserole and set aside in a bowl.

2 Add the chopped onion to the ghee and stir over a high heat for 3–4 minutes.

3 Grind together the garlic, ginger, chilies, cardamom, cloves, coriander, cumin, paprika, and salt. Add the spice paste and bay leaf to the casserole and stir until fragrant.

4 Return the meat and any juices in the bowl to the casserole and simmer for 2–3 minutes. Gradually stir the yogurt into the casserole keeping the sauce simmering.

5 Stir in the cinnamon stick and hot water, and pepper to taste.

6 Cover the casserole and cook in a preheated oven, 350°F, for 1¼ hours until the meat is very tender and the sauce is slightly reduced. Discard the cinnamon stick and stir in the garam masala. Remove surplus oil from the surface of the casserole before serving.

Tamarind Beef Balti

Tamarind has been used in Asian cooking for centuries and gives a sour fruity flavor to the sauce.

NUTRITIONAL INFORMATION

Calories	280	Sugars	.........7g
Protein	........35g	Fat	..........12g
Carbohydrate	....7g	Saturates	......4g

12 HOURS   🕐 35 MINS

SERVES 4

I N G R E D I E N T S

4½ oz tamarind block, broken into pieces

⅔ cup water

2 tbsp tomato paste

1 tbsp granulated sugar

1 inch piece gingerroot, chopped

1 garlic clove, chopped

½ tsp salt

1 onion, chopped

2 tbsp oil

1 tsp cumin seeds

1 tsp coriander seeds

1 tsp brown mustard seeds

4 curry leaves

1 lb 10 oz lean braising steak, cut into
   1 inch cubes and par-cooked

1 red bell pepper, cut in half, sliced

2 fresh green chilies, seeded and sliced

1 tsp garam masala

1 tbsp chopped fresh cilantro,
   to garnish

1 Soak the tamarind overnight in the water. Strain the soaked tamarind, keeping the liquid.

2 Put the tamarind, tomato paste, sugar, ginger, garlic, salt, and onion into a food processor or blender and mix to a smooth purée. Alternatively, mash the ingredients together in a bowl.

3 Heat the oil in a Balti pan or wok, add the cumin, coriander seeds, mustard seeds, and curry leaves, and cook until the spices start popping.

4 Stir the beef into the spices and stir-fry for 2–4 minutes until the meat is browned.

5 Add the red bell pepper, chilies, garam masala, tamarind mixture and reserved tamarind, liquid and cook for 20–25 minutes.

6 Serve the beef balti garnished with fresh cilantro.

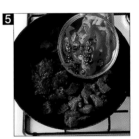

Beef Goulash

Slow, gentle cooking is the secret to this superb goulash–it really brings out the flavor of the ingredients.

NUTRITIONAL INFORMATION

Calories ....386 Sugars 10g
Protein ....44g Fat 16g
Carbohydrate ...17g Saturates 5g

 10 MINS   ⏱ 2¼ HOURS

SERVES 4

I N G R E D I E N T S

2 tbsp vegetable oil

1 large onion, chopped

1 garlic clove, minced

1 lb 10 oz lean stewing steak

2 tbsp paprika

15 oz can chopped tomatoes

2 tbsp tomato paste

1 large red bell pepper, seeded and chopped

6 oz mushrooms, sliced

2½ cups beef stock

1 tbsp cornstarch

1 tbsp water

4 tbsp low-fat unsweetended yogurt

salt and pepper

paprika for sprinkling

chopped fresh parsley, to garnish

long grain rice and wild rice, to serve

1 Heat the vegetable oil in a large skillet and cook the onion and garlic for 3–4 minutes.

2 Cut the stewing steak into chunks and cook over a high heat for 3 minutes until browned all over. Add the paprika and stir well, then add the chopped tomatoes, tomato paste, bell pepper and mushrooms. Cook for 2 minutes, stirring frequently.

3 Pour in the beef stock. bring to a boil, then reduce the heat. Cover and simmer for 1½–2 hours until the meat is tender.

4 Blend the cornstarch with the water, then add to the saucepan, stirring until thickened and smooth. Cook for 1 minute, then season with salt and pepper to taste.

5 Put the unsweetened yogurt in a serving bowl and sprinkle with a little paprika.

6 Transfer the beef goulash to a warm serving dish, garnish with chopped fresh parsley, and serve with rice and yogurt.

Boiled Beef & Carrots

Serve this old favorite with vegetables and herby dumplings for a substantial one-pot meal.

NUTRITIONAL INFORMATION

Calories .... .459 Sugars 2g
Protein .... .31g Fat .... .22g
Carbohydrate ...35g Saturates ..... .10g

15 MINS 2³/₄ HOURS

SERVES 6

INGREDIENTS

about 3½ lb joint of salted silverside or topside

2 onions, quartered, or 5–8 small onions

8–10 cloves

2 bay leaves

1 cinnamon stick

2 tbsp brown sugar

4 large carrots, sliced thickly

1 turnip, quartered

½ rulabaga, sliced thickly

1 large leek, sliced thickly

2 tbsp butter or margarine

4 tbsp all purpose flour

½ tsp dried mustard powder

salt and pepper

DUMPLINGS

2 cups self-rising flour

½ tsp dried sage

½ cup slivered vegetable suet

about ⅔ cup water

1 Put the beef in a large saucepan, add the onions, cloves, bay leaves, cinnamon, and sugar and sufficient water to cover the meat. Bring slowly to a boil, remove any scum from the surface, cover and simmer gently for 1 hour.

2 Add the carrots, turnip, rulabaga, and leeks, cover and simmer for a further 1¼ hours until the beef is tender.

3 Meanwhile, make the dumplings. Sift the flour into a bowl, season well and mix in the herbs and suet. Add sufficient water to mix to a softish dough.

4 Divide the dough into 8 pieces, roughly shape into balls and place on

top of the beef and vegetables. Replace the lid and simmer for 15–20 minutes.

5 Place the beef, vegetables, and dumplings in a serving dish. Measure 1¼ cups of the cooking liquid into a pan. Blend the margarine with the flour then gradually whisk into the pan. Bring to a boil and simmer until thickened. Stir in the mustard, adjust the seasoning, and serve with the beef.

Shepherd's Pie

Ground lamb or beef cooked with onions, carrots, herbs, and tomatoes and with a topping of piped creamed potatoes.

NUTRITIONAL INFORMATION

Calories 378	Sugars 8g	
Protein 33g	Fat 12g	
Carbohydrate ...37g	Saturates 4g	

 10 MINS   1¹/₂ HOURS

SERVES 4–5

INGREDIENTS

1 lb 9 oz lean ground or lamb or beef

2 onions, chopped

8 oz carrots, diced

1–2 garlic cloves, minced

1 tbsp all purpose flour

scant 1 cup beef stock

7 oz can chopped tomatoes

1 tsp Worcestershire sauce

1 tsp chopped fresh sage or oregano or
  ½ tsp dried sage or oregano

1½–2 lb potatoes

2 tbsp margarine

3–4 tbsp skimmed milk

4½ oz button mushrooms, sliced (optional)

salt and pepper

1 Place the meat in a heavy-bottomed saucepan with no extra fat and cook gently, stirring frequently, until the meat begins to brown.

2 Add the onions, carrots, and garlic and continue to cook gently for about 10 minutes. Stir in the flour and cook for a minute or so, then gradually stir in the stock and tomatoes and bring to a boil.

3 Add the Worcestershire sauce, seasoning, and herbs, cover the pan and simmer gently for about 25 minutes, giving an occasional stir.

4 Cook the potatoes in boiling salted water until tender, then drain thoroughly and mash, beating in the margarine, seasoning, and sufficient milk to give a piping consistency. Place in a pastry bag fitted with a large star tip.

5 Stir the mushrooms (if using) into the meat and adjust the seasoning. Turn into a shallow ovenproof dish.

6 Pipe the potatoes evenly over the meat. Cook in a preheated oven at 400°F for about 30 minutes until very hot and the potatoes are golden brown.

VARIATION

If liked, a mixture of boiled potatoes and parsnips or rulabaga may be used for the topping.

Steak in a Wine Marinade

Fillet, sirloin, rump, and entrecôte are all suitable cuts for this dish, although rump retains the most flavor.

NUTRITIONAL INFORMATION

Calories 356	Sugars 2g	
Protein 41g	Fat 9g	
Carbohydrate 2g	Saturates 4g	

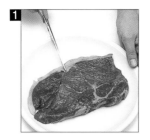  

 3 HOURS   15 MINS

SERVES 4

I N G R E D I E N T S

4 rump steaks, about 9 oz each

2½ cups red wine

1 onion, quartered

2 tbsp Dijon mustard

2 garlic cloves, minced

salt and pepper

4 large field mushrooms

olive oil for brushing

branch of fresh rosemary (optional)

1 Snip through the fat strip on the steaks in 3 places, so that the steak retains its shape when grilled.

2 Combine the red wine, onion, mustard, garlic, salt and pepper. Lay the steaks in a shallow non-porous dish and pour over the marinade. Cover and chill for 2–3 hours.

3 Remove the steaks from the refrigerator 30 minutes before you intend to cook them to let them come to room temperature. This is especially important if the steak is thick, so that it cooks more evenly and is not well done on the outside and raw in the middle.

4 Sear both sides of the steak–about 1 minute on each side–over a hot grill.

If it is about 1 inch thick, keep it over a hot grill, and cook for about 4 minutes on each side. This will give a medium-rare steak – cook it more or less, to suit your taste. If the steak is a thicker cut, move it to a less hot part of the grill or further away from the coals. To test the readiness of the meat while cooking, simply press it with your finger–the more the meat yields, the less it is cooked.

5 Brush the mushrooms with the olive oil and cook them alongside the steak, for 5 minutes, turning once. When you put the mushrooms on the grill, put the rosemary branch (if using) in the fire to flavor the meat slightly.

6 Remove the steak and leave to rest for a minute or two before serving. Slice the mushrooms and serve alongside the meat.

Beef Daube

This dish is very French but also very, very New Orleans, especially when the beef is perked up with Tabasco and Cajun spices.

NUTRITIONAL INFORMATION

Calories 251   Sugars 2g
Protein . . . . .31g   Fat 10g
Carbohydrate . . . .8g   Saturates 3g

 10 MINS   3¹/₄ HOURS

SERVES 6–8

INGREDIENTS

2 tbsp olive oil

1 large onion, cut into wedges

2 celery stalks, chopped

1 green bell pepper, cored, seeded and chopped

2 lb lean braising steak, cubed

½ cup all purpose flour, seasoned with salt and pepper

2½ cups beef stock

2 garlic cloves, minced

⅔ cup red wine

2 tbsp red wine vinegar

2 tbsp tomato paste

½ tsp Tabasco

1 tsp chopped fresh thyme

2 bay leaves

½ tsp Cajun Spice Mixture

French bread, to serve

1 Heat the oil in a large heavy-bottomed, flameproof casserole. Add the onion wedges and cook until browned on all sides. Remove with a draining spoon and set aside.

2 Add the celery and bell pepper to the pan and cook until softened. Remove the vegetables with a draining spoon and set aside.

3 Coat the meat in the seasoned flour, add to the pan and sauté until browned on all sides.

4 Add the stock, garlic, wine, vinegar, tomato paste, Tabasco, and thyme and heat gently.

5 Return the onions, celery, and peppers to the pan. Tuck in the bay leaves and sprinkle with the Cajun seasoning.

6 bring to a boil, transfer to the oven and cook for 2½–3 hours, or until the meat and vegetables are tender.

7 Serve the beef daube with French bread.

Beef Teriyaki

This Japanese-style teriyaki sauce complements grilled beef, but it can also be used to accompany chicken or salmon.

NUTRITIONAL INFORMATION

Calories 184   Sugars 6g
Protein ....24g   Fat 5g
Carbohydrate ....8g   Saturates 2g

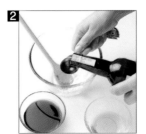

2¼ HOURS   15 MINS

SERVES 4

INGREDIENTS

1 lb extra thin lean beef steaks

8 scallions, trimmed and cut into short lengths

1 yellow bell pepper, seeded and cut into chunks

green salad, to serve

SAUCE

1 tsp cornstarch

2 tbsp dry sherry

2 tbsp white wine vinegar

3 tbsp soy sauce

1 tbsp dark muscovado sugar

1 clove garlic, minced

½ tsp ground cinnamon

½ tsp ground ginger

1 Place the meat in a shallow, non-metallic dish.

2 To make the sauce, combine the cornstarch with the sherry, then stir in the remaining sauce ingredients. Pour the sauce over the meat and leave to marinate for at least 2 hours.

3 Remove the meat from the sauce. Pour the sauce into a small saucepan.

4 Cut the meat into thin strips and thread these, concertina-style, on to pre-soaked wooden skewers, alternating each strip of meat with the prepared pieces of scallion and bell pepper.

5 Gently heat the sauce until it is just simmering, stirring occasionally.

6 Grill the kabobs over hot coals for 5–8 minutes, turning and basting the

beef and vegetables occasionally with the reserved teriyaki sauce.

7 Arrange the skewers on serving plates and pour the remaining sauce over the kabobs. Serve with a green salad.

Ginger Beef with Chili

Serve these fruity, hot and spicy steaks with noodles. Use a non-stick ridged skillet to cook with a minimum of fat.

NUTRITIONAL INFORMATION

Calories 179	Sugars 8g
Protein 21g	Fat 6g
Carbohydrate 8g	Saturates 2g

🍴 40 MINS 🕐 10 MINS

SERVES 4

INGREDIENTS

4 lean beef steaks (such as rump or sirloin), 3½ oz each

2 tbsp ginger wine

1 inch piece gingerroot ginger, finely chopped

1 garlic clove, minced

1 tsp ground chili

1 tsp vegetable oil

salt and pepper

red chili strips, to garnish

TO SERVE

freshly cooked noodles

2 scallions, shredded

RELISH

8 oz fresh pineapple

1 small red bell pepper

1 red chili

2 tbsp light soy sauce

1 piece stem ginger in syrup, drained and chopped

1 Trim any excess fat from the beef if necessary. Using a meat mallet or covered rolling pin, pound the steaks until ½ inch thick. Season on both sides and place in a shallow dish.

2 Mix the ginger wine, gingerroot, garlic, and chili and pour over the meat. Cover and chill for 30 minutes.

3 Meanwhile, make the relish. Peel and finely chop the pineapple and place it in a bowl. Halve, seed, and finely chop the bell pepper and chili. Stir into the pineapple together with the soy sauce and stem ginger. Cover and chill until required.

4 Brush a broiler pan with the oil and heat until very hot. Drain the beef and add to the pan, pressing down to seal. Lower the heat and cook for 5 minutes. Turn the steaks over and cook for a further 5 minutes.

5 Drain the steaks on paper towels and transfer to serving plates. Garnish with chili strips, and serve with noodles, scallions and the relish.

Pork with Fennel & Aniseed

Lean pork chops, stuffed with an aniseed and orange filling, are pan-cooked with fennel in an aniseed-flavored sweet sauce.

NUTRITIONAL INFORMATION

Calories	298	Sugars	........10g
Protein	........30g	Fat	..........10g
Carbohydrate	...18g	Saturates	......3g

20 MINS   35 MINS

SERVES 4

INGREDIENTS

4 lean pork chops, 4½ oz each

⅓ cup brown rice, cooked

1 tsp orange rind, grated

4 scallions, trimmed and finely chopped

½ tsp aniseed

1 tbsp olive oil

1 fennel bulb, trimmed and thinly sliced

2 cups unsweetened orange juice

1 tbsp cornstarch

2 tbsp Pernod

salt and pepper

fennel fronds, to garnish

cooked vegetables, to serve

1 Trim away any excess fat from the pork chops. Using a small, sharp knife, make a slit in the center of each chop to create a pocket.

2 Mix the rice, orange rind, scallions, seasoning and aniseed together in a bowl.

3 Push the rice mixture into the pocket of each chop, then press gently to seal.

4 Heat the oil in a skillet and fry the pork chops on each side for 2–3 minutes until lightly browned.

5 Add the sliced fennel and orange juice to the pan, bring to a boil and simmer for 15–20 minutes until the meat is tender and cooked through. Remove the pork and fennel with a draining spoon and transfer to a serving plate.

6 Blend the cornstarch and Pernod together in a small bowl. Add the cornstarch mixture to the pan and stir into the pan juices. Cook for 2–3 minutes, stirring, until the sauce thickens.

7 Pour the Pernod sauce over the pork chops, garnish with fennel fronds and serve with some cooked vegetables.

Fish-Flavored Pork

'Fish-flavored' is a Szechuan cookery term meaning that the dish is prepared with seasonings normally used in fish dishes.

NUTRITIONAL INFORMATION

Calories	183	Sugars	.......0.2g
Protein	........14g	Fat	..........13g
Carbohydrate	....3g	Saturates	.......3g

 25 MINS   10 MINS

SERVES 4

I N G R E D I E N T S

about 2 tbsp dried wood ears

9-10½ oz pork fillet

1 tsp salt

2 tsp cornstarch paste
(see page 15)

3 tbsp vegetable oil

1 garlic clove, finely chopped

½ tsp finely chopped gingerroot

2 scallions, finely chopped, with the white
and green parts separated

2 celery stalks, thinly sliced

½ tsp sugar

1 tbsp light soy sauce

1 tbsp chili bean sauce

2 tsp rice vinegar

1 tsp rice wine or dry sherry

a few drops of sesame oil

1 Soak the wood ears in warm water for about 20 minutes, then rinse in cold water until the water is clear. Drain well, then cut into thin shreds.

2 Cut the pork into thin shreds, then mix in a bowl with a pinch of salt and about half of the cornstarch paste until well coated.

3 Heat 1 tablespoon of vegetable oil in a preheated wok. Add the pork strips and stir-fry for about 1 minute, or until the color changes, then remove with a draining spoon and set aside until required.

4 Heat the remaining oil in the wok. Add the garlic, ginger, the white parts of the scallions, the wood ears, and celery and stir-fry for about 1 minute.

5 Return the pork strips together with the salt, sugar, soy sauce, chili bean sauce, vinegar, and wine or sherry. Blend well and continue stirring for 1 minute.

6 Finally, add the green parts of the scallions and blend in the remaining cornstarch paste and sesame oil. Stir until the sauce has thickened. Transfer the fish-flavored pork to a warm serving dish and serve immediately.

COOK'S TIP

Also known as cloud ears, wood ears are a dried grey-black fungus widely used in Szechuan cooking. They are always soaked in warm water before using. Wood ears have a crunchy texture and a mild flavor.

Red Roast Pork in Soy Sauce

In this traditional Chinese dish the pork turns 'red' during cooking because it is basted in dark soy sauce.

NUTRITIONAL INFORMATION

Calories ....268 Sugars 20g
Protein ....26g Fat 8g
Carbohydrate ...22g Saturates 3g

1¼ HOURS   1¼ HOURS

SERVES 4

INGREDIENTS

1 lb lean pork fillets

6 tbsp dark soy sauce

2 tbsp dry sherry

1 tsp five-spice powder

2 garlic cloves, minced

1 inch piece gingerroot, finely chopped

1 large red bell pepper

1 large yellow bell pepper

1 large orange bell pepper

4 tbsp superfine sugar

2 tbsp red wine vinegar

TO GARNISH

scallions, shredded

fresh chives, snipped

1 Trim away excess fat and silver skin from the pork and place in a shallow dish.

2 Mix together the soy sauce, sherry, five-spice powder, garlic, and ginger. Spoon over the pork, cover and marinate in the refrigerator for at least 1 hour or until required.

3 Preheat the oven to 375°F. Drain the pork, reserving the marinade.

4 Place the pork on a roasting rack over a roasting pan. Cook in the oven, occasionally basting with the marinade, for 1 hour or until cooked through.

5 Meanwhile, halve and seed the bell peppers. Cut each bell pepper half into 3 equal portions. Arrange them on a baking sheet and bake alongside the pork for the last 30 minutes of cooking time.

6 Place the superfine sugar and vinegar in a saucepan and heat gently until the sugar dissolves. bring to a boil and simmer for 3–4 minutes, until syrupy.

7 When the pork is cooked, remove it from the oven and brush with the sugar syrup. Leave for about 5 minutes, then slice and arrange on a serving platter with the bell peppers, garnished with the scallions and chives.

8 Serve garnished with the scallions and freshly snipped chives.

Pork Stroganoff

Tender, lean pork, cooked in a tasty, rich tomato sauce is flavored with the extra tang of unsweetened yogurt.

NUTRITIONAL INFORMATION

Calories 223	Sugars 7g	
Protein 22g	Fat 10g	
Carbohydrate ...12g	Saturates 3g	

🍲 2¼ HOURS   🕐 30 MINS

SERVES 4

I N G R E D I E N T S

12 oz lean pork fillet

1 tbsp vegetable oil

1 medium onion, chopped

2 garlic cloves, minced

1 oz all purpose flour

2 tbsp tomato paste

1¾ cups Fresh Chicken or Vegetable stock
(see page 14)

4½ oz button mushrooms, sliced

1 large green bell pepper, seeded and diced

½ tsp ground nutmeg

4 tbsp low-fat unsweetened yogurt, plus
extra to serve

salt and pepper

white rice, freshly boiled, to serve

ground nutmeg, to garnish

COOK'S TIP

You can buy ready-made stock
from leading supermarkets. Although
more expensive, they are more
nutritious than bouillon cubes, which
are high in salt and artificial flavorings.

1 Trim away any excess fat and silver skin from the pork, then cut the meat into slices 1 ½ inch thick.

2 Heat the oil in a large saucepan and gently fry the pork, onion, and garlic for 4–5 minutes until lightly browned.

3 Stir in the flour and tomato paste, pour in the stock and stir to mix thoroughly.

4 Add the mushrooms, bell pepper, seasoning, and nutmeg. bring to a boil, cover and simmer for 20 minutes until the pork is tender and cooked through.

5 Remove the saucepan from the heat and stir in the yogurt.

6 Serve the pork and sauce on a bed of rice with an extra spoonful of yogurt, and garnish with a dusting of ground nutmeg.

Pork with Ratatouille Sauce

Serve this delicious combination of meat and vegetables with baked potatoes for an appetizing supper dish.

NUTRITIONAL INFORMATION

Calories . . . . . . .230 Sugars 8g
Protein . . . . .29g Fat 9g
Carbohydrate . . . .8g Saturates 3g

 10 MINS    35 MINS

SERVES 4

I N G R E D I E N T S

4 lean, boneless pork chops, about
 4½ oz each

1 tsp dried mixed herbs

salt and pepper

baked potatoes, to serve

S A U C E

1 medium onion

1 garlic clove

1 small green bell pepper, seeded

1 small yellow bell pepper, seeded

1 medium zucchini, trimmed

3½ oz button mushrooms

14 oz can chopped tomatoes

2 tbsp tomato paste

1 tsp dried mixed herbs

1 tsp superfine sugar

COOK'S TIP

This vegetable sauce could
be served with any other broiled or
baked meat or fish. It would also
make an excellent alternative filling
for
savory crêpes.

1 To make the sauce, peel and chop the onion and garlic. Dice the bell peppers. Dice the zucchini. Wipe and halve the mushrooms.

2 Place all of the vegetables in a saucepan and stir in the chopped tomatoes and tomato paste. Add the dried herbs, sugar, and plenty of seasoning. bring to a boil, cover, and simmer for 20 minutes.

3 Meanwhile, preheat the broiler to medium. Trim away any excess fat from the chops, then season on both sides and rub in the dried mixed herbs. Cook the chops for 5 minutes, then turn over and cook for a further 6–7 minutes or until cooked through.

4 Drain the chops on absorbent paper towels and serve accompanied with the sauce and baked potatoes.

Fruity Pork Skewers

Prunes and apricots bring color and flavor to these tasty pork kabobs. They are delicious eaten straight off the grill.

NUTRITIONAL INFORMATION

Calories	205	Sugars	.........8g
Protein	........21g	Fat	..........10g
Carbohydrate	....8g	Saturates	......3g

 1¼ HOURS   15 MINS

MAKES 4

I N G R E D I E N T S

4 boneless lean pork loin steaks

8 ready-to-eat prunes

8 ready-to-eat dried apricots

4 bay leaves

slices of orange and lemon, to garnish

M A R I N A D E

4 tbsp orange juice

2 tbsp olive oil

1 tsp ground bay leaves

salt and pepper

1 Trim the visible fat from the pork and cut the meat into evenly-sized chunks.

2 Place the pork in a shallow, non-metallic dish and add the prunes and apricots.

3 To make the marinade, mix together the orange juice, oil, and bay leaves in a bowl. Season with salt and pepper to taste.

4 Pour the marinade over the pork and fruit and toss until well coated. Leave to marinate in the refrigerator for at least 1 hour or preferably overnight.

5 Soak 4 wooden skewers in cold water to prevent them from catching alight on the grill.

6 Remove the pork and fruit from the marinade, using a draining spoon, reserving the marinade for basting. Thread the pork and fruit on to the skewers, alternating with the bay leaves.

7 grill the skewers on an oiled rack over medium hot coals for 10–15 minutes, turning and frequently basting with the reserved marinade, or until the pork is cooked through.

8 Transfer the pork and fruit skewers to warm serving plates. Garnish with slices of orange and lemon and serve hot.

Pork & Apple Skewers

Flavored with mustard and served with a mustard sauce, these kabobs make an ideal lunch.

NUTRITIONAL INFORMATION

Calories 290	Sugars 11g
Protein 24g	Fat 17g
Carbohydrate 11g	Saturates 5g

 10 MINS   15 MINS

SERVES 4

INGREDIENTS

1 lb pork tenderloin

2 dessert apples

a little lemon juice

1 lemon

2 tsp wholegrain mustard

2 tsp Dijon mustard

2 tbsp apple or orange juice

2 tbsp sunflower oil

crusty brown bread, to serve

MUSTARD SAUCE

1 tbsp wholegrain mustard

1 tsp Dijon mustard

6 tbsp light cream

1 To make the mustard sauce, combine the wholegrain and Dijon mustards in a small bowl and slowly blend in the cream. Leave to stand until required.

2 Cut the pork fillet into bite-size pieces and set aside until required.

3 Core the apples, then cut them into thick wedges. Toss the apple wedges in a little lemon juice–this will prevent any discoloration. Slice the lemon.

4 Thread the pork, apple, and lemon slices alternately on to 4 metal or pre-soaked wooden skewers.

5 Mix together the mustards, apple or orange juice, and sunflower oil. Brush the mixture over the kabobs and grill over hot coals for 10–15 minutes, until cooked through, frequently turning and basting the kabobs with the mustard marinade.

6 Transfer the kabobs to warm serving plates and spoon over a little of the mustard sauce. Serve with the kabobs with fresh, crusty brown bread.

Pork with Plums

Plum sauce is often used in Chinese cooking with duck or rich meat to counteract the flavor.

NUTRITIONAL INFORMATION

Calories 281	Sugars 6g
Protein 25g	Fat 14g
Carbohydrate . . .10g	Saturates 4g

 35 MINS   🕑 25 MINS

SERVES 4

I N G R E D I E N T S

1 lb pork tenderloin

1 tbsp cornstarch

2 tbsp light soy sauce

2 tbsp Chinese rice wine

4 tsp light brown sugar

pinch of ground cinnamon

5 tsp vegetable oil

2 garlic cloves, minced

2 scallions, chopped

4 tbsp plum sauce

1 tbsp hoisin sauce

⅔ cup water

dash of chili sauce

fried plum quarters and scallions, to garnish

1 Cut the pork tenderloin into thin slices.

2 Combine the cornstarch, soy sauce, rice wine, sugar, and cinnamon in a small bowl.

3 Place the pork in a shallow dish and pour the cornstarch mixture over it. Toss the meat in the marinade until it is completely coated. Cover and leave to marinate for at least 30 minutes.

4 Remove the pork from the dish, reserving the marinade.

5 Heat the oil in a preheated wok or large skillet. Add the pork and stir-fry for 3–4 minutes, until a light golden color.

6 Stir in the garlic, scallions, plum sauce, hoisin sauce, water, and chili sauce. Bring the sauce to a boil. Reduce the heat, cover and leave to simmer for 8–10 minutes, or until the pork is cooked through and tender.

7 Stir in the reserved marinade and cook, stirring, for about 5 minutes.

8 Transfer the pork stir-fry to a warm serving dish and garnish with fried plum quarters and scallions. Serve immediately.

Pan-Cooked Pork Medallions

In this dish these lean and tender cuts of meat are perfectly complemented by the dessert apples and hard cider.

NUTRITIONAL INFORMATION

Calories 256   Sugars 12g
Protein ....21g   Fat 13g
Carbohydrate ...12g   Saturates 3g

2¹/₂ HOURS   40 MINS

SERVES 4

I N G R E D I E N T S

8 lean pork medallions, about 1¾ oz each

2 tsp vegetable oil

1 medium onion, finely sliced

1 tsp superfine sugar

1 tsp dried sage

⅔ cup hard cider

⅔ cup Fresh Chicken or Vegetable Stock
(see page 14)

1 green-skinned apple

1 red-skinned apple

1 tbsp lemon juice

salt and pepper

fresh sage leaves, to garnish

freshly cooked vegetables, to serve

1 Discard the string from the pork and trim away any excess fat. Re-tie with clean string and set aside until required.

2 Heat the oil in a skillet and gently fry the onion for about 5 minutes until soft. Add the sugar and cook for 3–4 minutes until golden. Add the pork to the pan and cook for 2 minutes on each side until browned.

3 Add the sage, cider, and stock. bring to a boil and then simmer for 20 minutes.

4 Meanwhile, core and cut each apple into 8 wedges. Toss the apple wedges in lemon juice so that they do not turn brown when exposed to the air.

5 Add the apples to the pork and mix gently. Season and cook for a further 3–4 minutes until tender.

6 Remove the string from the pork and serve immediately, garnished with fresh sage and accompanied with freshly cooked vegetables.

Tangy Pork Fillet

Grilled in a packet of kitchen foil, these tasty pork fillets are served with a tangy orange sauce.

NUTRITIONAL INFORMATION

Calories ....230 Sugars 16g
Protein ....19g Fat 9g
Carbohydrate ...20g Saturates 3g

 10 MINS   55 MINS

SERVES 4

INGREDIENTS

14 oz lean pork fillet

3 tbsp orange marmalade

grated rind and juice of 1 orange

1 tbsp white wine vinegar

dash of Tabasco sauce

salt and pepper

SAUCE

1 tbsp olive oil

1 small onion, chopped

1 small green bell pepper, seeded and thinly
  sliced

1 tbsp cornstarch

⅔ cup orange juice

TO SERVE

cooked rice

mixed salad leaves

1 Place a large piece of double thickness foil in a shallow dish. Put the pork fillet in the center of the foil and season.

2 Heat the marmalade, orange rind and juice, vinegar, and Tabasco sauce in a small pan, stirring until the marmalade melts and the ingredients combine. Pour the mixture over the pork and wrap the meat in foil, making sure that the parcel is well sealed so that the juices cannot run out. Place over hot coals and grill for about 25 minutes, turning the packet occasionally.

3 For the sauce, heat the oil and cook the onion for 2–3 minutes. Add the bell pepper and cook for 3–4 minutes.

4 Remove the pork from the kitchen foil and place on to the rack. Pour the juices into the pan with the sauce.

5 grill the pork for a further 10–20 minutes, turning, until cooked through and golden on the outside..

6 In a small bowl, mix the cornstarch with a little orange juice to form a paste. Add to the sauce with the remaining cooking juices. Cook, stirring, until the sauce thickens. Slice the pork, spoon over the sauce and serve with rice and mixed salad leaves.

Pork Chops & Spicy Beans

A tasty and substantial dish, and the spicy bean mixture, served on its own, also makes a good accompaniment to other meat or chicken dishes.

NUTRITIONAL INFORMATION

Calories ......388 Sugars 5g
Protein ....20g Fat 27g
Carbohydrate ...17g Saturates 8g

  5 MINS   50 MINS

SERVES 4

I N G R E D I E N T S

3 tbsp vegetable oil

4 lean pork chops, rind removed

2 onions, peeled and thinly sliced

2 garlic cloves, peeled and minced

2 fresh green chilies, seeded and
    chopped or use 1-2 tsp minced
    chili (from a jar)

1 in piece gingerroot, peeled and chopped

1½ tsp cumin seeds

1½ tsp ground coriander

2½ cups stock or water

2 tbsp tomato paste

½ eggplant, trimmed and cut into ½ inch
    dice

salt

1 x 14 oz can red kidney beans, drained

4 tbsp heavy cream

sprigs of cilantro, to garnish

2 Add the sliced onions, garlic, chilies, ginger, and spices and fry gently for 2 minutes. Stir in the stock or water, tomato paste, diced eggplant, and season with salt and pepper.

3 Bring the mixture to a boil, place the pork chops on top, then cover and simmer gently over medium heat for 30 minutes .

4 Remove the chops for a moment and stir the red kidney beans and heavy cream into the mixture. Return the chops to the pan, cover and heat through gently for 5 minutes.

5 Taste and adjust the seasoning, if necessary. Serve hot, garnished with cilantro sprigs.

1 Heat the ghee or vegetable oil in a large skillet, add the pork chops and fry until sealed and browned on both sides. Remove from the pan and set aside until required.

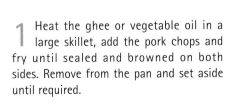   

Lamb with Rosemary

This is a pretty dish of pink tender lamb tenderloin served on a light green bed of mashed leeks and potatoes.

NUTRITIONAL INFORMATION

Calories ....388 Sugars 11g
Protein ....35g Fat 12g
Carbohydrate ...38g Saturates 5g

1¼ HOURS   55 MINS

SERVES 4

I N G R E D I E N T S

1 lb lean lamb tenderloin

4 tbsp redcurrant jelly

1 tbsp chopped fresh rosemary

1 garlic clove, minced

1 lb potatoes, diced

1 lb leeks, sliced

⅔ cup fresh vegetable stock, (see page 14)

4 tsp low-fat unsweetened fromage blanc

salt and pepper

freshly steamed vegetables, to serve

T O   G A R N I S H

chopped fresh rosemary

redcurrants

1 Put the lamb in a shallow baking pan. Blend 2 tablespoons of the redcurrant jelly with the rosemary, garlic, and seasoning. Brush over the lamb and cook in a preheated oven at 450°F, brushing occasionally with any cooking juices, for 30 minutes.

2 Meanwhile, place the potatoes in a saucepan and cover with water. bring to a boil, and cook for 8 minutes until soft. Drain well.

3 Put the leeks in a saucepan with the stock. Cover and simmer for 7–8 minutes or until soft. Drain, reserving the cooking liquid.

4 Place the potato and leeks in a bowl and mash with a potato masher. Season and stir in the fromage blanc. Transfer to a warmed platter and keep warm.

5 In a saucepan, melt the remaining redcurrant jelly and stir in the leek cooking liquid. Boil for 5 minutes.

6 Slice the lamb and arrange over the mash. Spoon the sauce over the top. Garnish the lamb with rosemary and redcurrants and serve with freshly steamed vegetables.

Turkish Lamb Stew

A delicious blend of flavors with lamb, onions, and tomatoes, complete with potatoes to make the perfect one-pot dish for two.

NUTRITIONAL INFORMATION

Calories 442   Sugars 5g
Protein . . . . .41g   Fat 17g
Carbohydrate . . .35g   Saturates 7g

  10 MINS   1¼ HOURS

SERVES 2

I N G R E D I E N T S

12 oz lean boneless lamb

1 large or 2 small onions

1 garlic clove, minced

½ red, yellow or green bell pepper, diced roughly

1¼ cups stock

1 tbsp balsamic vinegar

2 tomatoes, peeled and chopped roughly

1½ tsp tomato paste

1 bay leaf

½ tsp dried sage

½ tsp dried dill weed

12 oz potatoes

6–8 black olives, halved and pitted

salt and pepper

1 Cut the piece of lamb into cubes of about ³/₄ inch, discarding any excess fat or gristle.

2 Place in a non-stick saucepan with no extra fat and heat gently until the fat runs and the meat begins to seal.

3 Cut the onion into 8 wedges. Add to the lamb with the garlic and fry for a further 3–4 minutes.

4 Add the bell pepper, stock, vinegar, tomatoes, tomato paste, bay leaf, sage, dill weed, and seasoning. Cover and simmer gently for 30 minutes.

5 Peel the potatoes and cut into ³/₄ inch cubes. Add to the stew and stir well. If necessary, add a little more boiling stock or water if it seems a little dry. Cover the pan again and simmer for a further 25–30 minutes, or until quite tender.

6 Add the olives and adjust the seasoning. Simmer for a further 5 minutes and serve with vegetables or a salad and crusty bread.

COOK'S TIP

A good accompaniment would be a salad made of shredded white cabbage, Little Gem lettuce, coarsely grated carrot, diced avocado, or cucumber and scallions.

Lamb Hotch Potch

This classic recipe using lamb cutlets layered between sliced potatoes, kidneys, onions, and herbs makes a perfect meal on a cold winter's day.

NUTRITIONAL INFORMATION

Calories	420	Sugars	.........2g
Protein	........41g	Fat	..........15g
Carbohydrate	...31g	Saturates	......8g

15 MINS   2 HOURS

SERVES 4

INGREDIENTS

1½ lb lean lamb neck cutlets

2 lamb's kidneys

1½ lb waxy potatoes, scrubbed and sliced thinly

1 large onion, sliced thinly

2 tbsp chopped fresh thyme

⅔ cup lamb stock

2 tbsp butter, melted

salt and pepper

fresh thyme sprigs, to garnish

1 Remove any excess fat from the lamb. Skin and core the kidneys and cut them into slices.

2 Arrange a layer of potatoes in the base of a 3½ cup ovenproof dish.

3 Arrange the lamb neck cutlets on top of the potatoes and cover with the sliced kidneys, onion, and chopped thyme.

4 Pour the lamb stock over the meat and season to taste with salt and pepper.

VARIATION

Traditionally, oysters are also included in this tasty hotch potch. Add them to the layers along with the kidneys, if wished.

5 Layer the remaining potato slices on top, overlapping to completely cover the meat and sliced onion.

6 Brush the potato slices with the butter, cover the dish and cook in a preheated oven, 350°F, for 1½ hours.

7 Remove the lid and cook for a further 30 minutes until golden brown on top.

8 Garnish with fresh thyme sprigs and serve hot.

Sweet Lamb Fillet

Lamb fillet, enhanced by a sweet and spicy glaze, is cooked on the grill in a kitchen foil packet for deliciously moist results.

NUTRITIONAL INFORMATION

Calories ....258 Sugars 13g
Protein ....24g Fat 13g
Carbohydrate ...13g Saturates 5g

 5 MINS   1 HOUR

SERVES 4

I N G R E D I E N T S

2 fillets of neck of lean lamb, each 8 oz

1 tbsp olive oil

½ onion, chopped finely

1 clove garlic, minced

1 inch piece gingerroot, grated

5 tbsp apple juice

3 tbsp smooth apple sauce

1 tbsp light muscovado sugar

1 tbsp tomato catsup

½ tsp mild mustard

salt and pepper

green salad leaves, croûtons, and fresh
  crusty bread, to serve

1 Place the lamb fillet on a large piece of double thickness kitchen foil. Season with salt and pepper to taste.

2 Heat the oil in a small pan and fry the onion and garlic for 2–3 minutes until softened but not browned. Stir in the grated ginger and cook for 1 minute, stirring occasionally.

3 Stir in the apple juice, apple sauce, sugar, catsup, and mustard and bring to a boil. Boil rapidly for about 10 minutes until reduced by half. Stir the mixture occasionally so that it does not burn and stick to the base of the pan.

4 Brush half of the sauce over the lamb, then wrap up the lamb in the kitchen foil to completely enclose it. Grill the lamb packets over hot coals for about 25 minutes, turning the packet over occasionally.

5 Open out the kitchen foil and brush the lamb with some of the sauce. Continue to grill for a further 15–20 minutes or until cooked through.

6 Place the lamb on a chopping board, remove the foil, and cut into thick slices. Transfer to serving plates and spoon over the remaining sauce. Serve with green salad leaves, croûtons, and fresh crusty bread.

Stir-Fried Lamb with Orange

Oranges and lamb are a great combination because the tangy citrus flavor offsets the fuller flavor of the lamb.

NUTRITIONAL INFORMATION

Calories ....209 Sugars 4g
Protein ....25g Fat 10g
Carbohydrate ....5g Saturates 5g

5 MINS   30 MINS

SERVES 4

INGREDIENTS

1 lb ground lamb

2 cloves garlic, minced

1 tsp cumin seeds

1 tsp ground coriander

1 red onion, sliced

finely grated zest and juice of
    1 orange

2 tbsp soy sauce

1 orange, peeled and segmented

salt and pepper

snipped fresh chives, to garnish

1 Heat a wok or large, heavy-bottomed skillet, without adding any oil.

2 Add the ground lamb to the wok. Dry fry the ground lamb for 5 minutes, or until the lamb is evenly browned. Drain away any excess fat from the wok.

3 Add the garlic, cumin seeds, coriander, and red onion to the wok and stir-fry for a further 5 minutes.

4 Stir in the finely grated orange zest and juice and the soy sauce, mixing until thoroughly combined. Cover, reduce the heat, and leave to simmer, stirring occasionally, for 15 minutes.

5 Remove the lid, increase the heat, and add the orange segments. Stir to mix.

6 Season with salt and pepper to taste and heat through for a further 2–3 minutes.

7 Transfer the stir-fry to warm serving plates and garnish with snipped fresh chives. Serve immediately.

COOK'S TIP

If you wish to serve wine with your meal, try light, dry white wines and lighter Burgundy-style red wines as they blend well with Oriental food.

Savory Hotch Potch

This hearty lamb stew is full of vegetables and herbs, and is topped with a layer of crisp, golden potato slices.

NUTRITIONAL INFORMATION

Calories	365	Sugars 5g
Protein	........23g	Fat 11g
Carbohydrate	...48g	Saturates 4g

   15 MINS   2 HOURS

SERVES 4

I N G R E D I E N T S

8 middle neck lean lamb chops, neck of lamb or any lean stewing lamb on the bone

1–2 garlic cloves, minced

2 lamb's kidneys (optional)

1 large onion, sliced thinly

1 leek, sliced

2–3 carrots, sliced

1 tsp chopped fresh tarragon or sage, or ½ tsp dried tarragon or sage

2 lb potatoes, sliced thinly

1¼ cups stock

2 tbsp margarine, melted, or 1 tbsp vegetable oil

salt and pepper

chopped fresh parsley, to garnish

1 Trim any excess fat from the lamb, season well with salt and pepper and arrange in a large ovenproof casserole. Sprinkle with the garlic.

2 If using kidneys, remove the skin, halve and cut out the cores. Chop into small pieces and sprinkle over the lamb.

3 Place the vegetables over the lamb, allowing the pieces to slip in between the meat, then sprinkle with the herbs.

4 Arrange the potato slices over the meat and vegetables, in an overlapping pattern.

5 Bring the stock to a boil, season with salt and pepper to taste, then pour over the casserole.

6 Brush the potatoes with the melted margarine or vegetable oil, cover with greased foil or a lid and cook in a preheated oven at 350°F for 1½ hours.

7 Remove the foil or lid from the potatoes, increase the temperature to 425°F and return the casserole to the oven for about 30 minutes until the potatoes are browned.

8 Garnish the hotch potch with the chopped fresh parsley and serve immediately.

Kibbeh

This Lebanese grill dish is similar to the Turkish kofte and the Indian kofta, but the spices used to flavor the meat are quite different.

NUTRITIONAL INFORMATION

Calories 232	Sugars 3g
Protein 19g	Fat 13g
Carbohydrate 9g	Saturates 4g

  1 HOUR 15 MINS

SERVES 4

I N G R E D I E N T S

2¾ oz couscous

1 small onion

12 oz lean ground lamb

½ tsp ground cinnamon

¼ tsp cayenne pepper

4 tsp ground allspice

green salad and onion rings, to serve

B A S T E

2 tbsp tomato catsup

2 tbsp sunflower oil

1 Place the couscous in a large bowl, cover with cold water and leave to stand for 30 minutes or until the couscous has swelled and softened. Alternatively, soak the couscous according to the directions on the packet.

2 Drain the couscous through a strainer and squeeze out as much moisture as you can.

3 If you have a food processor, add the onion and chop finely. Add the lamb and process briefly to chop the ground lamb further. If you do not have a processor, grate the onion then add to the lamb.

4 Combine the couscous, lamb, and spices and mix well together. Divide the mixture into 8 equal sized portions. Press and shape the mixture around 8 skewers, pressing the mixture together firmly so that it holds it shape. Leave to chill for at least 30 minutes or until required.

5 To make the baste, combine the oil and catsup.

6 grill the kibbeh over hot coals for 10–15 minutes, turning and basting frequently. Serve with grilled onion rings and green salad leaves.

Minty Lamb Kabobs

These spicy lamb kabobs go well with the cool cucumber and yogurt dip. In the summer you can grill the kabobs outside.

NUTRITIONAL INFORMATION

Calories 295	Sugars 4g	
Protein 29g	Fat 18g	
Carbohydrate 4g	Saturates 9g	

5 MINS   20 MINS

SERVES 4

I N G R E D I E N T S

2 tsp coriander seeds

2 tsp cumin seeds

3 cloves

3 green cardamom pods

6 black peppercorns

½ inch piece gingerroot

2 garlic cloves

2 tbsp chopped fresh mint

1 small onion, chopped

1¾ cups ground lamb

½ tsp salt

lime slices to serve

D I P

⅔ cup low-fat unsweetened yogurt

2 tbsp chopped fresh mint

3 inch piece of cucumber, grated

1 tsp mango chutney

1 Heat a skillet and dry-fry the coriander, cumin, cloves, cardamom pods, and peppercorns until they turn a shade darker and release a roasted aroma.

2 Grind the spices in a coffee grinder, spice mill or a mortar and pestle.

3 Put the ginger and garlic into a food processor or blender and process to a purée. Add the ground spices, mint, onion, lamb, and salt and process until chopped finely. Alternatively, finely chop the garlic and ginger and mix with the ground spices and remaining kebab ingredients.

4 Mold the kabob mixture into small sausage shapes on 4 kabob skewers.

Cook under a preheated hot broiler for 10–15 minutes, turning the skewers occasionally.

5 To make the dip, mix together the yogurt, mint, cucumber, and mango chutney.

6 Serve the kabobs with lime slices and the dip.

Lamb Kabobs with Herbs

Serve the kabobs sizzling hot, and the cucumber and yogurt sauce as cool as can be–it is a delicious partnership.

NUTRITIONAL INFORMATION

Calories . . . . . . .238 Sugars 7g
Protein . . . . .21g Fat 14g
Carbohydrate . . . .7g Saturates 5g

2¼ HOURS   15 MINS

SERVES 4

INGREDIENTS

2 lb lean leg of lamb, trimmed
    of fat

3 tbsp olive oil

1 tbsp red wine vinegar

juice of ½ lemon

3 tbsp low-fat unsweetened yogurt

1 tbsp dried oregano

2 large garlic cloves, minced

2 dried bay leaves, crumbled

4 fresh bay leaves

2 tbsp chopped parsley

salt and pepper

SAUCE

1¼ cups low-fat unsweetened yogurt

1 garlic clove, minced

¼ tsp salt

½ small cucumber, peeled and finely
    chopped

3 tbsp finely chopped mint

pinch of paprika

1 Cut the lamb into cubes about 1½-2 inches square. Pat dry with paper towels to ensure that the meat stays crisp and firm on the outside when broiled.

2 Whisk together the olive oil, wine vinegar, lemon juice, and yogurt. Stir in the oregano, garlic, and crumbled bay leaves and season with salt and pepper. Place the meat cubes in the marinade and stir until well coated in the mixture. Cover and place in the refrigerator for at least 2 hours.

3 Meanwhile, make the sauce. Place the unsweetened yogurt in a large bowl. Stir in the garlic, salt, cucumber, and mint. Cover with plastic wrap and set aside in the refrigerator until required.

4 Heat the broiler to high. With a draining spoon, lift the meat from the marinade and shake off any excess liquid. Divide the meat into 4 equal portions. Thread the meat and the fresh bay leaves on to 4 skewers.

5 Broil the kabobs for about 4 minutes on each side, basting frequently with the marinade. At this stage the meat should be crisp on the outside and slightly pink on the inside. If you prefer lamb well done, cook the kabobs for a little longer.

6 Sprinkle the kabobs with parsley and serve at once. Sprinkle the paprika over the sauce and serve chilled.

Lamb & Potato Moussaka

Ground lamb makes a very tasty and authentic moussaka. For a change, use ground beef.

NUTRITIONAL INFORMATION

Calories 422   Sugars 8g
Protein . . . . .32g   Fat 18g
Carbohydrate . . .35g   Saturates 8g

45 MINS   1¼ HOURS

SERVES 4

I N G R E D I E N T S

1 large eggplant, sliced

1 tbsp olive or vegetable oil

1 onion, chopped finely

1 garlic clove, minced

12 oz lean ground lamb

9 oz mushrooms, sliced

15 oz can chopped tomatoes with herbs

⅔ cup lamb or vegetable stock

2 tbsp cornstarch

2 tbsp water

1 lb potatoes, parboiled for 10 minutes and sliced

2 eggs

½ cup low-fat soft cheese

⅔ cup low-fat unsweetened yogurt

½ cup grated low-fat sharp Cheddar cheese

salt and pepper

fresh flat-leaf parsley, to garnish

green salad, to serve

1 Lay the eggplant slices on a clean surface and sprinkle liberally with salt, to extract the bitter juices. Leave for 10 minutes then turn the slices over and repeat. Put in a colander, rinse and drain well.

2 Meanwhile, heat the oil in a saucepan and fry the onion and garlic for 3–4 minutes. Add the lamb and mushrooms and cook for 5 minutes, until browned. Stir in the tomatoes and stock, bring to a boil and simmer for 10 minutes. Mix the cornstarch with the water and stir into the pan. Cook, stirring, until thickened.

3 Spoon half the mixture into an ovenproof dish. Cover with the eggplant slices, then the remaining lamb mixture. Arrange the sliced potatoes on top.

4 Beat together the eggs, soft cheese, yogurt, and seasoning. Pour over the potatoes to cover them completely. Sprinkle with the grated cheese.

5 Bake in a preheated oven at 375°F for 45 minutes until the topping is set and golden brown. Garnish with flat-leaf parsley and serve with a green salad.

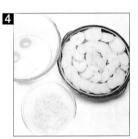

Masala Kabobs

Indian kabob dishes are not necessarily cooked on a skewer; they can also be served in a dish and are always dry dishes with no sauce.

NUTRITIONAL INFORMATION

Calories 294	Sugars 0g	
Protein 35g	Fat 17g	
Carbohydrate 0g	Saturates 7g	

1¼ HOURS   20 MINS

SERVES 4

INGREDIENTS

1 dried bay leaf

1 inch piece gingerroot, chopped

1 inch cinnamon stick

1 tsp coriander seeds

½ tsp salt

1 tsp fennel seeds

1 tsp chili powder

1 tsp garam masala

1 tsp lemon juice

1 tsp ground turmeric

1 tbsp oil

1 lb 10 oz lamb neck fillet

TO GARNISH

sprigs of fresh cilantro

lemon wedges

TO SERVE

bread

chutney

1 Use a food processor, blender or mortar and pestle to grind together the bay leaf, ginger, cinnamon, coriander seeds, salt, fennel seeds, and chili powder.

2 Combine this spice mix with the garam masala, lemon juice, turmeric, and oil in a large bowl.

3 Cut the lamb into ¼ inch slices. Add to the spice mix and leave to marinate at room temperature for about 1 hour, or in the refrigerator for 3 hours or overnight.

4 Spread out the pieces of lamb on a baking sheet and cook in a preheated oven, 400°F, for 20 minutes until well done. Transfer the pieces of lamb to paper towels to drain any excess fat.

5 Thread 3 or 4 pieces of meat on to each skewer and garnish with sprigs of fresh cilantro and lemon wedges.

6 Serve the masala kabobs hot with bread and chutney.

Lamb Couscous

Couscous is a dish that originated among the Berbers of North Africa. When steamed, it is a delicious plump grain, ideal for serving with stews.

NUTRITIONAL INFORMATION

Calories 537	Sugars 11g
Protein 32g	Fat 14g
Carbohydrate . . .73g	Saturates 4g

15 MINS   35 MINS

SERVES 4

INGREDIENTS

2 medium red onions, sliced

juice of 1 lemon

1 large red bell pepper, seeded and thickly sliced

1 large green bell pepper, seeded and thickly sliced

1 large orange bell pepper, seeded and thickly sliced

pinch of saffron strands

cinnamon stick, broken

1 tbsp clear honey

1¼ cups vegetable stock

2 tsp olive oil

12 oz lean lamb fillet, trimmed and sliced

1 tsp Harissa paste

7 oz can chopped tomatoes

15 oz can garbanzo beans, drained

12 oz precooked couscous

2 tsp ground cinnamon

salt and pepper

1 Toss the onions in the lemon juice and transfer to a saucepan. Mix in the bell peppers, saffron, cinnamon stick and honey. Pour in the stock, bring to a boil, cover and simmer for 5 minutes.

2 Meanwhile, heat the oil in a skillet and gently fry the lamb for 3–4 minutes until browned all over.

3 Using a draining spoon, drain the lamb and transfer it to the pan with the onions and peppers. Season and stir in the Harissa paste, tomatoes, and garbanzo beans. Mix well, bring back to a boil and simmer, uncovered, for 20 minutes.

4 Soak the couscous, following the packet directions. Bring a saucepan of water to a boil. Put the couscous in a steamer or strainer lined with cheesecloth over the pan of boiling water. Cover and steam.

5 Transfer the couscous to a serving plate and dust with ground cinnamon. Discard the cinnamon stick and spoon the stew over the couscous.

Lamb Dopiaza

Do Pyaza usually indicates a dish of meat cooked with plenty of onions, and in this recipe the onions are cooked in two different ways.

NUTRITIONAL INFORMATION

Calories	433	Sugars	.........6g
Protein	........42g	Fat	..........27g
Carbohydrate	....7g	Saturates	......8g

  10 MINS 🕐 1³/₄ HOURS

SERVES 4

INGREDIENTS

2 tbsp ghee or vegetable oil

2 large onions, sliced finely

4 garlic cloves, 2 of them minced

1 lb 10 oz lean boneless lamb, cut into 1 inch cubes

1 tsp chili powder

1 inch piece gingerroot, grated

2 fresh green chilies, chopped

½ tsp ground turmeric

½ cup low-fat unsweetened yogurt

2 cloves

1 inch piece cinnamon stick

1¼ cups water

2 tbsp chopped fresh cilantro

3 tbsp lemon juice

salt and pepper

naan bread, to serve

1 Heat the ghee or oil in a large saucepan and add 1 of the onions and all the garlic. Cook for 2–3 minutes, stirring constantly.

2 Add the lamb and brown all over. Remove and set aside. Add the chili powder, ginger, chilies, and turmeric and stir for a further 30 seconds.

3 Add plenty of salt and pepper, the yogurt, cloves, cinnamon, and water.

4 Return the lamb to the pan. bring to a boil then simmer for 10 minutes.

5 Transfer the mixture to an ovenproof dish and cook uncovered in a preheated oven, 350°F, for 40 minutes.

6 Adjust the seasoning, if necessary, stir in the remaining onion and cook uncovered for a further 40 minutes.

7 Add the fresh cilantro and lemon juice.

8 Transfer the lamb dopiaza to a warm serving dish and serve with naan bread.

Venison & Garlic Mash

Rich game is best served with a sweet fruit sauce. Here the venison steaks are cooked with sweet, juicy prunes and redcurrant jelly.

NUTRITIONAL INFORMATION

Calories 602   Sugars 18g
Protein . . . . .51g   Fat 14g
Carbohydrate . . .62g   Saturates 1g

 10 MINS   35 MINS

SERVES 4

I N G R E D I E N T S

8 medallions of venison, 2¾ oz each

1 tbsp vegetable oil

1 red onion, chopped

⅔ cup fresh beef stock

⅔ cup red wine

3 tbsp redcurrant jelly

3½ oz no-need-to-soak dried, pitted prunes

2 tsp cornstarch

2 tbsp brandy

salt and pepper

pattypans, to serve (optional)

GARLIC MASH

2 lb potatoes, peeled and diced

½ tsp garlic paste

2 tbsp low-fat unsweetened fromage blanc

4 tbsp fresh parsley, chopped

1 Trim off any excess fat from the meat and season with salt and pepper on both sides. Heat the oil in a skillet and fry the lamb with the onions for 2 minutes on each side until brown.

2 Lower the heat and pour in the stock and wine. Add the redcurrant jelly and prunes and stir until the jelly melts. Cover and simmer for 10 minutes.

3 Meanwhile, make the garlic mash. Place the potatoes in a saucepan and cover with water. bring to a boil and cook for 8–10 minutes. Drain well and mash until smooth. Add the garlic paste, fromage blanc, and parsley and blend thoroughly. Season, set aside and keep warm.

4 Remove the medallions from the skillet with a draining spoon and keep warm.

5 Blend the cornstarch with the brandy in a small bowl and add to the pan juices. Heat, stirring, until thickened. Season with salt and pepper to taste. Serve the venison with the redcurrant and prune sauce, garlic mash and pattypans (if using).

Poultry & Game

Chicken and turkey contain less fat than red meats, and even less if you remove the skin first. Duck is a rich meat with a distinctive flavor, and you only need a small amount

to create flavorsome dishes which are healthy too. Because chicken itself does not have a very strong flavor, it marries well with other ingredients and the recipes in this chapter exploit that quality. Fruit features heavily in low-fat diets and it works particularly well with chicken. In this chapter there are several examples. Broiling, or grilling, is a very healthy way to cook as it requires little or no fat, and it produces deliciously succulent meat with a cripsy coating,

Chicken with a Yogurt Crust

A spicy, Indian-style coating is baked around lean chicken to give a full flavor. Serve with a tomato, cucumber, and cilantro relish.

NUTRITIONAL INFORMATION

Calories 176   Sugars 5g
Protein ....30g   Fat 4g
Carbohydrate ....5g   Saturates 1g

 10 MINS   35 MINS

SERVES 4

INGREDIENTS

1 garlic clove, minced

1 inch piece gingerroot, finely chopped

1 fresh green chili, seeded and finely chopped

6 tbsp low-fat unsweetened yogurt

1 tbsp tomato paste

1 tsp ground turmeric

1 tsp garam masala

1 tbsp lime juice

4 boneless, skinless chicken breasts, each 4½ oz

salt and pepper

wedges of lime or lemon, to serve

RELISH

4 medium tomatoes

¼ cucumber

1 small red onion

2 tbsp fresh cilantro, chopped

1 Preheat the oven to 375°F

2 Place the garlic, ginger, chili, yogurt, tomato paste, spices, lime juice, and seasoning in a bowl and mix to combine all the ingredients.

3 Wash and pat dry the chicken breasts with absorbent paper towels and place them on a baking sheet.

4 Brush or spread the spicy yogurt mix over the chicken and bake in the oven for 30–35 minutes until the meat is tender and cooked through.

5 Meanwhile, make the relish. Finely chop the tomatoes, cucumber, and

onion and mix together with the cilantro. Season with salt and pepper to taste, cover and chill in the refrigerator until required.

6 Drain the cooked chicken on absorbent paper towels and serve hot with the relish and lemon or lime wedges. Alternatively, allow to cool, chill for at least 1 hour and serve sliced as part of a salad.

Chicken in Spicy Yogurt

Make sure the grill is really hot before you start cooking. The coals should be white and glow red when fanned.

NUTRITIONAL INFORMATION

Calories ....74 Sugars 2g
Protein ....9g Fat 4g
Carbohydrate ....2g Saturates 1g

4³/₄ HOURS   25 MINS

SERVES 6

INGREDIENTS

3 dried red chilies

2 tbsp coriander seeds

2 tsp turmeric

2 tsp garam masala

4 garlic cloves, minced

½ onion, chopped

1 inch piece fresh gingerroot,
    grated

2 tbsp lime juice

1 tsp salt

½ cup low-fat unsweetened yogurt

1 tbsp oil

4 lb 8 oz lean chicken, cut into
    6 pieces, or 6 chicken portions

TO SERVE

chopped tomatoes

diced cucumber

sliced red onion

cucumber and yogurt

1 Grind together the chilies, coriander seed, turmeric, garam masala, garlic, onion, ginger, lime juice, and salt with a mortar and pestle or grinder.

2 Gently heat a skillet and add the spice mixture. Stir until fragrant, about 2

minutes, and turn into a shallow non-porous dish.

3 Add the unsweetened yogurt and the oil to the spice paste and mix well to combine.

4 Remove the skin from the chicken portions and make three slashes in the flesh of each piece. Add the chicken to the dish containing the yogurt and spice mixture and coat the pieces completely in the marinade. Cover with plastic wrap and chill for at least 4 hours. Remove the dish from the refrigerator and leave covered at room temperature for 30 minutes before cooking.

5 Wrap the chicken pieces in foil, sealing well so the juices cannot escape.

6 Cook the chicken pieces over a very hot grill for about 15 minutes, turning once.

7 Remove the foil, with tongs, and brown the chicken on the grill for 5 minutes.

8 Serve the chicken with the chopped tomatoes, diced cucumber, sliced red onion, and the yogurt and cucumber mixture.

Spicy Tomato Chicken

These low-fat, spicy skewers are cooked in a matter of minutes–assemble ahead of time.

NUTRITIONAL INFORMATION

Calories	195	Sugars	........11g
Protein	........28g	Fat	...........4g
Carbohydrate	...12g	Saturates	......1g

10 MINS · 10 MINS

SERVES 4

I N G R E D I E N T S

1 lb skinless, boneless chicken breasts

3 tbsp tomato paste

2 tbsp clear honey

2 tbsp Worcestershire sauce

1 tbsp chopped fresh rosemary

9 oz cherry tomatoes

sprigs of rosemary, to garnish

couscous or rice, to serve

1 Cut the chicken into 1 inch chunks and place in a bowl.

2 Mix together the tomato paste, honey, Worcestershire sauce, and rosemary. Add to the chicken, stirring to coat evenly.

3 Alternating the chicken pieces and cherry tomatoes, thread them on to eight wooden skewers.

4 Spoon over any remaining glaze. Cook under a preheated hot broiler for 8–10 minutes, turning occasionally, until the chicken is thoroughly cooked.

5 Serve on a bed of couscous or rice and garnish with sprigs of rosemary.

COOK'S TIP

Couscous is made from semolina that has been made into separate grains. It usually just needs moistening or steaming before serving.

Karahi Chicken

A karahi is an extremely versatile two-handled metal pan, similar to a wok. Food is always cooked over a high heat in a karahi.

NUTRITIONAL INFORMATION

Calories	270	Sugars	....1g
Protein	....41g	Fat	....11g
Carbohydrate	....1g	Saturates	....2g

🥔 5 MINS   🕐 20 MINS

SERVES 4

INGREDIENTS

2 tbsp ghee

3 garlic cloves, minced

1 onion, chopped finely

2 tbsp garam masala

1 tsp coriander seeds, ground

½ tsp dried mint

1 bay leaf

1 lb 10 oz lean boneless chicken meat, diced

scant 1 cup chicken stock

1 tbsp fresh cilantro, chopped

salt

warm naan bread or chapatis, to serve

1 Heat the ghee in a karahi, wok or a large, heavy skillet. Add the garlic and onion. Stir-fry for about 4 minutes until the onion is golden.

2 Stir in the garam masala, ground coriander, mint, and bay leaf.

3 Add the chicken and cook over a high heat, stirring occasionally, for about 5 minutes. Add the stock and simmer for 10 minutes, until the sauce has thickened

and the chicken juices run clear when the meat is tested with a sharp knife.

4 Stir in the fresh cilantro and salt to taste, mix well, and serve immediately with warm naan bread or chapatis.

COOK'S TIP

Always heat a karahi or wok before you add the oil to help maintain the high temperature.

Chicken Tikka

Traditionally, chicken tikka is cooked in a clay tandoori oven, but it works well on the grill, too.

NUTRITIONAL INFORMATION

Calories 173	Sugars 6g
Protein 28g	Fat 4g
Carbohydrate 6g	Saturates 2g

2¼ HOURS   15 MINS

SERVES 4

I N G R E D I E N T S

4 chicken breasts, skinned and boned

½ tsp salt

4 tbsp lemon or lime juice

oil, for brushing

M A R I N A D E

⅔ cup low-fat unsweetened yogurt

2 cloves garlic, minced

1 inch piece gingerroot, peeled and grated

1 tsp ground cumin

1 tsp chili powder

½ tsp ground coriander

½ tsp ground turmeric

S A U C E

⅔ cup low-fat unsweetened yogurt

1 tsp mint sauce

1 Cut the chicken into 1 inch cubes. Sprinkle with the salt and the citrus juice. Set aside for 10 minutes.

2 To make the marinade, combine all the ingredients together in a small bowl until well mixed.

3 Thread the cubes of chicken on to skewers. Brush the marinade over the chicken. Cover and leave to marinate in the refrigerator for at least 2 hours, preferably overnight. Grill the chicken skewers over hot coals, brushing with oil and turning frequently, for 15 minutes or until cooked through.

4 Meanwhile, combine the yogurt and mint to make the sauce and serve with the chicken.

COOK'S TIP

Use the marinade to coat chicken portions, such as drumsticks, if you prefer. grill over medium hot coals for 30–40 minutes, until the juices run clear when the chicken is pierced with a skewer.

Chicken Tikka Kabobs

Chicken tikka is a low-fat Indian dish. Recipes vary but you can try your own combination of spices to suit your personal taste.

NUTRITIONAL INFORMATION

Calories	191	Sugars	. . . . .8g
Protein	. . . . .30g	Fat	. . . . .4g
Carbohydrate	. . . .8g	Saturates	. . . . . .2g

2¼ HOURS   15 MINS

SERVES 4

I N G R E D I E N T S

4 × 4½ oz boneless, skinless chicken breasts,

1 garlic clove, minced

1 tsp grated gingerroot

1 fresh green chili, seeded and chopped finely

6 tbsp low-fat unsweetened yogurt

1 tbsp tomato paste

1 tsp ground cumin

1 tsp ground coriander

1 tsp ground turmeric

1 large ripe mango

1 tbsp lime juice

salt and pepper

fresh cilantro leaves, to garnish

TO SERVE

boiled white rice

lime wedges

mixed salad

warmed naan bread

1 Cut the chicken into 1 inch cubes and place in a shallow dish.

2 Mix together the garlic, ginger, chili, yogurt, tomato paste, spices, and seasoning. Spoon over the chicken, cover and chill for 2 hours.

3 Using a vegetable peeler, peel the skin from the mango. Slice down either side of the pit and cut the mango flesh into cubes. Toss in lime juice, cover, and chill until required.

4 Thread the chicken and mango pieces alternately on to 8 skewers. Place the skewers on a broiler rack and brush the chicken with the yogurt marinade and the lime juice left from the mango.

5 Place under a preheated moderate broiler for 6–7 minutes. Turn over, brush again with the marinade and lime juice and cook for a further 6–7 minutes until the chicken juices run clear when pierced with a sharp knife.

6 Serve on a bed of rice on a warmed platter, garnished with fresh cilantro leaves and accompanied by lime wedges, salad, and naan bread.

Spiced Apricot Chicken

Spiced chicken legs are partially boned and packed with dried apricot.
A golden, spiced, low-fat yogurt coating keeps the chicken moist.

NUTRITIONAL INFORMATION

Calories ....305 Sugars 21g
Protein ....15g Fat 8g
Carbohydrate ...45g Saturates 1g

 10 MINS   40 MINS

SERVES 4

INGREDIENTS

4 large, lean skinless chicken leg quarters

finely grated rind of 1 lemon

1 cup ready-to-eat dried apricots

1 tbsp ground cumin

1 tsp ground turmeric

½ cup low-fat unsweetened yogurt

salt and pepper

TO SERVE

1½ cups brown rice

2 tbsp slivered hazelnuts, toasted

2 tbsp sunflower seeds, toasted

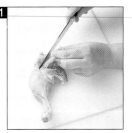  

1 Remove any excess fat from the chicken legs. Use a small sharp knife to carefully cut the flesh away from the thigh bone. Scrape the meat away down as far as the knuckle. Grasp the thigh bone firmly and twist it to break it away from the drumstick.

2 Open out the boned part of the chicken and sprinkle with lemon rind and pepper. Pack the dried apricots into each piece of chicken.

3 Fold over to enclose, and secure with tooth picks. Mix together the cumin, turmeric, yogurt and salt and pepper, then brush this mixture over the chicken to coat evenly. Place the chicken in an ovenproof dish and bake in a preheated oven, 375°F, for 35–40 minutes, or until the chicken juices run clear, not pink, when pierced through the thickest part with a skewer.

4 Meanwhile, cook the rice in boiling, lightly salted water until just tender, then drain well. Stir the hazelnuts and sunflower seeds into the rice and serve.

VARIATION

For a change use dried herbs instead of spices to flavor the coating. Use dried oregano, tarragon, or rosemary–but remember dried herbs are more powerful than fresh, so you will only need a little.

Thai Red Chicken

This is a really colorful dish, the red of the tomatoes perfectly complementing the orange of the sweet potato.

NUTRITIONAL INFORMATION

Calories 249	Sugars 14g	
Protein 26g	Fat 7g	
Carbohydrate ...22g	Saturates 2g	

10 MINS   35 MINS

SERVES 4

I N G R E D I E N T S

1 tbsp sunflower oil

1 lb lean boneless, skinless chicken

2 cloves garlic, minced

2 tbsp Thai red curry paste

2 tbsp fresh grated galangal or gingerroot

1 tbsp tamarind paste

4 lime leaves

8 oz sweet potato

2½ cups coconut milk

8 oz cherry tomatoes, halved

3 tbsp chopped fresh cilantro

cooked jasmine or Thai fragrant rice, to serve

1 Heat the sunflower oil in a large preheated wok.

2 Thinly slice the chicken. Add the chicken to the wok and stir-fry for 5 minutes.

3 Add the garlic, curry paste, galangal or gingerroot, tamarind, and lime leaves to the wok and stir-fry for about 1 minute.

4 Using a sharp knife, peel and dice the sweet potato. Add the coconut milk and sweet potato to the mixture in the wok and bring to a boil. Allow to bubble over a medium heat for 20 minutes, or until the juices start to thicken and reduce.

5 Add the cherry tomatoes and cilantro to the curry and cook for a further 5 minutes, stirring occasionally. Transfer to serving plates and serve hot with cooked jasmine or Thai fragrant rice.

COOK'S TIP

Galangal is a spice very similar to ginger and is used to replace the latter in Thai cuisine. It can be bought fresh from Oriental food stores but is also available dried and as a powder. The fresh root, which is not as pungent as ginger, needs to be peeled before slicing to use.

Thai-Style Chicken Skewers

The chicken is marinated in an aromatic sauce before being cooked on the grill. Use bay leaves if kaffir lime leaves are unavailable.

NUTRITIONAL INFORMATION

Calories 218   Sugars 4g
Protein . . . . .28g   Fat 10g
Carbohydrate . . . .5g   Saturates 2g

2¹/₄ HOURS   20 MINS

SERVES 4

I N G R E D I E N T S

4 lean chicken breasts, skinned and boned

1 onion, peeled and cut into wedges

1 large red bell pepper, seeded

1 large yellow bell pepper seeded

12 kaffir lime leaves

2 tbsp sunflower oil

2 tbsp lime juice

tomato halves, to serve

M A R I N A D E

1 tbsp Thai red curry paste

⅔ cup canned coconut milk

1 To make the marinade, place the red curry paste in a small pan over medium heat and cook for 1 minute. Add half of the coconut milk to the pan and bring the mixture to a boil. Boil for 2–3 minutes until the liquid has reduced by about two-thirds.

2 Remove the pan from the heat and stir in the remaining coconut milk. Set aside to cool.

3 Cut the chicken into 1 inch pieces. Stir the chicken into the cold marinade, cover and leave to chill for at least 2 hours.

4 Cut the onion into wedges and the bell peppers into 1 inch pieces.

5 Remove the chicken pieces from the marinade and thread them on to skewers, alternating the chicken with the vegetables and lime leaves.

6 Combine the oil and lime juice in a small bowl and brush the mixture over the kabobs. Grill the skewers over hot coals, turning and basting frequently for 10–15 minutes until the chicken is cooked through. grill the tomato halves and serve with the chicken skewers.

COOK'S TIP

Cooking the marinade first intensifies the flavor. It is important to allow the marinade to cool before adding the chicken, or bacteria may breed in the warm temperature.

Ginger Chicken & Corn

Chicken wings and corn in a sticky ginger marinade are designed to be eaten with the fingers–there's no other way!

NUTRITIONAL INFORMATION

Calories	123	Sugars	.........3g
Protein	........14g	Fat	...........6g
Carbohydrate	....3g	Saturates	......1g

10 MINS   20 MINS

SERVES 6

I N G R E D I E N T S

3 cobs fresh corn-on-the-cob

12 chicken wings

1 inch piece fresh gingerroot

6 tbsp lemon juice

4 tsp sunflower oil

1 tbsp golden superfine sugar

jacket potatoes or salad, to serve

1 Remove the husks and silks from the corn. Using a sharp knife, cut each cob into 6 slices.

2 Place the corn in a large bowl with the chicken wings.

3 Peel and grate the gingerroot or chop finely. Place in a bowl and add the lemon juice, sunflower oil, and golden superfine sugar. Mix together until well combined.

4 Toss the corn and chicken in the ginger mixture to coat evely.

5 Thread the corn and chicken wings alternately on to metal or pre-soaked wooden skewers, to make turning easier.

6 Cook under a preheated moderately hot broiler or grill for 15–20 minutes, basting with the gingery glaze and turning frequently until the corn is golden brown and tender and the chicken is cooked. Serve with jacket potatoes or salad.

COOK'S TIP

Cut off the wing tips before broiling as they burn very easily. Or you can cover them with small pieces of foil.

Steamed Chicken Packets

A healthy recipe with a delicate oriental flavor. Use large spinach leaves to wrap around the chicken, but make sure they are young leaves.

NUTRITIONAL INFORMATION

Calories 216   Sugars 7g
Protein . . . . .31g   Fat 7g
Carbohydrate . . . .7g   Saturates 2g

20 MINS   30 MINS

SERVES 4

I N G R E D I E N T S

4 lean boneless, skinless chicken
  breasts

1 tsp ground lemon grass

2 scallions, chopped finely

1 cup young carrots

1¾ cups young zucchini

2 stalks celery

1 tsp light soy sauce

¾ cup spinach leaves

2 tsp sesame oil

salt and pepper

1 With a sharp knife, make a slit through one side of each chicken breast to open out a large pocket.

2 Sprinkle the inside of the pocket with lemon grass, salt and pepper. Tuck the scallions into the chicken pockets.

3 Trim the carrots, zucchini and celery, then cut into small matchstalks. Plunge them into a pan of boiling water for 1 minute, then drain and toss in the soy sauce

4 Pack the mixture into the pockets in each chicken breast and fold over

firmly to enclose. Reserve the remaining vegetables. Wash and dry the spinach leaves then wrap the chicken breasts firmly in the leaves to enclose completely. If the leaves are too firm, steam them for a few seconds until they are softened and more flexible.

5 Place the wrapped chicken in a steamer and steam over rapidly boiling water for 20–25 minutes, depending on size.

6 Stir-fry any leftover vegetable stalks and spinach for 1–2 minutes in the sesame oil and serve with the chicken.

Crispy Stuffed Chicken

An attractive main course of chicken breasts filled with mixed bell peppers and set on a sea of red bell peppers and tomato sauce.

NUTRITIONAL INFORMATION

Calories 196   Sugars 4g
Protein .... 29g   Fat 6g
Carbohydrate .... 6g   Saturates 2g

20 MINS   50 MINS

SERVES 4

INGREDIENTS

4 boneless chicken breasts, about
   5½ oz each, skinned

4 sprigs fresh tarragon

½ small orange bell pepper, seeded and
   sliced

½ small green bell pepper, seeded and
   sliced

½ oz whole-wheat bread crumbs

1 tbsp sesame seeds

4 tbsp lemon juice

1 small red bell pepper, halved and seeded

7 oz can chopped tomatoes

1 small red chili, seeded and chopped

¼ tsp celery salt

salt and pepper

fresh tarragon, to garnish

1 Preheat the oven to 400°F. Slit the chicken breasts with a small, sharp knife to create a pocket in each. Season inside each pocket.

2 Place a sprig of tarragon and a few slices of orange and green bell peppers in each pocket. Place the chicken breasts on a non-stick baking sheet and sprinkle over the bread crumbs and sesame seeds.

3 Spoon 1 tablespoon lemon juice over each chicken breast and bake in the oven for 35–40 minutes until the chicken is tender and cooked through.

4 Meanwhile, preheat the broiler to hot. Arrange the red bell pepper halves, skin side up, on the rack and cook for 5–6 minutes until the skin blisters. Leave to cool for 10 minutes, then peel off the skins.

5 Put the red bell pepper in a blender, add the tomatoes, chili, and celery salt and process for a few seconds. Season to taste. Alternatively, finely chop the red bell pepper and press through a strainer with the tomatoes and chili.

6 When the chicken is cooked, heat the sauce, spoon a little on to a warm plate and arrange a chicken breast in the center. Garnish with tarragon and serve.

Teppanyaki

This simple, Japanese style of cooking is ideal for thinly-sliced breast of chicken. You can use thin turkey escalopes, if you prefer.

NUTRITIONAL INFORMATION

Calories	206	Sugars	........4g
Protein	........30g	Fat	..........7g
Carbohydrate	....6g	Saturates	......2g

5 MINS   10 MINS

SERVES 4

INGREDIENTS

4 boneless chicken breasts

1 red bell pepper

1 green bell pepper

4 scallions

8 baby corn-on-the-cob

½ cup mung bean sprouts

1 tbsp sesame or sunflower oil

4 tbsp soy sauce

4 tbsp mirin

1 tbsp grated fresh gingerroot

1 Remove the skin from the chicken and slice at a slight angle, to a thickness of about ¼ inch.

2 Seed and thinly slice the bell peppers and trim and slice the scallions and corn-on-the-cob.

3 Arrange the bell peppers, scallions, corn, and bean sprouts on a plate with the sliced chicken.

4 Heat a large griddle or heavy skillet then lightly brush with oil. Add the vegetables and chicken slices in small batches, allowing space between them so that they cook thoroughly.

5 Combine the soy sauce, mirin, and ginger and serve as a dip with the chicken and vegetables.

COOK'S TIP

Mirin is a rich, sweet rice wine which you can buy in oriental shops, but if it is not available add one 1 tablespoon of soft light brown sugar to the sauce instead.

Sweet and Sour Chicken

This sweet-citrusy chicken is delicious hot or cold. Sesame-flavored noodles are the ideal accompaniment for the hot version.

NUTRITIONAL INFORMATION

Calories 248   Sugars 8g
Protein ....30g   Fat 8g
Carbohydrate ...16g   Saturates 2g

 5 MINS   25 MINS

SERVES 4

INGREDIENTS

4 boneless chicken breasts, about
   4½ oz each

2 tbsp clear honey

1 tbsp dark soy sauce

1 tsp lemon rind, finely grated

1 tbsp lemon juice

salt and pepper

TO GARNISH

1 tbsp fresh chives, chopped

lemon rind, grated

NOODLES

8 oz rice noodles

2 tsp sesame oil

1 tbsp sesame seeds

1 tsp lemon rind, finely grated

1 Preheat the broiler to medium. Skin and trim the chicken breasts to remove any excess fat, then wash and pat them dry with absorbent paper towels Using a sharp knife, score the chicken breasts with a criss-cross pattern on both sides (making sure that you do not cut all the way through the meat).

2 Mix together the honey, soy sauce, lemon rind, and juice in a small bowl, and then season well with black pepper.

3 Arrange the chicken breasts on the broiler rack and brush with half the honey mixture. Cook for 10 minutes, turn over and brush with the remaining mixture. Cook for a further 8–10 minutes or until cooked through.

4 Meanwhile, prepare the noodles according to the directions on the packet. Drain well and transfer to a warm serving bowl. Mix the noodles with the sesame oil, sesame seeds, and the lemon rind. Season and keep warm.

5 Drain the chicken and serve with a small mound of noodles, garnished with chopped chives and grated lemon rind.

VARIATION

For a different flavor, replace the lemon with orange or lime. If you prefer, serve the chicken with boiled rice or pasta, which you can flavor with sesame seeds and citrus rind in the same way.

Chicken & Ginger Stir-Fry

The pomegranate seeds add a sharp Chinese flavor to this Indian stir-fry. Serve in the summer with a spicy rice salad or a mixed green salad.

NUTRITIONAL INFORMATION

Calories	.291	Sugars	.0g
Protein	.41g	Fat	.14g
Carbohydrate	.0g	Saturates	.3g

 10 MINS   25 MINS

SERVES 4

I N G R E D I E N T S

3 tbsp oil

1 lb 9 oz lean skinless, boneless chicken breasts, cut into 2 inch strips

3 garlic cloves, minced

1½ inch piece fresh gingerroot, cut into strips

1 tsp pomegranate seeds, minced

½ tsp ground turmeric

1 tsp garam masala

2 fresh green chilies, sliced

½ tsp salt

4 tbsp lemon juice

grated rind of 1 lemon

6 tbsp chopped fresh cilantro

½ cup chicken stock

naan bread, to serve

1 Heat the oil in a wok or large skillet and stir-fry the chicken until golden brown all over. Remove from the pan and set aside.

2 Add the garlic, ginger, and pomegranate seeds to the pan and fry in the oil for 1 minute taking care not to let the garlic burn.

3 Stir in the turmeric, garam masala and chilies, and fry for 30 seconds.

4 Return the chicken to the pan and add the salt, lemon juice, lemon rind, cilantro, and stock. Stir the chicken well to make sure it is coated in the sauce.

5 Bring the mixture to a boil, then lower the heat and simmer for 10–15 minutes until the chicken is thoroughly cooked. Serve with warm naan

COOK'S TIP

Stir-frying is perfect for low-fat diets as only a little oil is needed. Cooking the food over a high temperature ensures that food is sealed and cooked quickly to hold in the flavor.

Filipino Chicken

Tomato catsup is a very popular ingredient in Asian dishes, as it imparts a zingy sweet-sour flavor.

NUTRITIONAL INFORMATION

Calories 197   Sugars 7g
Protein ....28g   Fat 4g
Carbohydrate ....8g   Saturates 1g

2³/₄ HOURS   20 MINS

SERVES 4

I N G R E D I E N T S

1 can lemonade or lime-and-lemonade

2 tbsp gin

4 tbsp tomato catsup

2 tsp garlic salt

2 tsp Worcestershire sauce

4 lean chicken suprêmes or breast fillets

salt and pepper

TO SERVE

thread egg noodles

1 green chili, chopped finely

2 scallions, sliced

1 Combine the lemonade or lime-and-lemonade, gin, tomato catsup, garlic salt, Worcestershire sauce, and seasoning in a large non-porous dish.

2 Put the chicken supremes into the dish and make sure that the marinade covers them completely.

3 Leave to marinate in the refrigerator for 2 hours. Remove and leave covered at room temperature for 30 minutes.

4 Place the chicken over a medium grill and cook for 20 minutes.

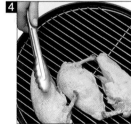

5 Turn the chicken once, halfway through the cooking time.

6 Remove from the grill and leave to rest for 3–4 minutes before serving.

7 Serve with egg noodles, tossed with a little green chili and scallions.

COOK'S TIP

Cooking the meat on the bone after it has reached room temperature means that it cooks in a shorter time, which ensures that the meat remains moist right through to the bone.

Poussin with Dried Fruits

Baby chickens are ideal for a one or two portion meal, and cook very easily and quickly for a special dinner–either in the oven or microwave.

NUTRITIONAL INFORMATION

Calories 316   Sugars 23g
Protein . . . . .23g   Fat 15g
Carbohydrate . . .23g   Saturates 2g

35 MINS   30 MINS

SERVES 2

INGREDIENTS

¾ cup dried apples, peaches, and prunes

½ cup boiling water

2 baby chickens

⅓ cup walnut halves

1 tbsp honey

1 tsp ground allspice

1 tbsp walnut oil

salt and pepper

vegetables and new potatoes, to serve

1 Place the fruits in a bowl, cover with the water and leave to stand for about 30 minutes.

2 Cut the chickens in half down the breastbone using a sharp knife, or leave whole.

3 Mix the fruit and any juices with the walnuts, honey, and allspice and divide between two small roasting bags or squares of foil.

4 Brush the chickens with walnut oil and sprinkle with salt and pepper then place on top of the fruits.

5 Close the roasting bags or fold the foil over to enclose the chickens and bake on a baking sheet in a preheated oven, 375°F, for 25–30 minutes or until the juices run clear. To cook in a microwave, use microwave roasting bags and cook on HIGH power for 6–7 minutes each, depending on size.

6 Transfer the poussin to a warm plate and serve hot with fresh vegetables and new potatoes.

VARIATION

Alternative dried fruits that can be used in this recipe are cherries, mangoes or papayas.

  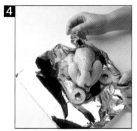

Pot-Roast Orange Chicken

This colorful, nutritious pot-roast could be served for a family meal or for a special dinner. Add more vegetables if you're feeding a crowd.

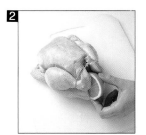

NUTRITIONAL INFORMATION

Calories 302	Sugar 17g	
Protein 29g	Fats 11g	
Carbohydrates ...22g	Saturates 2g	

 10 MINS   🕐 2 HOURS

SERVES 4

I N G R E D I E N T S

2 tbsp sunflower oil

1 chicken, weighing about 3 lb

2 large oranges

2 small onions, quartered

2 cups small whole carrots or thin carrots, cut into 2 inch lengths

⅔ cup orange juice

2 tbsp brandy

2 tbsp sesame seeds

1 tbsp cornstarch

salt and pepper

1 Heat the oil in a large flameproof casserole and fry the chicken, turning occasionally until evenly browned.

2 Cut one orange in half and place half inside the cavity of the chicken. Place the chicken in a large, deep casserole. Arrange the onions and carrots around the chicken. Season with salt and pepper and pour over the orange juice.

3 Cut the remaining oranges into thin wedges and tuck around the chicken, among the vegetables.

4 Cover and cook in a preheated oven, 350°F, for about 1½ hours, or until the chicken juices run clear when pierced, and the vegetables are tender. Remove the lid and sprinkle with the brandy and sesame seeds. Return to the oven for 10 minutes.

5 To serve, lift the chicken on to a large platter and add the vegetables. Skim any excess fat from the juices. Blend the cornstarch with 1 tablespoon of cold water, then stir into the juices and bring to a boil, stirring. Season to taste, then serve the sauce with the chicken.

Harlequin Chicken

This colorful dish will tempt the appetites of all the family–it is ideal for toddlers, who enjoy the fun shapes of the multi-colored bell peppers.

NUTRITIONAL INFORMATION

Calories ....183 Sugar 8g
Protein ....24g Fats 6g
Carbohydrates ....8g Saturates 1g

 5 MINS   25 MINS

SERVES 4

INGREDIENTS

10 skinless, boneless chicken thighs

1 medium onion

1 each medium red, green and yellow bell peppers

1 tbsp sunflower oil

14 oz can chopped tomatoes

2 tbsp chopped fresh parsley

pepper

whole-wheat bread and salad, to serve

1 Using a sharp knife, cut the chicken thighs into bite-sized pieces.

2 Peel and thinly slice the onion. Halve and seed the bell peppers and cut into small diamond shapes.

3 Heat the sunflower oil in a shallow pan then quickly fry the chicken and onion until golden.

4 Add the bell peppers, cook for 2–3 minutes, then stir in the tomatoes and chopped fresh parsley and season with pepper.

5 Cover tightly and simmer for about 15 minutes, until the chicken and vegetables are tender. Serve hot with whole-wheat bread and a green salad.

COOK'S TIP
If you are making this dish for small children, the chicken can be finely chopped or ground first.

Mediterranean Chicken

This recipe uses ingredients found in the Languedoc area of France, where cooking over hot embers is a way of life.

NUTRITIONAL INFORMATION

Calories ....143 Sugars 4g
Protein ....13g Fat 8g
Carbohydrate ....4g Saturates 2g

2³/₄ HOURS   40 MINS

SERVES 4

I N G R E D I E N T S

4 tbsp low-fat unsweetened yogurt

3 tbsp sun-dried tomato paste

1 tbsp olive oil

¼ cup fresh basil leaves, lightly minced

2 garlic cloves, chopped roughly

4 chicken quarters

green salad, to serve

1 Combine the yogurt, tomato paste, olive oil, basil leaves, and garlic in a small bowl and stir well to mix.

2 Put the marinade into a bowl large enough to hold the chicken quarters in a single layer. Add the chicken quarters. Make sure that the chicken pieces are thoroughly coated in the marinade.

3 Leave to marinate in the refrigerator for 2 hours. Remove and leave covered at room temperature for 30 minutes.

4 Place the chicken over a medium grill and cook for 30–40 minutes, turning frequently. Test for readiness by piercing the flesh at the thickest part–usually at the top of the drumstick. If the juices that run out are clear, it is cooked through.

5 Serve hot with a green salad. It is also delicious eaten cold.

VARIATION

For a marinade with an extra zingy flavor combine 2 garlic cloves, coarsely chopped, the juice of 2 lemons and 3 tbsp olive oil, and cook in the same way.

Chicken with Two Sauces

With its red and yellow bell pepper sauces, this quick and simple dish is colorful and healthy, and perfect for an impromptu lunch or supper.

NUTRITIONAL INFORMATION

Calories 257	Sugars 7g
Protein 29g	Fat 10g
Carbohydrate 8g	Saturates 2g

 10 MINS   1¹/₂ HOURS

SERVES 4

I N G R E D I E N T S

2 tbsp olive oil

2 medium onions, chopped finely

2 garlic cloves, minced

2 red bell peppers, chopped

good pinch cayenne pepper

2 tsp tomato paste

2 yellow bell peppers, chopped

pinch of dried basil

4 lean skinless, boneless chicken
  breasts

²/₃ cup dry white wine

²/₃ cup chicken stock

bouquet garni

salt and pepper

fresh herbs, to garnish

1 Heat 1 tablespoon of olive oil in each of two medium saucepans. Place half the chopped onions, 1 of the garlic cloves, the red bell peppers, the cayenne pepper, and the tomato paste in one of the saucepans. Place the remaining onion, garlic, yellow bell peppers, and basil in the other pan.

2 Cover each pan and cook over a very low heat for 1 hour until the bell peppers are very soft. If either mixture becomes dry, add a little water. Process then strain the contents of each pan separately.

3 Return to the pans and season with salt and pepper. Gently reheat the two sauces while the chicken is cooking.

4 Put the chicken breasts into a skillet and add the wine and stock. Add the bouquet garni and bring the liquid to simmer. Cook the chicken for about 20 minutes until tender.

5 To serve, put a pool of each sauce on to four serving plates, slice the chicken breasts and arrange on the plates. Garnish with fresh herbs.

Chicken with Whisky Sauce

After cooking with stock and vegetables, chicken breasts are served with a velvety sauce made from whisky and low-fat crème fraîche.

NUTRITIONAL INFORMATION

Calories ....337 Sugars 6g
Protein ....37g Fat 15g
Carbohydrate ....6g Saturates 8g

5 MINS   30 MINS

SERVES 4

I N G R E D I E N T S

2 tbsp butter

½ cup shredded leeks

⅓ cup diced carrot

¼ cup diced celery

4 shallots, sliced

2½ cups chicken stock

6 chicken breasts

¼ cup whisky

1 cup low-fat crème fraîche

2 tbsp freshly grated horseradish

1 tsp honey, warmed

1 tsp chopped fresh parsley

salt and pepper

parsley, to garnish

TO SERVE

vegetable patty

mashed potato

fresh vegetables

1 Melt the butter in a large saucepan and add the leeks, carrot, celery, and shallots. Cook for 3 minutes, add half the chicken stock and cook for about 8 minutes.

2 Add the remaining chicken stock, and bring to a boil. Add the chicken breasts and cook for about 10 minutes or until tender.

3 Remove the chicken with a draining spoon and cut into thin slices. Place on a large, hot serving dish and keep warm.

4 In another saucepan, heat the whisky until reduced by half. Strain the chicken stock through a fine strainer, add to the pan and heat until the liquid is reduced by half.

5 Add the crème fraîche, the horseradish, and the honey. Heat gently and add the chopped fresh parsley and salt and pepper to taste.

6 Pour a little of the whisky sauce around the chicken and pour the remaining sauce into a sauceboat to serve.

7 Serve with a vegetable patty made from the leftover vegetables, mashed potato, and fresh vegetables. Garnish with fresh parsley.

Two-in-One Chicken

Cook four chicken pieces and serve two hot, topped with a crunchy herb mixture. Serve the remainder as a salad in a delicious curry sauce.

NUTRITIONAL INFORMATION

Calories 421   Sugars 20g
Protein . . . . .31g   Fat 18g
Carbohydrate . . .34g   Saturates 4g

2¹/₂ HOURS   45 MINS

SERVES 2

INGREDIENTS

4 lean chicken thighs

oil for brushing

garlic powder

½ eating apple, grated coarsely

1½ tbsp dry parsley and thyme stuffing mix

salt and pepper

pasta shapes, to serve

SAUCE

1 tbsp butter or margarine

2 tsp all-purpose flour

5 tbsp skimmed milk

2 tbsp dry white wine or stock

½ tsp dried mustard powder

1 tsp capers or chopped gherkins

SPICED CHICKEN SALAD

½ small onion, chopped finely

1 tbsp oil

1 tsp tomato paste

½ tsp curry powder

1 tsp apricot jam

1 tsp lemon juice

2 tbsp low-fat mayonnaise

1 tbsp low-fat unsweetened fromage frais

¾ cup seedless grapes, halved

¼ cup white long-grain rice, cooked, to serve

1 Place the chicken in a shallow ovenproof dish. Brush with oil, sprinkle with garlic powder and season with salt and pepper. Place in a preheated oven, 400°F, for 25 minutes, or until almost cooked through. Combine the apple with the stuffing mix. Baste the chicken, then spoon the mixture over two of the pieces. Return all the chicken pieces to the oven for about 10 minutes until the chicken is cooked.

2 To make the sauce, melt the magarine in a pan, stir in the flour, and cook for 1–2 minutes. Add the milk gradually, then the wine or stock, and bring to a boil. Stir in the mustard, capers or gherkins, and seasoning. Simmer for 1 minute. Serve the two crunchy-topped pieces of chicken with the sauce and pasta shapes.

3 For the salad, fry the onion gently in the oil until barely colored. Add the tomato paste, curry powder, and jam, and cook for 1 minute. Leave the mixture to cool. Blend the mixture in a food processor, or press through a strainer . Beat in the lemon juice, mayonnaise and fromage frais. Season to taste with salt and pepper.

4 Cut the chicken into strips and add to the sauce with the grapes. Mix well, and chill. Serve with the rice.

Sticky Chicken Wings

These need to be eaten with your fingers so serve them at an informal supper.

NUTRITIONAL INFORMATION

Calories ....165 Sugars 12g
Protein ....14g Fat 7g
Carbohydrate ...12g Saturates 1g

3¼ HOURS   1 HOUR

SERVES 4–6

INGREDIENTS

2 tbsp olive oil

1 small onion, finely chopped

2 garlic cloves, minced

¾ pint sieved tomatoes

2 tsp dried thyme

1 tsp dried oregano

pinch fennel seeds

3 tbsp red wine vinegar

2 tbsp Dijon mustard

pinch ground cinnamon

2 tbsp brown sugar

1 tsp chili flakes

2 tbsp black treacle

16 chicken wings

salt and pepper

TO GARNISH

celery stalks

cherry tomatoes

1 Heat the olive oil in a large skillet and fry the onion and garlic for about 10 minutes.

2 Add the sieved tomatoes, dried herbs, fennel, red wine vinegar, mustard, and cinnamon to the skillet along with the sugar, chili flakes, treacle, and salt and pepper. Bring to a boil, then reduce the heat and simmer gently for about 15 minutes, until the sauce is slightly reduced.

3 Put the chicken wings in a large dish, and coat liberally with the sauce. Leave to marinate for 3 hours or as long as possible, turning the wings over often in the marinade.

4 Transfer the wings to a clean baking sheet, and roast in a preheated oven, 425°F, for 10 minutes. Reduce the heat to 375°F and cook for 20 minutes, basting often.

5 Serve the wings very hot, garnished with celery stalks and cherry tomatoes.

Jerk Chicken

This is perhaps one of the best-known Caribbean dishes. The 'jerk' in the name refers to the hot spicy coating.

NUTRITIONAL INFORMATION

Calories . . . . . . .158 Sugars 0.4g
Protein . . . . .29g Fat 4g
Carbohydrate . . . .2g Saturates 1g

 24 HOURS   30 MINS

SERVES 4

INGREDIENTS

4 lean chicken portions

1 bunch scallions, trimmed

1–2 Scotch Bonnet chilies, seeded

1 garlic clove

2 inch piece gingerroot, peeled and roughly chopped

½ tsp dried thyme

½ tsp paprika

¼ tsp ground allspice

pinch ground cinnamon

pinch ground cloves

4 tbsp white wine vinegar

3 tbsp light soy sauce

pepper

1 Rinse the chicken portions and pat them dry on absorbent paper towels Place them in a shallow dish.

2 Place the scallions, chilies, garlic, ginger, thyme, paprika, allspice, cinnamon, cloves, wine vinegar, soy sauce, and pepper to taste in a food processor and process until smooth.

3 Pour the spicy mixture over the chicken. Turn the chicken portions

over so that they are well coated in the marinade.

4 Transfer the chicken portions to the refrigerator and leave to marinate for up to 24 hours.

5 Remove the chicken from the marinade and grill over medium hot

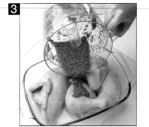

coals for about 30 minutes, turning the chicken over and basting occasionally with any remaining marinade, until the chicken is browned and cooked through.

6 Transfer the chicken portions to individual serving plates and serve at once.

Lime Fricassée of Chicken

The addition of lime juice and lime rind adds a delicious tangy flavor to this chicken stew.

NUTRITIONAL INFORMATION

Calories . . . . . . .235 Sugars 3g
Protein . . . . .20g Fat 6g
Carbohydrate . . .26g Saturates 1g

15 MINS   1¾ HOURS

SERVES 4

I N G R E D I E N T S

2 tbsp oil

1 large chicken, cut into small portions

½ cup flour, seasoned

1 lb baby onions or shallots, sliced

1 each green and red bell pepper, sliced thinly

⅔ cup chicken stock

juice and rind of 2 limes

2 chilies, chopped

2 tbsp oyster sauce

1 tsp Worcestershire sauce

salt and pepper

1 Heat the oil in a large skillet. Coat the chicken pieces in the seasoned flour and cook for about 4 minutes until browned all over.

2 Transfer the chicken to a large casserole. Sprinkle with the onions.

3 Slowly fry the bell peppers in the juices in the skillet.

4 Add the chicken stock, lime juice, and rind and cook for a further 5 minutes.

5 Add the chilies, oyster sauce, and Worcestershire sauce, mixing well.

6 Season to taste with salt and pepper, then pour the bell peppers and juices over the chicken and onions.

7 Cover the casserole with a lid or cooking foil.

8 Cook in the center of a preheated oven, 375°F for 1½ hours until the chicken is very tender, then serve.

COOK'S TIP

Try this casserole with a cheese biscuit topping. About 30 minutes before the end of cooking time, simply top with rounds cut from cheese biscuit pastry.

Mexican Chicken

Chili, tomatoes, and corn are typical ingredients in a Mexican dish. This is a quick and easy meal for unexpected guests.

NUTRITIONAL INFORMATION

Calories 207   Sugars 8g
Protein . . . . .18g   Fat 9g
Carbohydrate . . .13g   Saturates 2g

5 MINS   35 MINS

SERVES 4

INGREDIENTS

2 tbsp oil

8 chicken drumstalks

1 medium onion, finely chopped

1 tsp chili powder

1 tsp ground coriander

15 oz can chopped tomatoes

2 tbsp tomato paste

⅔ cup frozen corn-on-the-cob

salt and pepper

TO SERVE

boiled rice

mixed bell pepper salad

1 Heat the oil in a large skillet, add the chicken drumstalks and cook over a medium heat until lightly browned on all sides. Remove from the pan and set aside.

2 Add the onion to the pan and cook for 3–4 minutes until soft, then stir in the chili powder and coriander and cook for a few seconds.

3 Add the chopped tomatoes with their juice and the tomato paste paste.

4 Return the chicken to the pan and simmer gently for 20 minutes until the chicken is tender and thoroughly cooked. Add the corn-on-the-cob and cook a further 3–4 minutes. Season to taste.

5 Serve with boiled rice and mixed bell pepper salad.

COOK'S TIP

If you dislike the heat of the chilies, just leave them out–the chicken will still taste delicious.

Grilled Chicken

These chicken wings are brushed with a simple grill glaze, which can be made in minutes, but will be enjoyed by all.

NUTRITIONAL INFORMATION

Calories	143	Sugars	.........6g
Protein	........14g	Fat	...........7g
Carbohydrate	....6g	Saturates	......1g

 5 MINS   20 MINS

SERVES 4

I N G R E D I E N T S

8 chicken wings or 1 chicken cut into
  8 portions

3 tbsp tomato paste

3 tbsp brown fruity sauce

1 tbsp white wine vinegar

1 tbsp clear honey

1 tbsp olive oil

1 clove garlic, minced (optional)

salad leaves, to serve

1   Remove the skin from the chicken if you want to reduce the fat in the dish.

2   To make the grill glaze, place the tomato paste, brown fruity sauce, white wine vinegar, honey, oil, and garlic in a small bowl. Stir all of the ingredients together until they are thoroughly blended.

3   Brush the grill glaze over the chicken and broil over hot coals for 15–20 minutes. Turn the chicken portions over occasionally and baste frequently with the grill glaze.

4   If the chicken begins to blacken before it is cooked, raise the rack if possible or move the chicken to a cooler part of the grill to slow down the cooking.

5   Transfer the grilled chicken to warm serving plates and serve with fresh salad leaves.

COOK'S TIP

When poultry is cooked over a very hot grill the heat immediately seals in all of the juices, leaving the meat succulent. For this reason make sure that the coals are hot enough before starting to grill.

Festive Apple Chicken

The stuffing in this recipe is cooked under the breast skin so all the flavor sealed in, and the chicken stays really moist and succulent .

NUTRITIONAL INFORMATION

Calories	.219	Sugars	.7g
Protein	.29g	Fat	.8g
Carbohydrate	.9g	Saturates	.4g

🐚 🐚 🐚

🍲 10 MINS   🕐 2¹/₄ HOURS

SERVES 6

I N G R E D I E N T S

1 chicken, weighing 4½ lb

2 eating apples

1 tbsp butter

1 tbsp redcurrant jelly

parsley, to garnish

S T U F F I N G

1 tbsp butter

1 small onion, chopped finely

2 oz mushrooms, chopped finely

2 oz lean smoked ham, chopped finely

½ cup fresh bread crumbs

1 tbsp chopped fresh parsley

1 crisp eating apple

1 tbsp lemon juice

oil, to brush

salt and pepper

  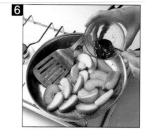

1 To make the stuffing, melt the butter and fry the onion gently, stirring until soft. Stir in the mushrooms and cook over a moderate heat for 2–3 minutes. Remove from the heat and stir in the ham, bread crumbs, and the chopped parsley.

2 Core the apple, leaving the skin on, and grate coarsely. Add the stuffing mixture to the apple with the lemon juice. Season to taste.

3 Loosen the breast skin of the chicken and carefully spoon the stuffing mixture under it, smoothing evenly with your hands.

4 Place the chicken in a roasting pan and brush lightly with oil.

5 Roast the chicken in a preheated oven, 375°F, for 25 minutes per 1 lb plus 25 minutes, or until there is no trace

of pink in the juices when the chicken is pierced through the thickest part with a skewer. If the breast starts to brown too much, cover the chicken with foil.

6 Core and slice the remaining apples and sauté in the butter until golden. Stir in the redcurrant jelly and warm through until melted. Serve the chicken garnished with the apple and parsley.

Roast Duck with Apple

The richness of the duck meat contrasts well with the apricot sauce. If duckling portions are unavailable, use a whole bird cut into joints.

NUTRITIONAL INFORMATION

Calories 316	Sugars 38g
Protein 25g	Fat 6g
Carbohydrate . . .40g	Saturates 1g

10 MINS   1¹/₂ HOURS

SERVES 4

I N G R E D I E N T S

4 duckling portions,12 oz each

4 tbsp dark soy sauce

2 tbsp light muscovado sugar

2 red-skinned apples

2 green-skinned apples

juice of 1 lemon

2 tbsp clear honey

few bay leaves

salt and pepper

assorted fresh vegetables, to serve

S A U C E

14 oz can apricots, in unsweetened juice

4 tbsp sweet sherry

1 Preheat the oven to 375°F. Wash the duck and trim away any excess fat. Place on a wire rack over a roasting pan and prick all over with a fork.

2 Brush the duck with the soy sauce. Sprinkle over the sugar and season with pepper. Cook in the oven, basting occasionally, for 50–60 minutes until the meat is cooked through–the juices should run clear when a skewer is inserted into the thickest part of the meat.

3 Meanwhile, core the apples and cut each into 6 wedges. Place in a small roasting pan and mix with the lemon juice and honey. Add a few bay leaves and season. Cook alongside the duck, basting occasionally, for 20–25 minutes until tender. Discard the bay leaves.

4 To make the sauce, place the apricots in a blender or food processor together with the juice from the can and the sherry. Process for a few seconds until smooth. Alternatively, mash the apricots with a fork until smooth and mix with the juice and sherry.

5 Just before serving, heat the apricot paste in a small pan. Remove the skin from the duck and pat the flesh with paper towels to absorb any fat. Serve the duck with the apple wedges, apricot sauce, and fresh vegetables.

VARIATION

Fruit complements duck perfectly. Use canned pineapple in unsweetened juice for a delicious alternative.

Citrus Duckling Skewers

The tartness of citrus fruit goes well with the rich meat of duckling.
Duckling makes a change from chicken for the grill.

NUTRITIONAL INFORMATION

Calories 205   Sugars 5g
Protein . . . . .24g   Fat 10g
Carbohydrate . . . .5g   Saturates 2g

45 MINS   20 MINS

SERVES 12

INGREDIENTS

3 duckling breasts, skinned, boned and cut into bite-size pieces

1 small red onion, cut into wedges

1 small eggplant, cut into cubes

lime and lemon wedges, to garnish (optional)

MARINADE

grated rind and juice of 1 lemon

grated rind and juice of 1 lime

grated rind and juice of 1 orange

1 clove garlic, minced

1 tsp dried oregano

2 tbsp olive oil

dash of Tabasco sauce

1 Cut the duckling into bite-sized pieces. Place in a non-metallic bowl together with the prepared vegetables.

2 To make the marinade, place the lemon, lime, and orange rinds and juices, garlic, oregano, oil, and Tabasco sauce in a screw-top jar and shake until well combined. Pour the marinade over the duckling and vegetables and toss to coat. Leave to marinate for 30 minutes.

3 Remove the duckling and vegetables from the marinade and thread them on to skewers, reserving the marinade.

4 Grilll the skewers on an oiled rack over medium hot coals, turning and basting frequently with the reserved marinade, for 15-20 minutes until the meat is cooked through. Serve the kabobs garnished with lemon and lime wedges for squeezing (if using).

COOK'S TIP

For more zing add 1 teaspoon of chili sauce to the marinade. The meat can be marinated for several hours, but it is best to marinate the vegetables separately for only about 30 minutes.

Turkey with Redcurrant

Prepare these steaks the day before they are needed and serve in toasted ciabatta bread, accompanied with crisp salad greens.

NUTRITIONAL INFORMATION

Calories 219   Sugars 4g
Protein . . . . .28g   Fat 10g
Carbohydrate . . . .4g   Saturates 1g

12 HOURS   15 MINS

SERVES 4

I N G R E D I E N T S

3½ oz redcurrant jelly

2 tbsp lime juice

3 tbsp olive oil

2 tbsp dry white wine

¼ tsp ground ginger

pinch grated nutmeg

4 turkey breast steaks

salt and pepper

T O   S E R V E

mixed salad leaves

vinaigrette dressing

1 ciabatta loaf

cherry tomatoes

1 Place the redcurrant jelly and lime juice in a saucepan and heat gently until the jelly melts. Add the oil, wine, ginger, and nutmeg.

2 Place the turkey steaks in a shallow, non-metallic dish and season with salt and pepper. Pour over the marinade, turning the meat so that it is well coated. Cover and refrigerate overnight.

3 Remove the turkey from the marinade, reserving the marinade for basting, and grill on an oiled rack over hot coals for about 4 minutes on each side.

Baste the turkey steaks frequently with the reserved marinade.

4 Meanwhile, toss the salad greens in the vinaigrette dressing. Cut the ciabatta loaf in half lengthwise and place, cut-side down, at the side of the barbecue. Grill until golden. Place each steak on top of a salad leaf, sandwich between 2 pieces of bread and serve with cherry tomatoes.

COOK'S TIP

Turkey and chicken escalopes are also ideal for cooking on the grill. Because they are thin, they cook through without burning on the outside. Leave them overnight in a marinade of your choice and cook, basting with a little lemon juice and oil.

Fish & Seafood

Naturally low in fat yet rich in minerals and proteins, white fish and shellfish are ideal to include in a low-fat diet. There are so many different textures and flavors

available that they lend themselves to a wide range of cooking methods, as you will see from the recipes that follow. White fish such as cod, haddock, halibut, angler fish, and mullet are readily available and easy to cook. Shellfish such as shrimp, oysters, crab, and lobster may take a little longer to prepare but are well worth the effort. Oily fish – like salmon, trout, tuna, and mackerel – are high in fat and should be eaten in moderation.

Oriental Shellfish Kabobs

These shellfish and vegetable kabobs are ideal for serving at parties. They are quick and easy to prepare and take next to no time to cook.

NUTRITIONAL INFORMATION

Calories 93   Sugars 1g
Protein . . . . .15g   Fat 2g
Carbohydrate . . . .2g   Saturates 0.3g

  2¹/₂ HOURS   5 MINS

MAKES 12

INGREDIENTS

12 oz raw tiger shrimp, peeled leaving tails intact

12 oz scallops, cleaned, trimmed, and halved (quartered if large)

1 bunch scallions, sliced into 1 inch pieces

1 medium red bell pepper, seeded and cubed

3½ oz baby-corn-on-the-cobs, trimmed and sliced into ½ inch pieces

3 tbsp dark soy sauce

½ tsp hot chili powder

½ tsp ground ginger

1 tbsp sunflower oil

1 red chili, seeded and sliced, to garnish

DIP

4 tbsp dark soy sauce

4 tbsp dry sherry

2 tsp clear honey

1 inch piece gingerroot, peeled and grated

1 scallion, trimmed and sliced very finely

1 Divide the shrimp, scallops, scallions, bell pepper, and baby corn into 12 portions and thread on to the skewers (soaked for 10 minutes in water to prevent them from burning). Cover the ends with foil so that they do not burn and place in a shallow dish.

2 Mix the soy sauce, chili powder, and ground ginger and coat the kabobs. Cover and chill for about 2 hours.

3 Preheat the broiler to hot. Arrange the kabobs on the rack, brush with oil and cook for 2–3 minutes on each side until the prawns shrimp turn pink, the scallops become opaque, and the vegetables soften.

4 Mix together the dip ingredients.

5 Remove the foil and transfer the kabobs to a warm serving plate. Garnish with sliced chili and serve with the dip.

Scallop Skewers

As the scallops are marinated, it is not essential that they are fresh; frozen shellfish are fine for a grill.

NUTRITIONAL INFORMATION

Calories ....182 Sugars 0g
Protein ....29g Fat 7g
Carbohydrate ....0g Saturates 1g

30 MINS   10 MINS

SERVES 4

INGREDIENTS

grated zest and juice of 2 limes

2 tbsp finely chopped lemon grass or 1 tbsp lemon juice

2 garlic cloves, minced

1 green chili, seeded and chopped

16 scallops, with corals

2 limes, each cut into 8 segments

2 tbsp sunflower oil

1 tbsp lemon juice

salt and pepper

TO SERVE

1 cup arugula

3 cups mixed salad greens

1 Soak 8 skewers in warm water for at least 10 minutes before you use them to prevent the food from sticking.

2 Combine the lime juice and zest, lemon grass, garlic, and chili together in a mortar and pestle or spice grinder to make a paste.

3 Thread 2 scallops on to each of the soaked skewers. Cover the ends with foil to prevent them from burning.

4 Alternate the scallops with the lime segments.

5 Whisk together the oil, lemon juice, salt, and pepper to make the dressing.

6 Coat the scallops with the spice paste and place over a medium barbecue, basting occasionally.

7 Cook for 10 minutes, turning once.

8 Toss the arugula, mixed salad greens, and dressing together well. Put into a serving bowl.

9 Serve the scallops very hot, 2 skewers on each plate, with the salad.

Salmon Yakitori

The Japanese sauce used here combines well with salmon, although it is usually served with chicken.

NUTRITIONAL INFORMATION

Calories	247	Sugars	........10g
Protein	........19g	Fat	...........11g
Carbohydrate	...12g	Saturates	......2g

20 MINS   15 MINS

SERVES 4

INGREDIENTS

12 oz chunky salmon fillet

8 baby leeks

YAKITORI SAUCE

5 tbsp light soy sauce

5 tbsp fish stock

2 tbsp superfine sugar

5 tbsp dry white wine

3 tbsp sweet sherry

1 clove garlic, minced

1 Skin the salmon and cut the flesh into 2 inch chunks. Trim the leeks and cut them into 2 inch lengths.

2 Thread the salmon and leeks alternately on to 8 pre-soaked wooden skewers. Leave to chill in the refrigerator until required.

3 To make the sauce, place all of the ingredients in a small pan and heat gently, stirring, until the sugar has dissolved.

4 Bring to the boil, then reduce the heat and simmer for 2 minutes. Strain the sauce through a fine strainer and leave to cool until it is required.

5 Pour about one-third of the sauce into a small dish and set aside to serve with the kabobs.

6 Brush plenty of the remaining sauce over the skewers and cook directly on the rack.

7 If preferred, place a sheet of oiled kitchen foil on the rack and cook the salmon on that.

8 Grill the salmon and leek kabobs over hot coals for about 10 minutes or until cooked though, turning once.

9 Use a brush to baste frequently during cooking with the remaining sauce in order to prevent the fish and vegetables from drying out. Transfer the kabobs to a large serving plate and serve with a small bowl of the reserved sauce for dipping.

Butterfly Shrimp

These shrimp look stunning when presented on the skewers, and they are an impressive prelude to the main meal.

NUTRITIONAL INFORMATION

Calories ....183 Sugars 0g
Protein ....28g Fat 8g
Carbohydrate ....0g Saturates 1g

4¹/₂ HOURS   10 MINS

SERVES 2–4

I N G R E D I E N T S

1 lb 2 oz or 16 raw shrimp, shelled, leaving
   tails intact

juice of 2 limes

1 tsp cardamom seeds

2 tsp cumin seeds, ground

2 tsp coriander seeds, ground

½ tsp ground cinnamon

1 tsp ground turmeric

1 garlic clove, minced

1 tsp cayenne pepper

2 tbsp oil

cucumber slices, to garnish

1 Soak 8 wooden skewers in water for 20 minutes. Cut the shrimp lengthways in half down to the tail and flatten out to form a symmetrical shape.

2 Thread a shrimp on to 2 wooden skewers, with the tail between them, so that, when laid flat, the skewers hold the shrimp in shape. Thread another 3 shrimp on to these 2 skewers in the same way.

3 Repeat until you have 4 sets of 4 shrimp each.

4 Lay the skewered shrimp in a non-porous, nonmetallic dish, and sprinkle over the lime juice.

5 Combine the spices and the oil, and coat the shrimp well in the mixture. Cover the shrimp and chill for 4 hours.

6 Cook over a hot grill or in a broiler pan lined with foil under a preheated broiler for 6 minutes, turning once.

7 Serve immediately, garnished with cucumber and accompanied by a sweet relish – walnut chutney is ideal.

Angler Fish with Coconut

This is a tasty kabob with a mild marinade. Allow the skewers to marinate for at least an hour before cooking.

NUTRITIONAL INFORMATION

Calories 193
Protein 39g
Carbohydrate 2g

Sugars 2g
Fat 3g
Saturates 1g

4 HOURS   30 MINS

SERVES 4

INGREDIENTS

1 lb monkfish tails

8 oz uncooked peeled shrimp

shredded coconut, toasted, to garnish (optional)

MARINADE

1 tsp sunflower oil

½ small onion, finely grated

1 tsp gingerroot, grated

⅔ cup canned coconut milk

2 tbsp chopped, fresh cilantro

1 To make the marinade, heat the oil in a wok or saucepan and fry the onion and ginger for 5 minutes until just softened but not browned.

2 Add the coconut milk to the pan and bring to a boil. Boil rapidly for about 5 minutes or until reduced to the consistency of light cream.

3 Remove the pan from the heat and allow to cool completely.

4 When cooled, stir the cilantro into the coconut milk and pour into a shallow dish.

5 Cut the fish into bite-sized chunks and stir gently into the coconut mixture together with the shrimp. Leave to chill for 1–4 hours.

6 Thread the fish and shrimp on to skewers and discard any remaining marinade. Grill the skewers over hot coals for 10–15 minutes, turning frequently. Garnish with toasted coconut (if using).

COOK'S TIP

Look out for uncooked shrimp in the freezer cabinet in large stores. If you cannot obtain them, you can use cooked shrimp, but remember they only need heating through.

Caribbean Shrimp

This is an ideal recipe for cooks who have difficulty in finding raw shrimp at their local store.

NUTRITIONAL INFORMATION

Calories 110	Sugars 15g
Protein 5g	Fat 4g
Carbohydrate . . .15g	Saturates 3g

40 MINS   15 MINS

SERVES 4

I N G R E D I E N T S

16 cooked tiger shrimp

1 small pineapple

slivered coconut, to garnish (optional)

M A R I N A D E

⅔ cup pineapple juice

2 tbsp white wine vinegar

2 tbsp dark muscovado sugar

2 tbsp shredded coconut

1 If they are unpeeled, peel the shrimp, leaving the tails attached if preferred.

2 Peel the pineapple and cut it in half lengthways. Cut one pineapple half into wedges then into chunks.

3 To make the marinade, mix together half of the pineapple juice and the vinegar, sugar, and coconut in a shallow, nonmetallic dish. Add the peeled shrimp and pineapple chunks and toss until well coated. Leave the shrimp and pineapple to marinate for at least 30 minutes.

4 Remove the pineapple and shrimp from the marinade and thread them on to skewers. Reserve the marinade.

5 Strain the marinade and place in a food processor. Roughly chop the remaining pineapple and add to the processor with the remaining pineapple juice. Process the pineapple for a few seconds to produce a thick sauce.

6 Pour the sauce into a small saucepan. Bring to a boil then simmer for about 5 minutes. If you prefer, you can heat up the sauce by the side of the grill.

7 Transfer the kabobs to the grill and brush with some of the sauce. Grillfor about 5 minutes until the kabobs are very hot. Turn the kabobs, brushing occasionally with the sauce.

8 Serve the kabobs with extra sauce, sprinkled with slivered coconut (if using).

Lemony Angler Fish Skewers

A simple basting sauce is brushed over these tasty kabobs. When served with crusty bread, they make a perfect light meal.

NUTRITIONAL INFORMATION

Calories 191	Sugars 2g
Protein 21g	Fat 11g
Carbohydrate 1g	Saturates 1g

10 MINS   15 MINS

SERVES 4

INGREDIENTS

1 lb angler fish tail

2 zucchini

1 lemon

12 cherry tomatoes

8 bay leaves

SAUCE

3 tbsp olive oil

2 tbsp lemon juice

1 tsp chopped, fresh thyme

½ tsp lemon pepper

salt

TO SERVE

green salad leaves

fresh, crusty bread

1 Cut the angler fish into 2 inch chunks.

2 Cut the zucchini into thick slices and the lemon into wedges.

3 Thread the monkfish, zucchini, lemon, tomatoes, and bay leaves on to 4 skewers.

4 To make the basting sauce, combine the oil, lemon juice, thyme, lemon pepper, and salt to taste in a small bowl.

5 Brush the basting sauce liberally all over the fish, lemon, tomatoes, and bay leaves on the skewers.

6 Cook the skewers on the grill for about 15 minutes over medium-hot coals, basting them frequently with the sauce, until the fish is cooked through. Transfer the skewers to plates and serve with green salad leaves and wedges of crusty bread.

VARIATION

Use flounder fillets instead of the angler fish, if you prefer. Allow two fillets per person, and skin and cut each fillet lengthways into two. Roll up each piece and thread them on to the skewers.

Balti Scallops

This is a wonderful recipe for a special occasion dish. Cooked with cilantro and tomatoes, the scallops have a spicy flavor.

NUTRITIONAL INFORMATION

Calories ....258 Sugars 2g
Protein ....44g Fat 8g
Carbohydrate ....3g Saturates 1g

1¼ HOURS   15 MINS

SERVES 4

INGREDIENTS

1 lb 10 oz shelled scallops

2 tbsp oil

2 onions, chopped

3 tomatoes, quartered

2 fresh green chilies, sliced

4 lime wedges, to garnish

MARINADE

3 tbsp chopped fresh cilantro

1 inch piece gingerroot, grated

1 tsp ground coriander

3 tbsp lemon juice

grated rind of 1 lemon

¼ tsp ground black pepper

½ tsp salt

½ tsp ground cumin

1 garlic clove, minced

1 To make the marinade, mix all the ingredients together in a bowl.

2 Put the scallops into a bowl. Add the marinade and turn the scallops until they are well coated.

3 Then cover and leave to marinate for 1 hour or overnight in the fridge.

4 Heat the oil in a Balti pan or wok, add the onions and stir-fry until softened.

5 Add the tomatoes and chilies and stir-fry for 1 minute.

6 Add the scallops and stir-fry for 6–8 minutes until the scallops are cooked through, but still succulent inside.

7 Serve garnished with lime wedges.

COOK'S TIP

It is best to buy the scallops fresh in the shell with the roe – you will need 3 lb 5 oz – a fish seller will clean them and remove the shell for you.

Seafood Stir-Fry

This combination of assorted seafood and tender vegetables flavored with ginger makes an ideal light meal served with thread noodles.

NUTRITIONAL INFORMATION

Calories	226	Sugars	.........5g
Protein	........35g	Fat	...........7g
Carbohydrate	....6g	Saturates	......1g

🦐 5 MINS   🕐 15 MINS

SERVES 4

I N G R E D I E N T S

3½ oz small, thin asparagus spears, trimmed

1 tbsp sunflower oil

1 inch piece gingeroot, cut into thin strips

1 medium leek, shredded

2 medium carrots, julienned

3½ oz baby-corn-on-the-cobs, quartered lengthwise

2 tbsp light soy sauce

1 tbsp oyster sauce

1 tsp clear honey

1 lb cooked, assorted shellfish, thawed if frozen

freshly cooked egg noodles, to serve

TO GARNISH

4 large cooked shrimp

small bunch fresh chives, freshly snipped

1 Bring a small saucepan of water to a boil and blanch the asparagus for 1–2 minutes.

2 Drain the asparagus, set aside and keep warm.

3 Heat the oil in a wok or large skillet and stir-fry the ginger, leek, carrot, and corn for about 3 minutes. Do not allow the vegetables to brown.

4 Add the soy sauce, oyster sauce, and honey to the wok or skillet.

5 Stir in the cooked shellfish and continue to stir-fry for 2–3 minutes until the vegetables are just tender and the shellfish are thoroughly heated through. Add the blanched asparagus and stir-fry for about 2 minutes.

6 To serve, pile the cooked noodles on to 4 warm serving plates and spoon the seafood and vegetable stir fry over them.

7 Garnish with the cooked shrimps and freshly snipped chives and serve immediately. Serve garnished with a large shrimp and freshly snipped chives.

Provençale-Style Mussels

These delicious large mussels are served hot with a tasty tomato and vegetable sauce. Mop up the delicious sauce with some crusty bread.

NUTRITIONAL INFORMATION

Calories	253	Sugars	........8g
Protein	........31g	Fat	..........8g
Carbohydrate	....9g	Saturates	......1g

5 MINS   50 MINS

SERVES 4

I N G R E D I E N T S

1 tbsp olive oil

1 large onion, finely chopped

1 garlic clove, finely chopped

1 small red bell pepper, seeded and finely chopped

sprig of rosemary

2 bay leaves

14 oz can chopped tomatoes

⅔ cup white wine

1 zucchini, diced finely

2 tbsp tomato paste

1 tsp superfine sugar

1¾ oz pitted black olives in brine, drained, and chopped

1½ lb cooked green-lippedmussels in their shells

1 tsp orange rind

salt and pepper

crusty bread, to serve

2 tbsp chopped, fresh parsley, to garnish

1 Heat the olive oil in a large saucepan and gently fry the chopped onion, garlic and bell pepper for 3–4 minutes until just softened.

2 Add the rosemary and bay leaves to the saucepan with the tomatoes and ⅓ cup wine. Season to taste, then bring to a boil and simmer for 15 minutes.

3 Stir in the zucchini, tomato paste, sugar and olives. Simmer for 10 minutes.

4 Meanwhile, bring a pan of water to a boil. Arrange the mussels in a steamer or a large strainer and place over the water. Sprinkle with the remaining wine and the orange rind. Cover and steam until the mussels open (discard any that remain closed).

5 Remove the mussels with a draining spoon and arrange on a serving plate. Discard the herbs and spoon the sauce over the mussels. Garnish with chopped parsley and serve with crusty bread.

Yucatan Fish

Herbs, onion, green bell pepper, and pumpkin seeds are used to flavor this baked fish dish, which is first marinated in lime juice.

NUTRITIONAL INFORMATION

Calories 248
Sugars 2g
Protein 33g
Fat 11g
Carbohydrate 3g
Saturates 1g

40 MINS   35 MINS

SERVES 4

INGREDIENTS

4 cod cutlets or steaks or hake cutlets
   (about 6 oz each)

2 tbsp lime juice

salt and pepper

1 green bell pepper

1 tbsp olive oil

1 onion, chopped finely

1–2 garlic cloves, minced

1½ oz green pumpkin seeds

grated rind of ½ lime

1 tbsp chopped fresh cilantro
   or parsley

1 tbsp chopped fresh mixed herbs

2 oz button mushrooms,
   sliced thinly

2–3 tbsp fresh orange juice or
   white wine

TO GARNISH

lime wedges

fresh mixed herbs

1 Wipe the fish, place in a shallow ovenproof dish, and pour the lime juice over. Turn the fish in the juice, season with salt and pepper, cover and leave in a cool place for 15–30 minutes.

2 Halve the bell pepper, remove the seeds and place under a preheated moderate broiler, skin-side upwards, until the skin burns and splits. Leave to cool slightly, then peel off the skin and chop the flesh.

3 Heat the oil in a pan and fry the onion, garlic, bell pepper, and pumpkin seeds gently for a few minutes until the onion is soft.

4 Stir in the lime rind, cilantro, or parsley, mixed herbs, mushrooms, and seasoning, and spoon over the fish.

5 Spoon or pour the orange juice or wine over the fish, cover with foil or a lid and place in a preheated oven at 350°F for about 30 minutes, or until the fish is just tender.

6 Garnish the fish with lime wedges and fresh herbs and serve.

Shrimp Bhuna

This is a fiery recipe with subtle undertones. As the flavor of the shrimp should be noticeable, the spices should not take over this dish.

NUTRITIONAL INFORMATION

Calories	141	Sugars	. . . . . . .0.4g
Protein	. . . . .19g	Fat	. . . . .7g
Carbohydrate	. . . .1g	Saturates	. . . . . .1g

15 MINS   20 MINS

SERVES 4–6

I N G R E D I E N T S

2 dried red chilies, seeded if liked

3 fresh green chilies, finely chopped

1 tsp ground turmeric

3 garlic cloves, minced

½ tsp pepper

1 tsp paprika

2 tsp white wine vinegar

½ tsp salt

1 lb 2 oz uncooked peeled colossal shrimp

3 tbsp oil

1 onion, chopped very finely

¾ cup water

2 tbsp lemon juice

2 tsp garam masala

sprigs of fresh cilantro,
    to garnish

COOK'S TIP

Garam masala should be used sparingly and is generally added to foods towards the end of their cooking time. It is also used sprinkled over cooked meats, vegetables and legumes as a garnish.

1 Combine the chilies, spices, vinegar, and salt in a nonmetallic bowl. Stir in the shrimp and leave for 10 minutes.

2 Heat the oil in a large skillet or wok, add the onion and fry for 3–4 minutes until soft.

3 Add the shrimp and the contents of the bowl to the pan and stir-fry over a high heat for 2 minutes. Reduce the heat, add the water and boil for 10 minutes, stirring occasionally, until the water is evaporated and the curry is fragrant.

4 Stir in the lemon juice and garam masala then transfer the mixture to a warm serving dish and garnish with fresh cilantro sprigs.

Charred Tuna Steaks

Tuna has a firm flesh, which is ideal for grilling, but it can be a little dry unless it is marinated first.

NUTRITIONAL INFORMATION

Calories	153	Sugars	.........1g
Protein	........29g	Fat	...........3g
Carbohydrate	....1g	Saturates	......1g

 2 HOURS   15 MINS

SERVES 4

INGREDIENTS

4 tuna steaks

3 tbsp soy sauce

1 tbsp Worcestershire sauce

1 tsp wholegrain mustard

1 tsp superfine sugar

1 tbsp sunflower oil

green salad, to serve

TO GARNISH

flat-leaf parsley

lemon wedges

1 Place the tuna steaks in a shallow dish.

2 Mix together the soy sauce, Worcestershire sauce, mustard, sugar, and oil in a small bowl.

3 Pour the marinade over the tuna steaks.

4 Gently turn over the tuna steaks, using your fingers or a fork. Make sure that the fish steaks are well coated with the marinade.

5 Cover and place the tuna steaks in the refrigerator. Leave to chill for between 30 minutes and 2 hours.

6 Grill the marinated fish over hot coals for 10–15 minutes, turning once.

7 Baste frequently with any of the marinade that is left in the dish.

8 Garnish with flat-leaf parsley and lemon wedges. Serve with a fresh green salad.

COOK'S TIP

If a marinade contains soy sauce, the marinating time should be limited, usually to 2 hours. If allowed to marinate for too long, the fish will dry out and become tough.

Poached Salmon

Salmon steaks, poached in a well-flavored stock and served with a piquant sauce, make a delicious summer lunch or supper dish.

NUTRITIONAL INFORMATION

Calories 712   Sugars 5g
Protein . . . . .66g   Fat 47g
Carbohydrate . . . .6g   Saturates 9g

🕐 10 MINS   🕐 30 MINS

SERVES 4

I N G R E D I E N T S

1 small onion, sliced

1 small carrot, sliced

1 stalk celery, sliced

1 bay leaf

pared rind and juice of ½ orange

a few stalks of parsley

salt

5-6 black peppercorns

3 cups water

4 salmon steaks, about 12 oz each

salad leaves, to serve

lemon twists, to garnish

S A U C E

1 large avocado, peeled, halved and stoned

½ cup low-fat natural yogurt

grated zest and juice of ½ orange

black pepper

a few drops of hot red pepper sauce

1 Put the onion, carrot, celery, bay leaf, orange rind, orange juice, parsley stalks, salt, and peppercorns in a pan just large enough to take the salmon steaks in a single layer. Pour on the water, cover the pan and bring to a boil. Simmer the stock for 20 minutes.

2 Arrange the salmon steaks in the pan, return the stock to a boil and simmer for 3 minutes. Cover the pan, remove from the heat and leave the salmon to cool in the stock.

3 Roughly chop the avocado and place it in a blender or food processor with the yogurt, orange zest, and orange juice. Process until smooth, then season to taste with salt, pepper and hot pepper sauce.

4 Remove the salmon steaks from the stock (reserve it to make fish soup or a sauce), skin them and pat dry with paper towels.

5 Cover the serving dish with salad leaves, arrange the salmon steaks on top and spoon a little of the sauce into the center of each one. Garnish the fish with lemon twists, and serve the remaining sauce separately.

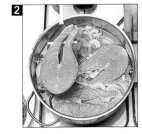

Salmon with Caper Sauce

The richness of salmon is beautifully balanced by the tangy capers in this creamy herb sauce.

NUTRITIONAL INFORMATION

Calories	302	Sugars	.........0g
Protein	........21g	Fat	.........24g
Carbohydrate	....1g	Saturates	......9g

 5 MINS 25 MINS

SERVES 4

I N G R E D I E N T S

4 salmon fillets, skinned

1 fresh bay leaf

few black peppercorns

1 tsp white wine vinegar

⅔ cup fish stock

3 tbsp heavy cream

1 tbsp capers

1 tbsp chopped fresh dill

1 tbsp chopped fresh chives

1 tsp cornstarch

2 tbsp skimmed milk

salt and pepper

new potatoes, to serve

T O G A R N I S H

fresh dill sprigs

chive flowers

1 Lay the salmon fillets in a shallow ovenproof dish. Add the bay leaf, peppercorns, vinegar, and stock.

2 Cover with foil and bake in a preheated oven at 350°F for 15–20 minutes until the flesh is opaque and flakes easily when tested with a fork.

3 Transfer the fish to warmed serving plates, cover and keep warm.

4 Strain the cooking liquid into a saucepan. Stir in the cream, capers, dill, and chives and seasoning to taste.

5 Blend the cornstarch with the milk. Add to the saucepan and heat, stirring, until thickened slightly. Boil for 1 minute.

6 Spoon the sauce over the salmon, garnish with dill sprigs and chive flowers.

7 Serve with new potatoes.

COOK'S TIP

Ask the fishstore to skin the fillets for you. The cooking time for the salmon will depend on the thickness of the fish: the thin tail end of the salmon takes the least time to cook.

Mackerel with Lime

The secret of this dish lies in the simple, fresh flavors which perfectly complement the fish.

NUTRITIONAL INFORMATION

Calories	302	Sugars	.........0g
Protein	........21g	Fat	.........24g
Carbohydrate	....0g	Saturates	......4g

 10 MINS · 10 MINS

SERVES 4

I N G R E D I E N T S

4 small mackerel

¼ tsp ground coriander

¼ tsp ground cumin

4 sprigs fresh cilantro

3 tbsp chopped, fresh cilantro

1 red chili, seeded and chopped

grated rind and juice of 1 lime

2 tbsp sunflower oil

salt and pepper

1 lime, sliced, to garnish

chili flowers (optional), to garnish

salad leaves, to serve

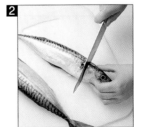

1 To make the chili flowers (if using), cut the tip of a small chili lengthways into thin strips, leaving the chili intact at the stem end. Remove the seeds and place in iced water until curled.

2 Clean and gut the mackerel, removing the heads if preferred. Transfer the mackerel to a chopping board.

3 Sprinkle the fish with the ground spices and salt and pepper to taste. Sprinkle 1 teaspoon of chopped cilantro inside the cavity of each fish.

4 Mix together the chopped cilantro, chili, lime rind and juice, and the oil in a small bowl. Brush the mixture liberally over the fish.

5 Place the fish in a hinged rack if you have one. Grill the fish over hot coals for 3–4 minutes on each side, turning once. Brush the fish frequently with the remaining basting mixture. Transfer to plates and garnish with chili flowers (if using) and lime slices, and serve with salad leaves.

COOK'S TIP

This recipe is suitable for other oily fish, such as trout, herring, or sardines.

Delicately Spiced Trout

The firm, sweet flesh of the trout is enhanced by the sweet-spicy flavor of the marinade and cooking juices.

NUTRITIONAL INFORMATION

Calories 374	Sugars 13g
Protein 38g	Fat 19g
Carbohydrate ...14g	Saturates 3g

45 MINS   20 MINS

SERVES 4

INGREDIENTS

4 trout, each weighing 6–9 oz, cleaned

3 tbsp oil

1 tsp fennel seeds

1tsp onion seeds

1 garlic clove, minced

⅔ cup coconut milk or fish stock

3 tbsp tomato paste

⅓ cup golden raisins

½ tsp garam masala

TO GARNISH

¼ cup chopped cashew nuts

lemon wedges

sprigs of fresh cilantro

MARINADE

4 tbsp lemon juice

2 tbsp chopped fresh cilantro

1 tsp ground cumin

½ tsp salt

½ tsp ground black pepper

1 Slash the trout skin in several places on both sides with a sharp knife.

2 To make the marinade, mix all the ingredients together in a bowl.

3 Put the trout in a shallow dish and pour over the marinade. Leave to marinate for 30–40 minutes; turn the fish over during the marinating time.

4 Heat the oil in a Balti pan or wok and fry the fennel seeds and onion seeds until they start popping.

5 Add the minced garlic, coconut milk or fish stock, and tomato paste and bring the mixture in the wok to a boil.

6 Add the golden raisins, garam masala, and trout with the juices from the marinade. Cover and simmer for 5 minutes. Turn the trout over and simmer for a further 10 minutes.

7 Serve garnished with the nuts, lemon, and cilantro sprigs.

Baked Sea Bass

Sea Bass is often paired with subtle oriental flavors. For a special occasion, you may like to bone the fish.

NUTRITIONAL INFORMATION

Calories 140   Sugars 0.1g
Protein ....29g   Fat 1g
Carbohydrate ...0.1g   Saturates 0.2g

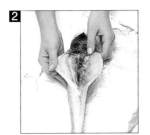  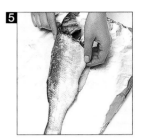

🍤 10 MINS   🕐 15 MINS

SERVES 4–6

I N G R E D I E N T S

2 sea bass, about 2 lb oz each, cleaned and scaled

2 scallions, green part only, cut into strips

2 inch piece ginger, peeled and cut into strips

2 garlic cloves, unpeeled, minced lightly

2 tbsp mirin or dry sherry

salt and pepper

TO SERVE

pickled sushi ginger (optional)

soy sauce

1 For each fish lay out a double thickness of foil and oil the top piece well, or lay a piece of silicon paper over the foil.

2 Place the fish in the middle and expose the cavity.

3 Divide the scallion and ginger between each cavity. Put a garlic clove in each cavity.

4 Pour over the mirin or dry sherry. Season the fish well.

5 Close the cavities and lay each fish on its side. Bring over the foil and fold the edges together to seal securely. Fold each end neatly.

6 Cook over a medium grill for 15 minutes, turning once.

7 To serve, remove the foil and cut each fish into 2 or 3 pieces.

8 Serve with the pickled ginger (if using) accompanied by soy sauce.

COOK'S TIP

Fresh sea bass is just as delicious when cooked very simply. Stuff the fish with garlic and chopped herbs, brush with olive oil and bake in the oven.

Indonesian-Style Spicy Cod

A delicious aromatic coating makes this dish rather special. Serve it with a crisp salad and crusty bread.

NUTRITIONAL INFORMATION

Calories 146	Sugars 2g
Protein 19g	Fat 7g
Carbohydrate 2g	Saturates 4g

🍲 🍲

🧊 10 MINS   🕐 15 MINS

SERVES 4

INGREDIENTS

4 cod steaks

1 stalk lemon grass

1 small red onion, chopped

3 cloves garlic, chopped

2 fresh red chilies, seeded and chopped

1 tsp grated gingerroot

¼ tsp turmeric

2 tbsp butter, cut into small cubes

8 tbsp canned coconut milk

2 tbsp lemon juice

salt and pepper

red chilies, to garnish (optional)

1 Rinse the cod steaks and pat them dry on absorbent paper towels.

2 Remove and discard the outer leaves from the lemon grass and thinly slice the inner section.

3 Place the lemon grass, onion, garlic, chilies, ginger, and turmeric in a food processor and blend until the ingredients are finely chopped. Season with salt and pepper to taste.

4 With the processor running, add the butter, coconut milk, and lemon juice and process until well blended.

5 Place the fish in a shallow, non-metallic dish. Pour over the coconut mixture and turn the fish until well coated.

6 If you have one, place the fish steaks in a hinged basket, which will make them easier to turn. Grill over hot coals for 15 minutes or until the fish is cooked through, turning once. Serve garnished with red chilies (if using).

COOK'S TIP

If you prefer a milder flavor, omit the chilies altogether. For a hotter flavor do not remove the seeds from the chilies.

Japanese Flounder

The marinade for this dish has a distinctly Japanese flavor. Its subtle flavor goes well with any white fish.

NUTRITIONAL INFORMATION

Calories . . . . .207 Sugars 9g
Protein . . . . .22g Fat 8g
Carbohydrate . . .10g Saturates 1g

6 HOURS   10 MINS

SERVES 4

I N G R E D I E N T S

4 small flounders

6 tbsp soy sauce

2 tbsp sake or dry white wine

2 tbsp sesame oil

1 tbsp lemon juice

2 tbsp light muscovado sugar

1 tsp gingerroot, grated

1 clove garlic, minced

TO GARNISH

1 small carrot

4 scallion

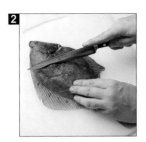
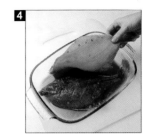
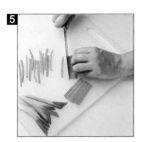

1 Rinse the fish and pat them dry on paper towels.

2 Cut a few slashes into the sides of the fish so that they absorb the marinade.

3 Mix together the soy sauce, sake or wine, oil, lemon juice, sugar, ginger, and garlic in a large, shallow dish.

4 Place the fish in the marinade and turn them over so that they are well coated on both sides. Leave to stand in the refrigerator for 1–6 hours.

5 Meanwhile, prepare the garnish. Cut the carrot into evenly-sized thin sticks and clean and shred the scallions.

6 Grill the fish over hot coals for about 10 minutes, turning once.

7 Scatter the chopped scallions and carrot over the fish and transfer the fish to a serving dish. Serve immediately.

VARIATION

Use sole instead of the flounders and scatter over some toasted sesame seeds instead of the carrot and scallions, if you prefer.

Herrings with Tarragon

The fish are filled with an orange-flavored stuffing and are wrapped in foil before being baked on the grill.

NUTRITIONAL INFORMATION

Calories 332	Sugars 4g
Protein 21g	Fat 24g
Carbohydrate 9g	Saturates 6g

 15 MINS   35 MINS

SERVES 4

INGREDIENTS

1 orange

4 scallions

1¾ oz fresh whole-wheat bread crumbs

1 tbsp fresh tarragon, chopped

4 herrings, cleaned and gutted

salt and pepper

green salad, to serve

TO GARNISH

2 oranges

1 tbsp light brown sugar

1 tbsp olive oil

sprigs of fresh tarragon

1 To make the stuffing, grate the rind from half of the orange, using a citrus zester.

2 Peel and chop all of the orange flesh on a plate in order to catch all of the juice.

3 Mix together the orange flesh, juice, rind, scallions, bread crumbs, and tarragon in a bowl. Season with salt and pepper to taste.

4 Divide the stuffing into 4 equal portions and use it to fill the body cavities of the fish.

5 Place each fish on to a square of lightly greased foil and wrap the foil around the fish so that it is completely enclosed. Grill over hot coals for 20–30 minutes until the fish are cooked through –the flesh should be white and firm to the touch.

6 Meanwhile make the garnish. Peel and thickly slice the 2 oranges and sprinkle over the sugar.

7 Just before the fish is cooked, drizzle a little oil over the orange slices and place them on the barbecue for about 5 minutes to heat through.

8 Transfer the fish to serving plates and garnish with the grilled orange slices and sprigs of fresh tarragon.

9 Serve the fish with a fresh green salad.

Steamed Stuffed Snapper

Red mullet may be used instead of the snapper, although they are a little more difficult to stuff because of their size. Use one mullet per person.

NUTRITIONAL INFORMATION

Calories . . . . .406 Sugar 4g
Protein . . . . .68g Fat 9g
Carbohydrate . . . .9g Saturates 0g

20 MINS   10 MINS

SERVES 4

I N G R E D I E N T S

3 lb whole snapper, cleaned and scaled

6 oz spinach

orange slices and shredded scallion, to
  garnish

S T U F F I N G

2 cups cooked long-grain rice

1 tsp grated fresh gingerroot

2 scallions, finely
  chopped

2 tsp light soy sauce

1 tsp sesame oil

½ tsp ground star anise

1 orange, segmented and chopped

1 Rinse the fish inside and out under cold running water and pat dry with paper towels.

2 Blanch the spinach for 40 seconds, rinse in cold water and drain well, pressing out as much moisture as possible.

3 Arrange the spinach on a heatproof plate and place the fish on top.

4 To make the stuffing, mix together the cooked rice, grated ginger, scallions, soy sauce, sesame oil, star anise, and orange in a bowl.

5 Spoon the stuffing into the body cavity of the fish, pressing it in well with a spoon.

6 Cover the plate and cook in a steamer for 10 minutes, or until the fish is cooked through.

7 Transfer the fish to a warmed serving dish, garnish with orange slices and shredded scallion and serve.

COOK'S TIP

The name snapper covers a family of tropical and subtropical fish that vary in color. They may be red, orange, pink, grey, or blue-green. Some are striped or spotted and they range in size from about 6 inches to 3 ft.

Crab-Stuffed Red Snapper

This popular fish is pinkish-red in color and has moist, tender flesh. For this recipe it is steamed, but it can also be baked or braised.

NUTRITIONAL INFORMATION

Calories 205	Sugars 0.1g
Protein 36g	Fat 6g
Carbohydrate ...0.1g	Saturates 1g

10 MINS   25 MINS

SERVES 4

INGREDIENTS

4 red snappers, cleaned and scaled, about 6 oz each

2 tbsp dry sherry

salt and pepper

wedges of lime, to garnish

red chili strips, to garnish

stir-fried shredded vegetables, to serve

STUFFING

1 small red chili

1 garlic clove

1 scallion

½ tsp finely grated lime rind

1 tbsp lime juice

3½ oz white crabmeat, slivered

1 Rinse the fish and pat dry on paper towels. Season inside and out and place in a shallow dish. Spoon over the sherry and set aside.

2 Meanwhile, make the stuffing. Carefully halve, seed and finely chop the chili. Place in a small bowl.

3 Peel and finely chop the garlic. Trim and finely chop the scallion. Add to the chili together with the grated lime rind, lime juice and the slivered crab meat.

4 Season with salt and pepper to taste and combine.

5 Spoon some of the stuffing into the cavity of each fish.

6 Bring a large saucepan of water to a boil. Arrange the fish in a steamer lined with baking parchment or in a large strainer and place over a boiling water.

7 Cover and steam for 10 minutes. Turn the fish over and steam for a further 10 minutes or until the fish is cooked

8 Drain the fish and transfer to serving plates.

9 Garnish with wedges of lime and strips of chilli, and serve the fish on a bed of stir-fried vegetables.

Pan-Seared Halibut

Liven up firm steaks of white fish with a spicy, colorful relish. Use red onions for a slightly sweeter flavor.

NUTRITIONAL INFORMATION

Calories ....197 Sugars 1g
Protein ....31g Fat 7g
Carbohydrate ....2g Saturates 1g

55 MINS   30 MINS

SERVES 4

INGREDIENTS

1 tsp olive oil

4 halibut steaks, skinned, 6 oz each

½ tsp cornstarch mixed with
　2 tsp cold water

salt and pepper

2 tbsp fresh chives, snipped, to garnish

RED ONION RELISH

2 tsp olive oil

2 medium red onions

6 shallots

1 tbsp lemon juice

2 tbsp red wine vinegar

2 tsp superfine sugar

⅔ cup Fresh Fish Stock
　(see page 15)

1 To make the relish, peel and thinly shred the onions and shallots. Place in a small bowl and toss in the lemon juice.

2 Heat the oil in a pan and fry the onions and shallots for 3–4 minutes until just softened.

3 Add the vinegar and sugar and continue to cook for a further 2 minutes over a high heat. Pour in the stock and season well. Bring to a boil and simmer gently for a further 8–9 minutes until the sauce has thickened and is slightly reduced.

4 Brush a non-stick, ridged skillet with oil and heat until hot. Press the fish steaks into the pan to seal, lower the heat and cook for 4 minutes. Turn the fish over and cook for 4–5 minutes until cooked through. Drain on paper towels and keep warm.

5 Stir the cornstarch paste into the onion sauce and heat through, stirring, until thickened. Season to taste.

6 Pile the relish on to 4 warm serving plates and place a halibut steak on top of each. Garnish with chives.

COOK'S TIP

If raw onions make your eyes water, try peeling them under cold, running water. Alternatively, stand or sit well back from the onion so that your face isn't directly over it.

Sole Paupiettes

A delicate dish of sole fillets rolled up with spinach and shrimps, served in a creamy ginger sauce.

NUTRITIONAL INFORMATION

Calories ....253 Sugars 7g
Protein ....24g Fat 14g
Carbohydrate ....9g Saturates 5g

🥘 10 MINS   🕐 45 MINS

SERVES 4

I N G R E D I E N T S

4½ oz fresh young spinach leaves

2 Dover soles or large lemon soles or plaice, filleted

4½ oz peeled shrimp, defrosted if frozen

2 tsp sunflower oil

2-4 scallions, finely sliced diagonally

2 thin slices gingerroot, finely chopped

⅔ cup fish stock or water

2 tsp cornstarch

4 tbsp single cream

6 tbsp low-fat unsweetened yogurt

salt and pepper

whole shrimp, to garnish (optional)

1 Strip the stalks off the spinach, wash and dry on paper towels. Divide the spinach between the seasoned fish fillets, laying the leaves on the skin side. Divide half the shrimp between them. Roll up the fillets from head to tail and secure with wooden tooth picks. Arrange the rolls on a plate in the base of a bamboo steamer.

2 Stand a low metal trivet in the wok and add enough water to come almost to the top of it. Bring to a boil. Place the bamboo steamer on the trivet,
cover with the steamer lid and then the wok lid, or cover tightly with a domed piece of foil. Steam gently for 30 minutes until the fish is tender and cooked through.

3 Remove the fish rolls and keep warm. Empty the wok and wipe dry with paper towels. Heat the oil in the wok, swirling it around until really hot. Add the scallions and ginger and stir-fry for 1-2 minutes.

4 Add the stock to the wok and bring to a boil. Blend the cornstarch with the
cream. Add the yogurt and remaining shrimp to the wok and heat gently until boiling. Add a little sauce to the blended cream and return it all to the wok. Heat gently until thickened and season to taste. Serve the paupiettes with the sauce spooned over and garnished with whole shrimp, if using.

Smoky Fish Pie

This flavorsome and colorful fish pie is perfect for a light supper. The addition of smoked salmon gives it a touch of luxury.

NUTRITIONAL INFORMATION

Calories 523	Sugars 15g
Protein 58g	Fat 6g
Carbohydrate ...63g	Saturates 2g

🥘 15 MINS   🕐 1 HOUR

SERVES 4

I N G R E D I E N T S

2 lb smoked haddock or
 cod fillets

2½ cups skimmed milk

2 bay leaves

4 oz button mushrooms, quartered

4 oz frozen English peas

4 oz frozen corn kernels

1½ lb potatoes, diced

5 tbsp low-fat unsweetened
 yogurt

4 tbsp chopped fresh parsley

2 oz smoked salmon, sliced into
 thin strips

3 tbsp cornstarch

1 oz smoked cheese, grated

salt and pepper

1 Preheat the oven to 400°F. Place the fish in a pan and add the milk and bay leaves. Bring to a boil, cover, and then simmer for 5 minutes.

2 Add the mushrooms, peas, and corn, bring back to a simmer, cover and cook for 5–7 minutes. Leave to cool.

3 Place the potatoes in a saucepan, cover with water, boil and cook for 8 minutes. Drain well and mash with a fork or a potato masher. Stir in the yogurt, parsley, and seasoning. Set aside.

4 Using a draining spoon, remove the fish from the pan. Flake the cooked fish away from the skin and place in an ovenproof gratin dish. Reserve the cooking liquid.

5 Drain the vegetables, reserving the cooking liquid, and gently stir into the fish with the salmon strips.

6 Blend a little cooking liquid into the cornstarch to make a paste. Transfer the rest of the liquid to a saucepan and add the paste. Heat through, stirring, until thickened. Discard the bay leaves and season to taste. Pour the sauce over the fish and vegetables and mix. Spoon over the mashed potato so that the fish is covered, sprinkle with cheese and bake for 25–30 minutes.

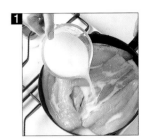

COOK'S TIP

If possible, use smoked haddock or cod that has not been dyed bright yellow or artificially flavored to give the illusion of having been smoked.

Seafood Pizza

Make a change from the standard pizza toppings–this dish is piled high with seafood baked with a red bell pepper and tomato sauce.

NUTRITIONAL INFORMATION

Calories ....248 Sugars 7g
Protein ....27g Fat 6g
Carbohydrate ...22g Saturates 2g

 25 MINS   55 MINS

SERVES 4

INGREDIENTS

5 oz standard pizza base mix

4 tbsp chopped fresh dill or 2 tbsp dried dill

fresh dill, to garnish

SAUCE

1 large red bell pepper

14 oz can chopped tomatoes with onion and herbs

3 tbsp tomato paste

salt and pepper

TOPPING

12 oz assorted cooked seafood, thawed if frozen

1 tbsp capers in brine, drained

1 oz pitted black olives in brine, drained

1 oz low-fat Mozzarella cheese, grated

1 tbsp grated, fresh Parmesan cheese

1 Preheat the oven to 400°F. Place the pizza base mix in a bowl and stir in the dill. Make the dough according to the directions on the packet.

2 Press the dough into a round measuring 10 inches across on a baking sheet lined with baking parchment. Set aside to prove rise.

3 Preheat the broiler to hot. To make the sauce, halve and seed the bell pepper and arrange on a broiler rack. Cook for 8–10 minutes until softened and charred. Leave to cool slightly, peel off the skin and chop the flesh.

4 Place the tomatoes and bell pepper in a saucepan. Bring to a boil and simmer for 10 minutes. Stir in the tomato paste and season to taste.

5 Spread the sauce over the pizza base and top with the seafood. Sprinkle over the capers and olives, top with the cheeses and bake for 25–30 minutes.

6 Garnish with sprigs of dill and serve hot.

Green Fish Curry

This dish has a wonderful fresh, hot, exotic taste resulting from the generous amount of fresh herbs, sharp fresh chilies, and coconut milk.

NUTRITIONAL INFORMATION

Calories 223   Sugars 2g
Protein ....44g   Fat 5g
Carbohydrate ....2g   Saturates 1g

5 MINS   20 MINS

SERVES 4

I N G R E D I E N T S

1 tbsp oil

2 scallions, sliced

1 tsp cumin seeds, ground

2 fresh green chilies, chopped

1 tsp coriander seeds, ground

4 tbsp chopped fresh cilantro

4 tbsp chopped fresh mint

1 tbsp chopped chives

⅔ cup coconut milk

4 white fish fillets, about 8 oz each

salt and pepper

basmati rice, to serve

1 mint sprig, to garnish

1 Heat the oil in a large skillet or shallow saucepan and add the scallions.

2 Stir-fry the scallions over a medium heat until they are softened but not colored.

3 Stir in the cumin, chilies, and ground coriander, and cook until fragrant.

4 Add the fresh cilantro, mint, chives, and coconut milk and season liberally.

5 Carefully place the fish in the pan and poach for 10–15 minutes until the flesh flakes when tested with a fork.

6 Serve the fish fillets in the sauce with the rice. Garnish with a mint sprig.

COOK'S TIP

Never overcook fish–it is surprising how little time it takes compared to meat. It will continue to cook slightly while keeping warm in the oven and while being dished up and brought to the table.

Vegetables
& Salads

There is more to the vegetarian diet than lentil roast and nut cutlets. For those of you who have cut out meat and fish completely from your diet or if you just want to

reduce your intake of these ingredients, this chapter offers an exciting assortment of vegetarian dishes, ranging from pizzas to curries and bakes. The advantage of vegetable

dishes is that very often the ingredients can be varied according to personal preference or seasonal availability, but always remember to buy the freshest vegetables available to ensure maximum flavor.

Stuffed Tomatoes

These grilled tomato cups are filled with a delicious Greek-style combination of herbs, nuts, and raisins.

NUTRITIONAL INFORMATION

Calories 156   Sugars 10g
Protein . . . . .3g   Fat 7g
Carbohydrate . . .22g   Saturates 0.7g

25 MINS   10 MINS

SERVES 4

INGREDIENTS

4 beefsteak tomatoes

4½ cups cooked rice

8 scallions, chopped

3 tbsp chopped fresh mint

2 tbsp chopped fresh parsley

3 tbsp pine nuts

3 tbsp raisins

2 tsp olive oil

salt and pepper

1 Cut the tomatoes in half, then scoop out the seeds and discard.

2 Stand the tomatoes upside down on absorbent paper towels for a few moments in order for the juices to drain out.

3 Turn the tomatoes the right way up and sprinkle the insides with salt and pepper.

4 Mix together the rice, scallions, mint, parsley, pine nuts and raisins.

5 Spoon the mixture into the tomato cups.

6 Drizzle over a little olive oil, then grill the tomatoes on an oiled rack over medium hot coals for about 10 minutes until they are tender and cooked through.

7 Transfer the tomatoes to serving plates and serve immediately while still hot.

COOK'S TIP

Tomatoes are a popular grill vegetable. Try broiling slices of beefsteak tomato and slices of onion, brushed with a little oil and topped with sprigs of fresh herbs. Or thread cherry tomatoes on to skewers and grill for 5–10 minutes.

Risotto Verde

Risotto is an Italian dish which is easy to make and uses arborio rice, onion, and garlic as a base for a range of savory recipes.

NUTRITIONAL INFORMATION

Calories	374	Sugars	.........5g
Protein	........10g	Fat	...........9g
Carbohydrate	...55g	Saturates	......2g

5 MINS   45 MINS

SERVES 4

I N G R E D I E N T S

7½ cups vegetable stock

2 tbsp olive oil

2 garlic cloves, minced

2 leeks, shredded

1¼ cups arborio rice

1¼ cups dry white wine

4 tbsp chopped mixed herbs

8 oz baby spinach

3 tbsp low-fat unsweetened yogurt

salt and pepper

shredded leek, to garnish

1 Pour the stock into a large saucepan and bring to the boil. Reduce the heat to a simmer.

2 Meanwhile, heat the oil in a separate pan and sauté the garlic and leeks for 2–3 minutes until softened.

3 Stir in the rice and cook for 2 minutes, stirring until well coated.

4 Pour in half of the wine and a little of the hot stock. Cook over a gentle heat until all of the liquid has been absorbed.

5 Add the remaining stock and wine and cook over a low heat for 25 minutes or until the rice is creamy.

6 Stir in the chopped mixed herbs and baby spinach, season well with salt and pepper and cook for 2 minutes.

7 Stir in the unsweetened yogurt, garnish with the shredded leek, and serve immediately.

COOK'S TIP

Do not hurry the process of cooking the risotto as the rice must absorb the liquid slowly in order for it to reach the correct consistency.

Fragrant Asparagus Risotto

Soft, creamy rice combines with the flavors of citrus and light aniseed to make this a delicious supper for four or a substantial starter for six.

NUTRITIONAL INFORMATION

Calories	223	Sugars	.........9g
Protein	.........6g	Fat	...........6g
Carbohydrate	...40g	Saturates	......1g

 10 MINS 45 MINS

SERVES 4

I N G R E D I E N T S

4 oz fine asparagus spears, trimmed

5 cups vegetable stock

2 bulbs fennel

1 oz low-fat spread

1 tsp olive oil

2 stalks celery, trimmed and chopped

2 medium leeks, trimmed and shredded

2 cups arborio rice

3 medium oranges

salt and pepper

1 Bring a small saucepan of water to a boil and cook the asparagus for 1 minute. Drain the asparagus and set aside until required.

2 Pour the stock into a saucepan and bring to a boil. Reduce the heat to maintain a gentle simmer.

3 Meanwhile, trim the fennel, reserving the fronds. Use a sharp knife to cut into thin slices.

4 Carefully melt the low-fat spread with the oil in a large saucepan, taking care that the water in the low-fat spread does not evaporate, and gently fry the fennel, celery, and leeks for 3–4 minutes until just softened. Add the rice

and cook, stirring, for a further 2 minutes until mixed.

5 Add a ladleful of stock to the pan and cook gently, stirring, until absorbed.

6 Continue ladling the stock into the rice until the rice becomes creamy, thick, and tender. This process will take about 25 minutes and should not be hurried.

7 Finely grate the rind and extract the juice from 1 orange and mix in to the rice. Carefully remove the peel and pith from the remaining oranges. Holding the fruit over the saucepan, cut out the orange segments and add to the rice, along with any juice that falls.

8 Stir the orange into the rice along with the asparagus spears. Season to taste and garnish with the fennel fronds.

Mexican-Style Pizzas

Ready-made pizza bases are topped with a chili-flavored tomato sauce and topped with kidney beans, cheese, and jalapeño chilies.

NUTRITIONAL INFORMATION

Calories 350	Sugars 8g
Protein 18g	Fat 10g
Carbohydrate ...49g	Saturates 3g

   10 MINS   20 MINS

SERVES 4

INGREDIENTS

4 x ready-made individual pizza bases

1 tbsp olive oil

7 oz can chopped tomatoes with garlic and herbs

2 tbsp tomato paste

7 oz can kidney beans, drained and rinsed

4 oz corn kernels, thawed if frozen

1–2 tsp chili sauce

1 large red onion, shredded

3½ oz reduced-fat sharp Cheddar cheese, grated

1 large green chili, sliced into rings

salt and pepper

1 Preheat the oven to 425°F. Arrange the pizza bases on a baking sheet and brush them lightly with the oil.

2 In a bowl, mix together the chopped tomatoes, tomato paste, kidney beans and sweetcorn, and add chili sauce to taste. Season with salt and pepper.

3 Spread the tomato and kidney bean mixture evenly over each pizza base to cover.

4 Top each pizza with shredded onion and sprinkle with some grated cheese and a few slices of green chili to taste.

5 Bake in the oven for about 20 minutes until the vegetables are tender, the cheese has melted and the base is crisp and golden.

6 Remove the pizzas from the baking sheet and transfer to serving plates. Serve immediately.

COOK'S TIP

Serve a Mexican-style salad with this pizza. Arrange sliced tomatoes, fresh cilantro leaves and a few slices of a small, ripe avocado on a plate. Sprinkle with fresh lime juice and coarse sea salt.

Potato & Tomato Calzone

These pizza dough Italian pasties are best served hot with a salad for a delicious lunch or supper dish.

NUTRITIONAL INFORMATION

Calories ....524 Sugars 8g
Protein ....17g Fat 8g
Carbohydrate ..103g Saturates 2g

  1½ HOURS   35 MINS

SERVES 4

I N G R E D I E N T S

D O U G H

4 cups white bread flour

1 tsp easy blend dried yeast

1¼ cups vegetable stock

1 tbsp clear honey

1 tsp caraway seeds

simmed milk, for glazing

F I L L I N G

1 tbsp vegetable oil

8 oz waxy potatoes, diced

1 onion, halved and sliced

2 garlic cloves, minced

1½ oz sun-dried tomatoes

2 tbsp chopped fresh basil

2 tbsp tomato paste

2 celery stalks, sliced

1¾ oz Mozzarella cheese, grated

1 To make the dough, sift the flour into a large mixing bowl and stir in the yeast. Make a well in the center of the mixture. Stir in the vegetable stock, honey and caraway seeds and bring the mixture together to form a dough.

2 Turn the dough out on to a lightly floured surface and knead for 8 minutes until smooth. Place the dough in a lightly oiled mixing bowl, cover and leave to rise in a warm place for 1 hour or until it has doubled in size.

3 Meanwhile, make the filling. Heat the oil in a skillet and add all the remaining ingredients except for the cheese. Cook for about 5 minutes, stirring.

4 Divide the risen dough into 4 pieces. On a lightly floured surface, roll them out to form four 7 inch circles. Spoon equal amounts of the filling on to one half of each circle. Sprinkle the cheese over the filling. Brush the edge of the dough with milk and fold the dough over to form 4 semi-circles, pressing to seal the edges.

5 Place on a non-stick baking sheet and brush with milk. Cook in a preheated oven, 425°F, for 30 minutes until golden and risen.

Potato Hash

This is a variation of the American dish, beef hash, which was made with salt beef and leftovers, and served to seagoing New Englanders.

NUTRITIONAL INFORMATION

Calories ....302 Sugars 5g
Protein ....15g Fat 10g
Carbohydrate ...40g Saturates 4g

5 MINS   30 MINS

SERVES 4

INGREDIENTS

2 tbsp butter

1 red onion, halved and sliced

1 carrot, diced

1 oz green beans, halved

3 large waxy potatoes, diced

2 tbsp all purpose flour

1¼ cups vegetable stock

8 oz bean curd, diced

salt and pepper

chopped fresh parsley, to garnish

1 Melt the butter in a skillet.

2 Add the onion, carrot, green beans, and potatoes and fry gently, stirring, for 5-7 minutes or until the vegetables begin to brown.

3 Add the flour to the skillet and cook for 1 minute, stirring constantly.

4 Gradually pour in the stock.

5 Reduce the heat and leave the mixture to simmer for 15 minutes or until the potatoes are tender.

6 Add the diced bean curd to the mixture and cook for a further 5 minutes.

7 Season to taste with salt and pepper.

8 Sprinkle the chopped parsley over the top of the potato hash to garnish, then serve hot from the skillet.

COOK'S TIP

A traditional hash dish is made from chopped fresh ingredients, such as roast beef or corned beef, bell peppers, onion and celery, often served with gravy.

Chinese Vegetable Pancakes

Chinese pancakes are made with hardly any fat–they are simply flattened white flour dough.

NUTRITIONAL INFORMATION

Calories	312	Sugars	.........5g
Protein	........13g	Fat	..........19g
Carbohydrate	...25g	Saturates	......7g

 5 MINS   10 MINS

SERVES 4

INGREDIENTS

1 tbsp vegetable oil

1 garlic clove, minced

1 inch piece gingerroot, grated

1 bunch scallions, trimmed and shredded lengthwise

3½ oz snow peas, topped, tailed and shredded

8 oz bean curd, drained and cut into ½ inch pieces

2 tbsp dark soy sauce, plus extra to serve

2 tbsp hoisin sauce, plus extra to serve

2 oz canned bamboo shoots, drained

2 oz canned water chestnuts, drained and sliced

3½ oz mung bean sprouts

1 small red chili, seeded and sliced thinly

1 small bunch fresh chives

12 soft Chinese pancakes

TO SERVE

shredded Chinese cabbage

1 cucumber, sliced

strips of red chili

2 Add the scallions, mangetout, tofu bean curd, soy and hoisin sauces. Stir-fry for 2 minutes.

3 Add the bamboo shoots, water chestnuts, bean sprouts, and sliced red chili to the pan.

1 Heat the oil in a non-stick wok or a large skillet and stir-fry the garlic and ginger for 1 minute.

4 Stir-fry gently for a further 2 minutes until the vegetables are just tender.

5 Snip the chives into 1 inch lengths and stir into the mixture.

6 Heat the pancakes according to the packet directions and keep warm.

7 Divide the vegetables and bean curd among the pancakes. Roll up and serve with the Chinese cabbage, cucumber, chili, and extra sauce for dipping.

Oriental Vegetable Noodles

This dish has a mild, nutty flavor from the peanut butter and dry-roasted peanuts.

NUTRITIONAL INFORMATION

Calories 193	Sugars 5g	
Protein 7g	Fat 12g	
Carbohydrate ...14g	Saturates 2g	

10 MINS   15 MINS

SERVES 4

INGREDIENTS

1½ cups green thread noodles or multi-colored spaghetti

1 tsp sesame oil

2 tbsp crunchy peanut butter

2 tbsp light soy sauce

1 tbsp white wine vinegar

1 tsp clear honey

4½ oz mooli, grated

1 large carrot, grated

4½ oz cucumber, shredded finely

1 bunch scallions, shredded finely

1 tbsp dry-roasted peanuts, minced

TO GARNISH

carrot flowers

scallion tassels

1 Bring a large saucepan of water to a boil, add the noodles or spaghetti and cook according to the packet directions. Drain well and rinse in cold water. Leave in a bowl of cold water until required.

2 To make the peanut butter sauce, put the sesame oil, peanut butter, soy sauce, vinegar, honey, and seasoning into a small screw-top jar. Seal and shake well to mix thoroughly.

3 Drain the noodles or spaghetti well, place in a large serving bowl and mix in half the peanut sauce.

4 Using 2 forks, toss in the mooli, carrot, cucumber, and scallions. Sprinkle with minced peanuts and garnish with carrot flowers and scallion tassels. Serve the noodles with the remaining peanut sauce.

COOK'S TIP

There are many varieties of oriental noodles available from oriental markets, delicatessens, and supermarkets. Try rice noodles, which contain very little fat and require little cooking; usually soaking in boiling water is sufficient.

Biryani with Onions

An assortment of vegetables cooked with tender rice, is flavored and colored with bright yellow turmeric and other warming Indian spices.

NUTRITIONAL INFORMATION

Calories	223	Sugars	........18g
Protein	.........8g	Fat	...........4g
Carbohydrate	...42g	Saturates	......1g

1¹/₄ HOURS   25 MINS

SERVES 4

INGREDIENTS

1 cup Basmati rice, rinsed

⅓ cup red lentils, rinsed

1 bay leaf

6 cardamom pods, split

1 tsp ground turmeric

6 cloves

1 tsp cumin seeds

1 cinnamon stick, broken

1 onion, chopped

8 oz cauliflower, broken into small florets

1 large carrot, diced

3½ oz frozen English peas

2 oz golden raisins

2½ cups Fresh Vegetable Stock
(see page 14)

salt and pepper

naan bread, to serve

CARAMELIZED ONIONS

2 tsp vegetable oil

1 medium red onion, shredded

1 medium onion, shredded

2 tsp superfine sugar

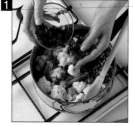

1 Place the rice, lentils, bay leaf, spices, onion, cauliflower, carrot, peas, and golden raisins in a large saucepan. Season with salt and pepper and mix well.

2 Pour in the stock, bring to a boil, cover and simmer for 15 minutes, stirring occasionally, until the rice is tender. Remove from the heat and leave to stand, covered, for 10 minutes to allow the stock to be absorbed. Discard the bay leaf, cardamom pods, cloves and cinnamon stick.

3 Heat the oil in a skillet and fry the onions over a medium heat for 3–4 minutes until just softened. Add the superfine sugar, raise the heat and cook, stirring, for a further 2–3 minutes until the onions are golden.

4 Gently mix the rice and vegetables and transfer to warm serving plates. Spoon over the caramelized onions and serve with plain, warmed naan bread.

Balti Dal

Chang dal is the husked, split, black garbanzo bean, which is yellow on the inside and has a nutty taste.

NUTRITIONAL INFORMATION

Calories ....132 Sugars 2g
Protein ....6g Fat 6g
Carbohydrate ...15g Saturates 1g

5 MINS   1¼ HOURS

SERVES 4

INGREDIENTS

1 cup chang dal or yellow split peas, washed

½ tsp ground turmeric

1 tsp ground coriander

1 tsp salt

4 curry leaves

2 tbsp oil

½ tsp asafetida powder (optional)

1 tsp cumin seeds

2 onions, chopped

2 garlic cloves, minced

½ inch piece gingerroot, grated

½ tsp garam masala

1 Put the chang dal in a large saucepan. Pour in enough water to cover by 1 inch.

2 Bring to a boil and use a spoon to remove the scum that has formed.

3 Add the turmeric, ground coriander, salt, and curry leaves. Simmer for 1 hour. The chang dal should be tender, but not mushy.

4 Heat the oil in a Balti pan or wok, Add the asafetida (if using) and fry for 30 seconds.

5 Add the cumin seeds and fry until they start popping.

6 Add the onions and stir-fry until golden brown.

7 Add the garlic, ginger, garam masala, and chang dal to the pan or wok and stir-fry for 2 minutes. Serve the balti hot as a side dish with a curry meal or store in the refrigerator for later use.

COOK'S TIP

Dal keeps well so it is a good idea to make a large amount and store it in the refrigerator or freezer in small portions. Reheat before serving.

Vegetable Curry

Vegetables are cooked in a mildly spiced curry sauce with yogurt and fresh cilantro stirred in just before serving.

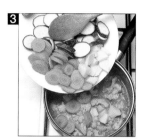

NUTRITIONAL INFORMATION

Calories 423	Sugars 24g	
Protein 16g	Fat 19g	
Carbohydrate ...50g	Saturates 7g	

 10 MINS   30 MINS

SERVES 4

I N G R E D I E N T S

2 tbsp sunflower oil

1 onion, sliced

2 tsp cumin seeds

2 tbsp ground coriander

1 tsp ground turmeric

2 tsp ground ginger

1 tsp chopped fresh red chili

2 garlic cloves, chopped

14 oz can chopped tomatoes

3 tbsp powdered coconut mixed with
1¼ cups boiling water

1 small cauliflower, broken into florets

2 zucchini, sliced

2 carrots, sliced

1 potato, diced

14 oz can garbanzo beans, drained and
rinsed

⅔ cup thick yogurt

2 tbsp mango chutney

3 tbsp chopped fresh cilantro

salt and pepper

fresh cilantro sprigs to garnish

T O   S E R V E

onion relish

banana raita

basmati rice and naan bread

1 Heat the oil in a saucepan and fry the onion until softened. Add the cumin, ground coriander, turmeric, ginger, chili and garlic and fry for 1 minute.

2 Add the tomatoes and coconut mixture and mix well.

3 Add the cauliflower, zucchini, carrots, potato, garbanzo beans, and seasoning. Cover and simmer for 20 minutes until the vegetables are tender.

4 Stir in the yogurt, mango chutney, and fresh cilantro and heat through gently, but do not boil.

5 Garnish the curry with cilantro sprigs and serve with onion relish, banana raita, basmati rice, and naan bread.

Eggplant Cake

This dish would make a stunning dinner party dish, yet it contains simple ingredients and is easy to make.

NUTRITIONAL INFORMATION

Calories 201   Sugars 4g
Protein . . . . .14g   Fat 7g
Carbohydrate . . .22g   Saturates 4g

 55 MINS   🕐 35 MINS

SERVES 4

I N G R E D I E N T S

1 medium eggplant

10½ oz tricolor pasta shapes

4½ oz low-fat soft cheese with garlic and herbs

1⅓ cups sieved tomatoes

4 tbsp grated Parmesan cheese

1½ tsp dried oregano

2 tbsp dry white bread crumbs

salt and pepper

1 Preheat the oven to 375°F. Grease and line a 8 inch round springform pan.

2 Trim the eggplant and slice lengthwise into slices about ¼ inch thick. Place in a bowl, sprinkle with salt, and set aside for 30 minutes to remove any bitter juices. Rinse well under cold running water and drain.

3 Bring a saucepan of water to a boil and blanch the eggplant slices for 1 minute. Drain and pat dry with paper towels. Set aside.

4 Cook the pasta shapes according to the directions on the packet; for best results, the pasta should be slightly undercooked. Drain well and return to the

saucepan. Add the soft cheese and allow it to melt over the pasta.

5 Stir in the sieved tomatoes, Parmesan cheese, oregano, and salt and pepper. Set aside.

6 Arrange the eggplant over the base and sides of the pan, overlapping the slices and making sure there are no gaps.

7 Pile the pasta mixture into the pan, packing down well, and sprinkle with the breadcrumbs. Bake for 20 minutes and leave to stand for 15 minutes.

8 Loosen the cake round the edge with a spatula and release from the pan. Turn out the pasta cake, eggplant-side uppermost, and serve hot.

Spicy Mexican Beans

These stewed beans form the basis of many Mexican recipes. Do not add salt until the beans are tender–it prevents them from softening.

NUTRITIONAL INFORMATION

Calories	234	Sugars	.........6g
Protein	........11g	Fat	..........13g
Carbohydrate	...20g	Saturates	......2g

12 HOURS   4 HOURS

SERVES 4

I N G R E D I E N T S

8 oz pinto beans or cannellini beans

1 large onion, sliced

2 garlic cloves, minced

1¾ pints water

salt

chopped fresh cilantro or parsley, to garnish

B E A N   S T E W

1 large onion, sliced

2 garlic cloves, minced

8 rashers lean streaky bacon, diced

2 tbsp oil

14 oz can chopped tomatoes

1 tsp ground cumin

1 tbsp sweet chili sauce

R E F R I E D   B E A N S

1 onion, chopped

2 garlic cloves, minced

2 tbsp oil

1 Soak the beans in a saucepan of cold water overnight. Drain the beans and put into a saucepan with the onion, garlic, and water, bring to a boil, cover and simmer gently for 1½ hours. Stir well, add more boiling water if necessary, and simmer, covered, for a further 1–1½ hours, or until the beans are tender.

2 When the beans are tender, add salt to taste (about 1 tsp) and continue to cook, uncovered, for about 15 minutes to allow most of the liquor to evaporate to form a thick sauce. Serve the basic beans hot sprinkled with chopped cilantro or parsley; or cool then store in the refrigerator for up to 1 week.

3 To make a bean stew, fry the onion, garlic and bacon for 3–4 minutes in the oil, add the other ingredients and bring to a boil. Cover and simmer very gently for 30 minutes, then season.

4 To make refried beans, fry the onion and garlic in the oil until golden brown. Add a quarter of the basic beans with a little of their liquor and mash. Continue adding and mashing the beans, while simmering gently until thick. Adjust the seasoning and serve hot.

Mixed Bean Stir-Fry

Any type of canned beans can be used–lima beans, black-eyed peas etc–but rinse under cold water and drain well before use.

NUTRITIONAL INFORMATION

Calories ....326 Sugars 16g
Protein ....18g Fat 7g
Carbohydrate ...51g Saturates 1g

10 MINS   10 MINS

SERVES 4

I N G R E D I E N T S

1 x 14 oz can red kidney beans

1 x 14 oz can cannellini beans

6 scallions

1 x 7 oz can pineapple rings or pieces in unsweetened juice, chopped

2 tbsp pineapple juice

3-4 pieces stem ginger

2 tbsp ginger syrup from the jar

thinly pared rind of ½ lime or lemon, cut into julienne strips

2 tbsp lime or lemon juice

2 tbsp soy sauce

1 tsp cornstarch

1 tbsp sesame oil

4½ oz French beans, cut into 1½ inch lengths

1 x 8 oz can bamboo shoots

salt and pepper

1 Drain all the beans, rinse under cold water, and drain again very thoroughly.

2 Cut 4 scallions into narrow slanting slices. Thinly slice the remainder and reserve for garnish.

3 Combine the pineapple and juice, ginger and syrup, lime rind and juice, soy sauce and cornstarch in a bowl.

4 Heat the oil in the wok, swirling it around until really hot. Add the scallions and stir-fry for about a minute, then add the green beans. Drain and thinly slice the bamboo shoots, add to the pan and continue to stir-fry for 2 minutes.

5 Add the pineapple and ginger mixture and bring just to a boil. Add the canned beans and stir until very hot–for about a minute.

6 Season to taste, sprinkled with the reserved chopped scallions; or serve as a vegetable accompaniment.

COOK'S TIP

Be sure to drain and rinse the beans before using, as they are usually canned in salty water, which will spoil the flavor of the finished dish.

Lemony Spaghetti

Steaming vegetables helps to preserve their nutritional content and allows them to retain their bright, unsweetened colors

NUTRITIONAL INFORMATION

Calories	 133	Sugars 8g
Protein	.... 8g	Fat 1g
Carbohydrate	... 25g	Saturates 0.2g

10 MINS   25 MINS

SERVES 4

INGREDIENTS

8 oz celeriac

2 medium carrots

2 medium leeks

1 small red bell pepper

1 small yellow bell pepper

2 garlic cloves

1 tsp celery seeds

1 tbsp lemon juice

10½ oz spaghetti

celery leaves, chopped, to garnish

LEMON DRESSING

1 tsp finely grated lemon rind

1 tbsp lemon juice

4 tbsp low-fat unsweetened fromage blanc

salt and pepper

2 tbsp snipped fresh chives

1 Peel the celeriac and carrots, cut into thin matchstalks and place in a bowl. Trim and slice the leeks, rinse under running water to flush out any trapped dirt, then shred finely. Halve, seed and slice the bell peppers. Peel and thinly slice the garlic.

2 Add all of the vegetables to the bowl with the celeriac and the carrots. Toss the vegetables with the celery seeds and lemon juice.

3 Bring a large saucepan of water to a boil and cook the spaghetti according to the directions on the packet. Drain and keep warm.

4 Meanwhile, bring another large saucepan of water to a boil, put the vegetables in a steamer or strainer and place over the boiling water. Cover and steam for 6–7 minutes or until tender.

5 While the spaghetti and vegetables are cooking, mix the ingredients for the lemon dressing together.

6 Transfer the spaghetti and vegetables to a warm serving bowl and mix with the dressing. Garnish with chopped celery leaves and serve.

Basil & Tomato Pasta

Roasting the tomatoes gives a sweeter and smoother flavor to this sauce. Italian tomatoes, such as plum or flavia, have the best flavor.

NUTRITIONAL INFORMATION

Calories	177	Sugars	........4g
Protein	.........5g	Fat	..........4g
Carbohydrate	...31g	Saturates	......1g

10 MINS   35 MINS

SERVES 4

I N G R E D I E N T S

1 tbsp olive oil

2 sprigs rosemary

2 cloves garlic, unpeeled

1 lb tomatoes, halved

1 tbsp sun-dried tomato paste

12 fresh basil leaves, plus extra to garnish

salt and pepper

1½ lb fresh farfalle or 12 oz dried farfalle

1 Place the oil, rosemary, garlic, and tomatoes, skin side up, in a shallow roasting pan.

2 Drizzle with a little oil and cook under a preheated broiler for 20 minutes or until the tomato skins are slightly charred.

3 Peel the skin from the tomatoes. Roughly chop the tomato flesh and place in a pan.

4 Squeeze the pulp from the garlic cloves and mix with the tomato flesh and sun-dried tomato paste.

5 Roughly tear the fresh basil leaves into smaller pieces and then stir them into the sauce. Season with a little salt and pepper to taste.

6 Cook the farfalle in a saucepan of boiling water according to the directions on the packet or until it is just cooked through. Drain

7 Gently heat the tomato and basil sauce.

8 Transfer the farfalle to serving plates and garnish with the basil. Serve with the tomato sauce.

COOK'S TIP

This sauce tastes just as good when mixed in with the pasta and served cold as a salad. Sprinkle some chopped parsley on top for added flavor and color.

Pesto Pasta

Italian pesto is usually laden with fat. This version has just as much flavor but is much healthier.

NUTRITIONAL INFORMATION

Calories 283   Sugars 5g
Protein ....14g   Fat 3g
Carbohydrate ...37g   Saturates 1g

1 HOUR   30 MINS

SERVES 4

INGREDIENTS

8 oz chestnut mushrooms, sliced

¾ cup fresh vegetable stock

6 oz asparagus, trimmed and cut into 2 inch lengths

10½ oz green and white tagliatelle

14 oz canned artichoke hearts, drained and halved

Grissini, to serve

TO GARNISH

basil leaves, shredded

Parmesan shavings

PESTO

2 large garlic cloves, minced

½ oz fresh basil leaves, washed

6 tbsp low-fat unsweetened fromage blanc

2 tbsp freshly grated Parmesan cheese

salt and pepper

1 Place the mushrooms in a saucepan with the stock. Bring to a boil, cover and simmer for 3–4 minutes until just tender. Drain and set aside, reserving the liquor to use in soups if wished.

2 Bring a small saucepan of water to a boil and cook the asparagus for 3–4 minutes until just tender. Drain and set aside until required.

3 Bring a large pan of lightly salted water to a boil and cook the tagliatelle according to the directios on the packet. Drain, return to the pan and keep warm.

4 Meanwhile, make the pesto. Place all of the ingredients in a blender or food processor and process for a few seconds until smooth. Alternatively, finely chop the basil and mix all the ingredients together.

5 Add the mushrooms, asparagus, and artichoke hearts to the pasta and cook, stirring, over a low heat for 2–3 minutes.

6 Remove from the heat and mix with the pesto.

7 Transfer to a warm bowl. Garnish with shredded basil leaves and Parmesan shavings and serve.

Mushroom Cannelloni

Thick pasta tubes are filled with a mixture of seasoned chopped mushrooms, and baked in a rich fragrant tomato sauce.

NUTRITIONAL INFORMATION

Calories	156	Sugar	.........8g
Protein	.........6g	Fats	...........1g
Carbohydrates	...21g	Saturates	.....0.2g

35 MINS   1¹/₂ HOURS

SERVES 4

I N G R E D I E N T S

12 oz chestnut mushrooms

1 medium onion, chopped finely

1 garlic clove, minced

1 tbsp chopped fresh thyme

½ tsp ground nutmeg

4 tbsp dry white wine

4 tbsp fresh white breadcrumbs

12 dried 'quick-cook' cannelloni

Parmesan shavings, to garnish (optional)

TOMATO SAUCE

1 large red bell pepper

¾ cup dry white wine

2 cups sieved tomatoes

2 tbsp tomato paste

2 bay leaves

1 tsp superfine sugar

1 Preheat the oven to 400°F. Finely chop the mushrooms and place in a pan with the onion and garlic. Stir in the thyme, nutmeg, and 4 tbsp wine. Bring to a boil, cover, and simmer for 10 minutes.

2 Stir in the breadcrumbs to bind the mixture together and season. Cool for 10 minutes.

3 Preheat the broiler to hot. To make the sauce, halve and deseed the bell pepper, place on the broiler rack and cook for 8–10 minutes until charred. Leave to cool for 10 minutes.

4 Once the bell pepper has cooled, peel off the charred skin. Chop the flesh and place in a food processor with the wine. Blend until smooth, and pour into a pan.

5 Mix the remaining sauce ingredients with the bell pepper and wine. Bring to a boil and simmer for 10 minutes. Discard the bay leaves.

6 Cover the base of an ovenproof dish with a thin layer of sauce. Fill the cannelloni with the mushroom mixture and place in the dish. Spoon over the remaining sauce, cover with foil, and bake for 35–40 minutes.

COOK'S TIP

For a more filling meal, add some flaked tuna or diced cooked chicken or ham to the stuffing mixture.

Beet & Orange Salad

Use freshly cooked beet in this unusual combination of colors and flavors, as beet soaked in vinegar will spoil the delicate balance.

NUTRITIONAL INFORMATION

Calories 240	Sugars 29g
Protein 10g	Fat 2g
Carbohydrate . . .49g	Saturates 0.3g

🥘 2¹/₄ HOURS 🕐 1 HOUR

SERVES 4

INGREDIENTS

1⅓ cups long-grain and wild rices

4 large oranges

1 lb cooked beet, peeled and drained (if necessary)

2 heads of chicory

salt and pepper

fresh snipped chives, to garnish

DRESSING

4 tbsp low-fat unsweetened fromage blanc

1 garlic clove, minced

1 tbsp whole-grain mustard

½ tsp finely grated orange rind

2 tsp clear honey

1 Cook the rices according to the packet directions. Drain and set aside to cool.

2 Meanwhile, slice the top and bottom off each orange. Using a sharp knife, remove the skin and pith. Holding the orange over a bowl to catch the juice, carefully slice between each segment. Place the segments in a separate bowl. Cover the juice and leave to chill.

   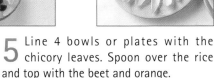

3 Dice the beet into small cubes. Mix with the orange segments, cover and chill.

4 When the rice has cooled, mix in the reserved orange juice until thoroughly incorporated and season with salt and pepper to taste.

5 Line 4 bowls or plates with the chicory leaves. Spoon over the rice and top with the beet and orange.

6 Mix all the dressing ingredients together and spoon over the salad, or serve separately in a bowl, if preferred. Garnish with fresh snipped chives.

Mexican Potato Salad

This dish is full of Mexican flavors, where potato slices are topped with tomatoes, chilies and ham, and served with a guacamole dressing.

NUTRITIONAL INFORMATION

Calories	260	Sugars	.........6g
Protein	.........6g	Fat	..........9g
Carbohydrate	...41g	Saturates	......2g

🫑 10 MINS   🕐 15 MINS

SERVES 4

INGREDIENTS

4 large waxy potatoes, sliced

1 ripe avocado

1 tsp olive oil

1 tsp lemon juice

1 garlic clove, minced

1 onion, chopped

2 large tomatoes, sliced

1 green chili, chopped

1 yellow bell pepper, sliced

2 tbsp chopped fresh cilantro

salt and pepper

lemon wedges, to garnish

1 Cook the potato slices in a saucepan of boiling water for 10-15 minutes or until tender. Drain and leave to cool.

2 Meanwhile, cut the avocado in half and remove the pit. Using a spoon, scoop the avocado flesh from the 2 halves and place in a mixing bowl.

3 Mash the avocado flesh with a fork and stir in the olive oil, lemon juice, garlic, and chopped onion. Cover the bowl and set aside.

4 Mix the tomatoes, chili and yellow bell pepper together and transfer to a salad bowl with the potato slices.

5 Spoon the avocado mixture on top and sprinkle with the cilantro. Season to taste and serve garnished with lemon wedges.

COOK'S TIP

Mixing the avocado flesh with lemon juice prevents it from turning brown once exposed to the air.

Grapefruit & Coconut Salad

This salad is deceptively light—although it is, in fact, quite filling. Reserve the grapefruit juices and add to the coconut dressing.

NUTRITIONAL INFORMATION

Calories 201	Sugars 13g
Protein 3g	Fat 15g
Carbohydrate . . .14g	Saturates 9g

 15 MINS   🕐 5 MINS

SERVES 4

INGREDIENTS

1 cup grated coconut

2 tsp light soy sauce

2 tbsp lime juice

2 tbsp water

2 tsp sunflower oil

1 garlic clove, halved

1 onion, chopped finely

2 large ruby grapefruits, peeled and segmented

1½ cups alfalfa sprouts

1 Toast the coconut in a dry skillet, stirring constantly, until golden brown, about 3 minutes. Transfer to a bowl.

2 Add the light soy sauce, lime juice and water.

3 Heat the oil in a saucepan and fry the garlic and onion until soft. Remove the garlic. Stir the onion into the coconut mixture.

4 Divide the grapefruit segments between 4 plates.

5 Sprinkle each with a quarter of the alfalfa sprouts and spoon over a quarter of the coconut mixture.

VARIATION

Try replacing the grapefruit with other citrus fruits belonging to the grapefruit family, such as pomelos, ugli fruit and mineolas.

  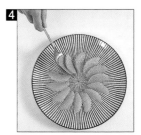

Hot & Spicy Rice Salad

Serve this spicy Indian-style dish with a low-fat unsweetened yogurt salad for a refreshing contrast.

NUTRITIONAL INFORMATION

Calories	329	Sugars 27g
Protein	. . . . .8g	Fat 8g
Carbohydrate	. . .59g	Saturates 1g

30 MINS   25 MINS

SERVES 4

I N G R E D I E N T S

2 tsp vegetable oil

1 onion, chopped finely

1 fresh red chili, seeded and chopped finely

8 cardamom pods

1 tsp ground turmeric

1 tsp garam masala

1¾ cups basmati rice, rinsed

3 cups boiling water

1 orange bell pepper, chopped

8 oz cauliflower florets, divided into small sprigs

4 ripe tomatoes, skinned, deseeded, and chopped

¾ cup seedless raisins

¼ cup toasted slivered almonds

salt and pepper

salad of low-fat unsweetened yogurt, onion, cucumber and mint, to serve

1 Heat the oil in a large non-stick saucepan, add the onion, chili, cardamom pods, turmeric, and garam masala and fry gently for 2–3 minutes until the vegetables are just softened.

2 Stir in the rice, boiling water, seasoning, bell pepper, and cauliflower.

3 Cover with a tight-fitting lid, bring to a boil, then cook over a low heat for 15 minutes without lifting the lid.

4 Uncover, fork through and stir in the tomatoes and raisins.

5 Cover again, turn off the heat and leave for 15 minutes. Discard the cardamom pods.

6 Pile on to a warmed serving platter and sprinkle over the toasted slivered almonds.

7 Serve the rice salad with the yogurt salad.

Melon and Mango Salad

A little freshly grated gingerroot mixed with creamy yogurt and clear honey makes a perfect dressing for this refreshing salad.

NUTRITIONAL INFORMATION

Calories 189	Sugars 30g
Protein 5g	Fat 7g
Carbohydrate ...30g	Saturates 1g

15 MINS   0 MINS

SERVES 4

I N G R E D I E N T S

1 cantaloupe melon

½ cup black grapes, halved and pipped

½ cup green grapes

1 large mango

1 bunch of watercress, trimmed

iceberg lettuce leaves, shredded

2 tbsp olive oil

1 tbsp cider vinegar

1 passion fruit

salt and pepper

D R E S S I N G

⅔ cup low-fat thick unsweetened yogurt

1 tbsp clear honey

1 tsp grated fresh gingerroot

1 To make the dressing for the melon, mix together the yogurt, honey, and ginger.

2 Halve the melon and scoop out the seeds. Slice, peel, and cut into chunks. Mix with the grapes.

3 Slice the mango on each side of its large flat pit. On each mango half, slash the flesh into a criss-cross pattern down to, but not through, the skin. Push the skin from underneath to turn the mango halves inside out. Now remove the flesh and add to the melon mixture.

4 Arrange the watercress and lettuce on 4 serving plates.

5 Make the dressing for the salad greens by mixing together the olive oil and cider vinegar with a little salt and pepper. Drizzle over the watercress and lettuce.

6 Divide the melon mixture between the 4 plates and spoon over the yogurt dressing.

7 Scoop the seeds out of the passion fruit and sprinkle them over the salads. Serve immediately or chill in the refrigerator until required.

Cool Cucumber Salad

This cooling salad is another good foil for a highly spiced meal. Omit the green chili, if preferred.

NUTRITIONAL INFORMATION

Calories 11	Sugars 2g
Protein 0.4g	Fat 0g
Carbohydrate 2g	Saturates 0g

 1¼ HOURS   0 MINS

SERVES 4

I N G R E D I E N T S

8 oz cucumber

1 green chili (optional)

fresh cilantro leaves, finely chopped

2 tbsp lemon juice

½ tsp salt

1 tsp sugar

fresh mint leaves and red bell pepper
  strips, to garnish

1 Using a sharp knife, slice the cucumber thinly. Arrange the cucumber slices on a round serving plate.

2 Using a sharp knife, chop the green chili (if using). Scatter the chopped chili over the cucumber.

3 To make the dressing, mix together the cilantro, lemon juice, salt, and sugar.

4 Place the cucumber in the refrigerator and leave to chill for at least 1 hour, or until required.

5 When ready to serve, transfer the cucumber to a serving dish. Pour the salad dressing over the cucumber just before serving and garnish with mint and red bell pepper.

Moroccan Couscous Salad

Couscous is a type of semolina made from durum wheat. It is wonderful in salads as it readily takes up the flavor of the dressing.

NUTRITIONAL INFORMATION

Calories ....195 Sugars 15g
Protein ....8g Fat 2g
Carbohydrate ...40g Saturates 0.3g

🥗 15 MINS   🕐 15 MINS

SERVES 6

I N G R E D I E N T S

2 cups couscous

1 bunch scallions, trimmed and chopped finely

1 small green bell pepper, cored, seeded, and chopped

4 inch piece cucumber, chopped

7 oz can garbanzo beans, rinsed and drained

⅔ cup golden raisins

2 oranges

salt and pepper

lettuce leaves, to serve

sprigs of fresh mint, to garnish

D R E S S I N G

finely grated rind of 1 orange

1 tbsp chopped fresh mint

⅔ cup low-fat unsweetened yogurt

1 Put the couscous into a bowl and cover with boiling water. Leave it to soak for about 15 minutes to swell the grains, then stir with a fork to separate them.

2 Add the scallions, green bell pepper, cucumber, garbanzo beans and golden raisins to the couscous, stirring to combine. Season well with salt and pepper.

3 To make the dressing, mix the orange rind, mint, and yogurt. Pour over the couscous mixture and stir well.

4 Using a sharp serrated knife, remove the peel and pith from the oranges. Cut the flesh into segments, removing all the membrane.

5 Arrange the lettuce leaves on serving plates. Divide the couscous mixture between the plates and arrange the orange segments on top.

6 Garnish with sprigs of fresh mint and serve.

VARIATION

As an alternative, use bulghur wheat instead of the couscous. Rinse thoroughly until the water runs clear, then soak in boiling water for 1 hour. Strain if necessary.

Coleslaw

Home-made coleslaw tastes far superior to any that you can buy. If you make it in advance, add the sunflower seeds just before serving.

NUTRITIONAL INFORMATION

Calories	224	Sugars	.........8g
Protein	.........3g	Fat	..........20g
Carbohydrate	....8g	Saturates	......3g

10 MINS   5 MINS

SERVES 4

I N G R E D I E N T S

⅔ cup low-fat mayonnaise

⅔ cup low-fat unsweetened yogurt

dash of Tabasco sauce

1 medium head white cabbage

4 carrots

1 green bell pepper

2 tbsp sunflower seeds

salt and pepper

1 To make the dressing, combine the mayonnaise, yogurt, Tabasco sauce, and salt and pepper to taste in a small bowl. Leave to chill until required.

2 Cut the cabbage in half and then into quarters. Remove and discard the tough center stalk. Shred the cabbage leaves finely. Wash the leaves and dry them thoroughly.

3 Peel the carrots and shred using a food processor or mandolin. Alternatively, coarsely grate the carrot.

4 Quarter and seed the bell pepper and cut the flesh into thin strips.

5 Combine the vegetables in a large mixing bowl and toss to mix. Pour over the dressing and toss until the vegetables are well coated. Leave to chill in the refrigerator until required.

6 Just before serving, place the sunflower seeds on a baking sheet, and toast them in the oven or under the broiler until golden brown. Transfer the salad to a large serving dish, scatter with sunflower seeds and serve.

VARIATION

For a slightly different taste, add one or more of the following ingredients to the coleslaw: raisins, grapes, grated apple, chopped walnuts, cubes of cheese or roasted peanuts.

Green Bean & Carrot Salad

This colorful salad of crisp vegetables is tossed in a delicious sun-dried tomato dressing.

NUTRITIONAL INFORMATION

Calories 104   Sugars 9g
Protein . . . . .2g   Fat 6g
Carbohydrate . . .10g   Saturates 1g

 10 MINS   5 MINS

SERVES 4

INGREDIENTS

12 oz green beans

8 oz carrots

1 red bell pepper

1 red onion

DRESSING

2 tbsp extra virgin olive oil

1 tbsp red wine vinegar

2 tsp sun-dried tomato paste

¼ tsp superfine sugar

salt and pepper

1 Top and tail the green beans and blanch them in boiling water for 4 minutes, until just tender. Drain the beans and rinse them under cold water until they are cool. Drain again thoroughly.

2 Transfer the beans to a large salad bowl.

3 Peel the carrots and cut them into thin matchstalks, using a mandolin if you have one.

4 Halve and seed the bell pepper and cut the flesh into thin strips.

5 Peel the onion and cut it into thin slices.

6 Add the carrot, bell pepper, and onion to the beans and toss to mix.

7 To make the dressing, place the oil, wine vinegar, sun-dried tomato paste, sugar, and salt and pepper to taste in a small screw-top jar and shake well.

8 Pour the dressing over the vegetables and serve immediately or leave to chill in the refrigerator until required.

COOK'S TIP

Use canned beans if fresh ones are unavailable. Rinse off the salty liquid and drain well. There is no need to blanch canned beans.

Spinach & Orange Salad

This is a refreshing and very nutritious salad. Add the dressing just before serving so that the leaves do not become soggy.

NUTRITIONAL INFORMATION

Calories . . . . . . .126 Sugars 10g
Protein . . . . .3g Fat 9g
Carbohydrate . . .10g Saturates 1g

 10 MINS   0 MINS

SERVES 4

INGREDIENTS

8 oz baby spinach leaves

2 large oranges

½ red onion

DRESSING

3 tbsp extra virgin olive oil

2 tbsp freshly squeezed orange juice

2 tsp lemon juice

1 tsp clear honey

½ tsp wholegrain mustard

salt and pepper

1 Wash the spinach leaves under cold running water and then dry them thoroughly on absorbent paper towels. Remove any tough stalks and tear the larger leaves into smaller pieces.

2 Slice the top and bottom off each orange with a sharp knife, then remove the peel. Carefully slice between the membranes of the orange to remove the segments. Reserve any juices for the salad dressing.

3 Using a sharp knife, finely chop the onion.

4 Mix together the salad greens and orange segments and arrange in a serving dish.

5 Scatter the chopped onion over the salad.

6 To make the dressing, whisk together the olive oil, orange juice, lemon juice, honey, mustard, and salt and pepper to taste in a small bowl.

7 Pour the dressing over the salad just before serving. Toss the salad well to coat the leaves with the dressing.

VARIATION

Use a mixture of spinach and watercress leaves, if you prefer a slightly more peppery flavor.

Minted Fennel Salad

This is a very refreshing salad. The subtle liquorice flavor of fennel combines well with the cucumber and mint.

NUTRITIONAL INFORMATION

Calories 90	Sugars 7g
Protein 4g	Fat 5g
Carbohydrate 7g	Saturates 1g

 25 MINS   0 MINS

SERVES 4

I N G R E D I E N T S

1 bulb fennel

2 small oranges

1 small or ½ large cucumber

1 tbsp chopped mint

1 tbsp virgin olive oil

2 eggs, hard cooked

1 Using a sharp knife, trim the outer leaves from the fennel. Slice the fennel bulb thinly into a bowl of water and then sprinkle with lemon juice (see Cook's Tip).

2 Grate the rind of the oranges over a bowl. Using a sharp knife, pare away the orange peel, then segment the orange by carefully slicing between each line of pith. Do this over the bowl in order to retain the juice.

3 Using a sharp knife, cut the cucumber into ½ inch rounds and then cut each round into quarters.

4 Add the cucumber to the fennel and orange mixture together with the mint.

5 Pour the olive oil over the fennel and cucumber salad and toss well.

6 Peel and quarter the eggs and use these to decorate the top of the salad. Serve at once.

COOK'S TIP

Fennel will discolor if it is left for any length of time without a dressing. To prevent any discoloration, place it in a bowl of water and sprinkle with lemon juice.

Pear & Roquefort Salad

The sweetness of the pear is a perfect partner to the 'bite' of the radicchio.

NUTRITIONAL INFORMATION

Calories 94   Sugars 10g
Protein ....5g   Fat 4g
Carbohydrate ...10g   Saturates 3g

 10 MINS   0 MINS

SERVES 4

INGREDIENTS

1¾ oz Roquefort cheese

⅔ cup low-fat unsweetened yogurt

2 tbsp snipped chives

few leaves of lollo rosso

few leaves of radicchio

few leaves of corn salad

2 ripe pears

pepper

whole chives, to garnish

1 Place the cheese in a bowl and mash with a fork. Gradually blend the yogurt into the cheese to make a smooth dressing. Add the chives and season with pepper to taste.

2 Tear the lollo rosso, radicchio, and corn salad leaves into manageable pieces. Arrange the salad leaves on a serving platter or on individual serving plates.

3 Quarter and core the pears and then cut them into slices.

4 Arrange the pear slices over the salad leaves.

5 Drizzle the dressing over the pears and garnish with a few whole chives.

COOK'S TIP

Look out for bags of mixed salad leaves as these are generally more economical than buying lots of different leaves separately.

Desserts

The healthiest ending to a meal would be fresh fruit topped with low-fat yogurt or fromage blanc. Fruit contains no fat and is naturally rich in sugar, vitamins, and fiber—perfect for the low-fat diet. However, there are many other ways to use fruit as the basis for a range of delicious desserts. Experiment with the unusual and exotic

fruits that are increasingly available in supermarkets. In this chapter there is a mouthwatering range of hot and cold fruit desserts, sophisticated mousses and fools and satisfying cakes, as well as variations on the traditional fruit salad. There are also a number of non-fruit based desserts and some low-fat treats for chocoholics.

Summer Pudding

Use whatever summer fruit you have available. Avoid strawberries as they do not give a good result, but cherries are delicious.

NUTRITIONAL INFORMATION

Calories ....174 Sugars 42g
Protein ....2g Fat 0.4g
Carbohydrate ...43g Saturates 0g

 12 HOURS   0 MINS

SERVES 4–6

INGREDIENTS

2 lb mixed summer fruit,
    such as blackberries, redcurrants,
    blackcurrants, raspberries,
    loganberries, and cherries

¾ cup superfine
    sugar

8 small slices white bread

low-fat fromage blanc, to serve

1 Stir the fruit and superfine sugar together in a large saucepan, cover and bring to a boil. Simmer for 10 minutes, stirring once.

2 Cut the crusts off the bread slices.

3 Line a 4¹/₂ cup pudding bowl with the bread, ensuring there are no gaps between the bread slices.

4 Add the fruit and as much of the cooking juices as will fit into the bread-lined bowl.

5 Cover the fruit with the remaining bread slices.

6 Put the pudding bowl on to a large plate or a shallow baking sheet. Place a plate on top and weigh it down with cans. Leave to chill in the refrigerator.

7 When ready to serve, turn the summer pudding out on to a serving plate or shallow bowl, cut into slices and serve cold with low-fat fromage blanc.

COOK'S TIP

To give the pudding a more lasting set, dissolve 2 enveloes or 2 tablespoons of powdered gelatine in water and stir into the fruit mixture. This enables you to turn it out on to the serving plate a couple of hours before serving.

Summer Fruit Clafoutis

Serve this mouth-watering French-style fruit-in-batter pudding hot or cold with low-fat fromage blanc or yogurt.

NUTRITIONAL INFORMATION

Calories 228	Sugars 26g
Protein 9g	Fat 2g
Carbohydrate ...42g	Saturates 1g

 1³/₄ HOURS   50 MINS

SERVES 6

INGREDIENTS

1 lb prepared fresh assorted soft fruits such as blackberries, raspberries, strawberries, blueberries, cherries, gooseberries, redcurrants, blackcurrants

4 tbsp soft fruit liqueur such as crème de cassis, kirsch, or framboise

4 tbsp skimmed milk powder

1 cup all-purpose flour

pinch of salt

¼ cup superfine sugar

2 eggs, size 2, beaten

1¼ cups skimmed milk

1 tsp vanilla extract

2 tsp superfine sugar to dust

TO SERVE

assorted soft fruits

low-fat yogurt or unsweetened fromage blanc

1 Place the assorted fruits in a mixing bowl and spoon over the fruit liqueur. Cover and chill for 1 hour for the fruit to macerate.

2 In a large bowl, mix the skimmed milk powder, flour, salt, and sugar. Make a well in the center and gradually whisk in the eggs, milk, and vanilla extract, using a balloon whisk, until smooth. Transfer to a jug, and set aside for 30 minutes.

3 Line the base of a 9 inch round ovenproof baking dish with baking parchment and spoon in the fruits and juices.

4 Re-whisk the batter and pour over the fruits, stand the dish on a baking sheet and bake in a preheated oven at 400°F for 50 minutes until firm, risen, and golden brown.

5 Dust with superfine sugar. Serve immediately with extra fruits, low-fat unsweetened yogurt or fromage blanc.

Fruit Bread Pudding

This is like a summer pudding, but it uses fruits which appear later in the year, such as apples, pears, and blackberries, as a succulent filling.

NUTRITIONAL INFORMATION

Calories	178	Sugars	........31g
Protein	.........3g	Fat	...........1g
Carbohydrate	...42g	Saturates	.....0.1g

12 HOURS   10 MINS

SERVES 8

I N G R E D I E N T S

4 cups mixed blackberries, chopped apples, chopped pears

¾ cup soft light brown sugar

1 tsp cinnamon

8 oz white bread, thinly sliced, crusts removed

1 Place the prepared fruit in a large saucepan with the soft light brown sugar, cinnamon and 3½ fl oz of water, stir and bring to a boil.

2 Reduce the heat and simmer for 5–10 minutes so that the fruits soften but still hold their shape.

3 Meanwhile, line the base and sides of a 1½ cups pudding bowl with the bread slices, ensuring that there are no gaps between the pieces of bread.

4 Spoon the fruit into the center of the bread-lined bowl and cover the fruit with the remaining bread.

5 Place a saucer on top of the bread and weight it down. Leave the pudding to chill in the refrigerator overnight.

6 Turn the autumn fruit bread pudding out on to a serving plate and serve immediately.

VARIATION

You can use thin slices of plain sponge cake instead of the sliced bread. The sponge will turn a pinkish color from the fruit juices and the brown edges of the cake will form an attractive pattern of irregular brown lines.

Winter Puddings

An interesting alternative to the familiar Summer Pudding, which uses dried fruits and a tasty malt loaf.

🍮 12 HOURS   🕐 15 MINS

SERVES 4

INGREDIENTS

11½ oz fruit malt loaf

1 cup no-need-to-soak dried apricots, chopped coarsely

½ cup dried apple, chopped coarsely

2 cups orange juice

1 tsp grated orange rind

2 tbsp orange liqueur

grated orange rind, to decorate

low-fat crème fraîche or low-fat unsweetened fromage blanc, to serve

1 Cut the malt loaf into ½ inch slices.

2 Place the apricots, apple, and orange juice in a saucepan. Bring to a boil, then simmer for 10 minutes. Remove the fruit using a draining spoon and reserve the liquid. Place the fruit in a dish and leave to cool. Stir in the orange rind and liqueur.

3 Line 4 × 1¾ cup pudding bowls or ramekin dishes with baking parchment.

4 Cut 4 circles from the malt loaf slices to fit the tops of the molds and cut the remaining slices to line them.

5 Soak the malt loaf slices in the reserved fruit syrup, then arrange around the base and sides of the molds. Trim away any crusts which overhang the edges. Fill the centers with the chopped fruit, pressing down well, and place the malt loaf circles on top.

6 Cover with baking parchment and weigh each bowl down with a 8 oz weight or a food can. Chill in the refrigerator overnight.

7 Remove the weight and baking parchment. Carefully turn the puddings out on to 4 serving plates. Remove the lining paper.

8 Decorate with orange rind and serve with crème fraîche or fromage blanc.

Crispy-Topped Fruit Bake

The sugar cubes give a lovely crunchy taste to this easy-to-make pudding.

NUTRITIONAL INFORMATION

Calories ....227 Sugars 30g
Protein ....5g Fat 1g
Carbohydrate ...53g Saturates 0.2g

15 MINS   1 HOUR

SERVES 10

I N G R E D I E N T S

12 oz cooking apples

3 tbsp lemon juice

10½ oz self-raising whole wheat flour

½ tsp baking powder

1 tsp ground cinnamon, plus extra for dusting

6 oz prepared blackberries, thawed if frozen, plus extra to decorate

6 oz light muscovado sugar

1 medium egg, beaten

¾ cup low-fat unsweetened fromage blanc

2 oz white or brown sugar cubes, lightly crushed

sliced eating apple, to decorate

1 Preheat the oven to 375°F. Grease and line a 2 lb loaf pan. Core, peel, and finely dice the apples. Place them in a saucepan with the lemon juice, bring to a boil, cover and simmer for 10 minutes until soft and pulpy. Beat well and set aside to cool.

2 Sift the flour, baking powder and 1 tsp cinnamon into a bowl, adding any husks that remain in the sifter Stir in 4 oz blackberries and the sugar.

3 Make a well in the center of the ingredients and add the egg, fromage blanc and cooled apple purée. Mix well to incorporate thoroughly. Spoon the mixture into the prepared loaf pan and smooth over the top.

4 Sprinkle with the remaining blackberries, pressing them down into the cake mixture, and top with the crushed sugar lumps. Bake for 40–45 minutes. Leave to cool in the pan.

5 Remove the cake from the pan and peel away the lining paper. Serve dusted with cinnamon and decorated with extra blackberries and apple slices.

VARIATION

Try replacing the blackberries with blueberries. Use the canned or frozen variety if fresh blueberries are unavailable.

Fruit & Nut Loaf

This loaf is like a fruit bread which may be served warm or cold, perhaps spread with a little margarine or butter or topped with jam.

NUTRITIONAL INFORMATION

Calories	531	Sugars	.......53g
Protein	........12g	Fat	..........14g
Carbohydrate	...96g	Saturates	......2g

1 HOUR   40 MINS

SERVES 4

I N G R E D I E N T S

1¾ cups white bread flour, plus extra for dusting

½ tsp salt

1 tbsp margarine, plus extra for greasing

2 tbsp soft light brown sugar

⅔ cup golden raisins

½ cup no-need to soak dried apricots, chopped

½ cup chopped hazelnuts

2 tsp easy-blend dried yeast

6 tbsp orange juice

6 tbsp low-fat unsweetened yogurt

2 tbsp strained apricot jam

1 Sieve the flour and salt into a mixing bowl. Rub in the margarine and stir in the sugar, golden raisins, apricots, nuts, and yeast.

2 Warm the orange juice in a saucepan but do not allow to boil.

3 Stir the warm orange juice into the flour mixture with the unsweetened yogurt and bring the mixture together to form a dough.

4 Knead the dough on a lightly floured surface for 5 minutes until smooth and elastic. Shape into a round and place on a lightly greased baking sheet. Cover with a clean dish cloth and leave to rise in a warm place until doubled in size.

5 Cook the loaf in a preheated oven, 425°F, for 35–40 minutes until cooked through. Transfer to a cooling rack and brush the cake with the apricot jam. Leave the cake to cool before serving.

COOK'S TIP

To test whether bread or cake is cooked, tap the tin from underneath. If it sounds hollow, the bread or cake is ready.

Fruit Loaf with Apple Spread

This sweet, fruity loaf is ideal served for tea or as a healthy snack. The fruit spread can be made quickly while the cake is in the oven.

NUTRITIONAL INFORMATION

Calories . . . . . . .733 Sugars 110g
Protein . . . . .12g Fat 5g
Carbohydrate . . .171g Saturates 1g

1¼ HOURS   2 HOURS

SERVES 4

I N G R E D I E N T S

6 oz oatmeal

3½ oz light muscovado sugar

1 tsp ground cinnamon

4½ oz golden raisins

6 oz seedless raisins

2 tbsp malt extract

1¼ cups unsweetened apple juice

6 oz self-rising whole-wheat flour

1½ tsp baking powder

strawberries and apple wedges, to serve

FRUIT SPREAD

8 oz strawberries, washed and hulled

2 eating apples, cored, chopped and mixed with 1 tbsp lemon juice to prevent browning

1¼ cups unsweetened apple juice

1 Preheat the oven to 350°F. Grease and line a 2 lb loaf pan.

2 Place the oatmeal, sugar, cinnamon, golden raisins, raisins, and malt extract in a mixing bowl. Pour in the apple juice, stir well and leave to soak for 30 minutes.

3 Sift in the flour and baking powder, adding any husks that remain in the sifter, and fold in using a metal spoon.

4 Spoon the mixture into the prepared pan and bake for 1½ hours until firm or until a skewer inserted into the center comes out clean.

5 Leave to cool for 10 minutes, then turn on to a rack and leave to cool.

6 Meanwhile, make the fruit spread. Place the strawberries and apples in a saucepan and pour in the apple juice. Bring to a boil, cover and simmer for 30 minutes. Beat the sauce well and spoon into a clean, warmed jar. Leave to cool, then seal and label.

7 Serve the loaf with 1–2 tablespoons of the fruit spread and an assortment of strawberries and apple wedges.

New Age Spotted Dick

This is a deliciously moist low-fat pudding. The sauce is in the center of the pudding, and will spill out when the pudding is cut.

NUTRITIONAL INFORMATION

Calories .... .529	Sugars .... .41g	
Protein 9g	Fat .... .31g	
Carbohydrate ... 58g	Saturates 4g	

🧺 25 MINS   🕐 1¹/₄ HOURS

SERVES 6–8

I N G R E D I E N T S

¾ cup raisins

generous ½ cup corn oil,
  plus a little for brushing

generous ½ cup superfine sugar

¼ cup ground almonds

2 eggs, lightly beaten

1½ cups self-rising flour

S A U C E

½ cup walnuts, chopped

½ cup ground almonds

1¼ cups semi-skimmed milk

4 tbsp granulated sugar

1 Put the raisins in a saucepan with ¹/₂ cup water. Bring to a boil, then remove from the heat. Leave to steep for 10 minutes, then drain.

2 Whisk together the oil, sugar, and ground almonds until thick and syrupy; this will need about 8 minutes of beating (on medium speed if using an electric whisk).

3 Add the eggs, one at a time, beating well after each addition. Combine the flour and raisins. Stir into the mixture. Brush a 4 cup pudding bowl with oil, or line with baking parchment.

4 Put all the sauce ingredients into a saucepan. Bring to a boil, stir and simmer for 10 minutes.

5 Transfer the sponge mixture to the greased bowl and pour on the hot sauce. Place on a baking sheet.

6 Bake in a preheated oven at 340°F for about 1 hour. Lay a piece of baking parchment across the top if it starts to brown too fast.

7 Leave to cool for 2–3 minutes in the bowl before turning out on to a serving plate.

COOK'S TIP

Always soak raisins before baking them, as they retain their moisture nicely and you taste the flavor of them instead of biting on a dried-out raisin.

Rich Fruit Cake

Serve this moist, fruit-laden cake for a special occasion. It would also make an excellent Christmas cake.

NUTRITIONAL INFORMATION

Calories	772	Sugars	.......137g
Protein	........14g	Fat	..........5g
Carbohydrate	..179g	Saturates	......1g

35 MINS   1³/₄ HOURS

SERVES 4

INGREDIENTS

6 oz unsweetened pitted dates

4½ oz no-need-to-soak dried prunes

¾ cup unsweetened orange juice

2 tbsp molasses

1 tsp finely grated lemon rind

1 tsp finely grated orange rind

8 oz self-rising whole-wheat flour

1 tsp mixed spice

4½ oz seedless raisins

4½ oz golden raisins

4½ oz currants

4½ oz dried cranberries

3 large eggs, separated

TO DECORATE

1 tbsp apricot jam, softened

6 oz sugarpaste

strips of orange rind

strips of lemon rind

1 Preheat the oven to 325°F. Grease and line a deep 8 inch round cake pan. Chop the dates and prunes and place in a pan. Pour over the orange juice and simmer for 10 minutes. Remove the pan from the heat and beat the fruit mixture until puréed. Add the molasses and rinds. Cool.

2 Sift the flour and spice into a bowl, adding any husks that remain in the sieve. Add the dried fruits. When the date and prune mixture is cool, whisk in the egg yolks. In a clean bowl, whisk the egg whites until stiff. Spoon the fruit mixture into the dry ingredients and mix together.

3 Gently fold in the egg whites using a metal spoon. Transfer to the prepared tin and bake for 1½ hours. Leave to cool.

4 Remove the cake from the pan and brush the top with jam. Dust the work counter with confectioners' sugar and roll out the sugarpaste thinly. Lay the sugarpaste over the top of the cake and trim the edges. Decorate with orange and lemon rind.

Chocolate & Pineapple Cake

Decorated with thick yogurt and canned pineapple, this is a low-fat cake, but it is by no means lacking in flavor.

10 MINS   25 MINS

SERVES 9

INGREDIENTS

⅔ cup low-fat spread

4½ oz superfine sugar

¾ cup self-rising flour, sifted

3 tbsp cocoa powder, sifted

1½ tsp baking powder

2 eggs

8 oz can pineapple pieces in unsweetened juice

½ cup low-fat thick unsweetened yogurt

about 1 tbsp confectioners' sugar

grated chocolate, to decorate

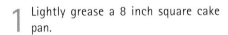

1 Lightly grease a 8 inch square cake pan.

2 Place the low-fat spread, superfine sugar, flour, cocoa powder, baking powder, and eggs in a large mixing bowl. Beat with a wooden spoon or electric hand whisk until smooth.

3 Pour the cake mixture into the prepared pan and level the surface. Bake in a preheated oven, 325°F, for 20-25 minutes or until springy to the touch. Leave to cool slightly in the pan before transferring to a wire rack to cool completely.

4 Drain the pineapple, chop the pineapple pieces, and drain again. Reserve a little pineapple for decoration, stir the rest into the yogurt and sweeten with confectioners' sugar.

5 Spread the pineapple and yogurt mixture over the cake and decorate with the reserved pineapple pieces. Sprinkle with the grated chocolate.

Carrot & Ginger Cake

This melt-in-the-mouth version of a favorite cake has a fraction of the fat of the traditional cake.

NUTRITIONAL INFORMATION

Calories	249	Sugars	........28g
Protein	.........7g	Fat	...........6g
Carbohydrate	...46g	Saturates	......1g

15 MINS   1¹/₄ HOURS

SERVES 10

INGREDIENTS

8 oz all-purpose flour

1 tsp baking powder

1 tsp bicarbonate of soda

2 tsp ground ginger

½ tsp salt

6 oz light muscovado sugar

8 oz carrots, grated

2 pieces stem ginger in syrup, drained and chopped

1 oz gingerroot, grated

2 oz seedless raisins

2 medium eggs, beaten

3 tbsp corn oil

juice of 1 medium orange

FROSTING

8 oz low-fat soft cheese

4 tbsp confectioners' sugar

1 tsp vanilla extract

TO DECORATE

grated carrot

fresh ginger

ground ginger

1 Preheat the oven to 350°F. Grease and line a 8 inch round cake pan with baking parchment.

2 Sift the flour, baking powder, bicarbonate of soda, ground ginger, and salt into a bowl. Stir in the sugar, carrots, gingerroot, fresh ginger, and raisins. Beat together the eggs, oil, and orange juice, then pour into the bowl. Mix the ingredients together well.

3 Spoon the mixture into the pan and bake in the oven for 1–1¹/₄ hours until firm to the touch, or until a skewer inserted into the center of the cake comes out clean.

4 To make the frosting, place the soft cheese in a bowl and beat to soften. Sift in the confectioners' sugar and add the vanilla extract. Mix well.

5 Remove the cake from the pan and smooth the frosting over the top. Decorate the cake and serve.

Banana & Lime Cake

A substantial cake that is ideal served for tea. The mashed bananas help to keep the cake moist, and the lime icing gives it extra zing and zest.

NUTRITIONAL INFORMATION

Calories 235	Sugars 31g
Protein 5g	Fat 1g
Carbohydrate . . .55g	Saturates 0.3g

35 MINS   45 MINS

SERVES 10

INGREDIENTS

10½ oz all-purpose flour

1 tsp salt

1½ tsp baking powder

6 oz light muscovado sugar

1 tsp lime rind, grated

1 medium egg, beaten

1 medium banana, mashed with 1 tbsp lime juice

⅔ cup low-fat unsweetened fromage blanc

4 oz golden raisins

banana chips, to decorate

lime rind, finely grated, to decorate

TOPPING

4 oz confectioners' sugar

1–2 tsp lime juice

½ tsp lime rind, finely grated

1 Preheat the oven to 350° Grease and line a deep 7 inch round cake with baking parchment.

2 Sift the flour, salt, and baking powder into a mixing bowl and stir in the sugar and lime rind.

3 Make a well in the center of the dry ingredients and add the egg, banana, fromage blanc and golden raisins. Mix well until thoroughly incorporated.

4 Spoon the mixture into the pan and smooth the surface. Bake for 40–45 minutes until firm to the touch or until a skewer inserted in the center comes out clean. Leave to cool for 10 minutes, then turn out on to a wire rack.

5 To make the topping, sift the confectioners' sugar into a small bowl and mix with the lime juice to form a soft, but not too runny, frosting. Stir in the grated lime rind. Drizzle the frosting over the cake, letpang it run down the sides.

6 Decorate the cake with banana chips and lime rind. Let the cake stand for 15 minutes so that the frosting sets.

VARIATION

For a delicious alternative, replace the lime rind and juice with orange and the golden raisins with chopped apricots.

Strawberry Roulade

Serve this moist, light sponge rolled up with an almond and strawberry fromage blanc filling for a delicious tea-time treat.

NUTRITIONAL INFORMATION

Calories 166	Sugars 19g
Protein 6g	Fat 3g
Carbohydrate ...30g	Saturates 1g

30 MINS   10 MINS

SERVES 8

INGREDIENTS

3 large eggs

4½ oz superfine sugar

4½ oz all-purpose flour

1 tbsp hot water

FILLING

¾ cup low-fat unsweetened fromage blanc

1 tsp almond extract

8 oz small strawberries

½ oz toasted almonds,
    slivered

1 tsp confectioners' sugar

1 Preheat the oven to 425°F . Line a 14 x 10 inch Jelly pan with baking parchment. Place the eggs in a mixing bowl with the superfine sugar. Place the bowl over a pan of hot water and whisk until pale and thick.

2 Remove the bowl from the pan. Sift in the flour and fold into the eggs with the hot water. Pour the mixture into the pan and bake for 8–10 minutes, until golden and set.

3 Transfer the mixture to a sheet of baking parchment. Peel off the lining

paper and roll up the sponge tightly along with the baking parchment. Wrap in a dish towel and let cool.

4 Mix together the fromage blanc and the almond extract. Reserving a few strawberries for decoration, wash, hull, and slice the rest. Leave the mixture to chill in the refrigerator until required.

5 Unroll the sponge, spread the fromage blanc mixture over the sponge and sprinkle with strawberries. Roll the sponge up again and transfer to a serving plate. Sprinkle with almonds and lightly dust with confectioners' sugar. Decorate with the reserved strawberries.

Fruity Potato Cake

Sweet potatoes mix beautifully with fruit and brown sugar in this unusual cake. Add a few drops of rum or brandy to the recipe if you like.

NUTRITIONAL INFORMATION

Calories 275	Sugars 44g
Protein 6g	Fat 5g
Carbohydrate ...55g	Saturates 2g

15 MINS   1½ HOURS

SERVES 6

INGREDIENTS

1½ lb sweet potatoes, diced

1 tbsp butter, melted

4½ oz demerara sugar

3 eggs

3 tbsp skimmed milk

1 tbsp lemon juice

grated rind of 1 lemon

1 tsp caraway seeds

4½ oz dried fruits, such as apple, pear or mango, chopped

2 tsp baking powder

1 Lightly grease an 7 inch square cake pan.

2 Cook the sweet potatoes in boiling water for 10 minutes or until soft. Drain and mash until smooth.

3 Transfer the mashed sweet potatoes to a mixing bowl whilst still hot and add the butter and sugar, mixing to dissolve.

4 Beat in the eggs, lemon juice and rind, caraway seeds, and chopped dried fruit. Add the baking powder and mix well.

5 Pour the mixture into the prepared cake pan.

6 Cook in a preheated oven, 325°F, for 1-1¼ hours or until cooked through.

7 Remove the cake from the pan and transfer to a wire rack to cool. Cut into thick slices to serve.

COOK'S TIP

This cake is ideal as a special occasion dessert. It can be made in advance and frozen until required. Wrap the cake in plastic wrap and freeze. Thaw at room temperature for 24 hours and warm through in a moderate oven before serving.

Fruity Muffins

Perfect for those on a low-fat diet, these little cakes contain no butter, just a little corn oil.

NUTRITIONAL INFORMATION

Calories	162	Sugars	. . . . .11g
Protein	. . . . .4g	Fat	. . . . .4g
Carbohydrate	. . .28g	Saturates	. . . . . .1g

 10 MINS 30 MINS

MAKES 10

I N G R E D I E N T S

8 oz self-raising whole-wheat flour

2 tsp baking powder

1 oz light muscovado sugar

3½ oz no-need-to-soak dried apricots, chopped finely

1 medium banana, mashed with 1 tbsp orange juice

1 tsp orange rind, grated finely

1¼ cups skimmed milk

1 medium egg, beaten

3 tbsp corn oil

2 tbsp oatmeal

fruit spread, honey, or maple syrup, to serve

1 Preheat the oven to 400°F . Place 10 paper muffin cases in a deep patty pan. Sift the flour and baking powder into a mixing bowl, adding any husks that remain in the sifter. Stir in the sugar and chopped apricots.

2 Make a well in the center of the dry ingredients and add the banana, orange rind, milk, beaten egg, and oil. Mix together well to form a thick batter. Divide the batter evenly among the 10 paper cases.

3 Sprinkle with a few oatmeal and bake for 25–30 minutes until well risen and firm to the touch, or until a skewer inserted into the center comes out clean. Transfer the muffins to a wire rack to cool slightly. Serve the muffins warm with a little fruit spread, honey, or maple syrup.

VARIATION

If you like dried figs, they make a deliciously crunchy alternative to the apricots; they also go very well with the flavor of orange. Other no-need-to-soak dried fruits, chopped up finely, can be used as well.

Paper-Thin Fruit Pies

The extra-crisp pastry cases, filled with slices of fruit and glazed with apricot jam, are best served hot with low-fat custard.

NUTRITIONAL INFORMATION

Calories	158	Sugars	........12g
Protein	.........2g	Fat	..........10g
Carbohydrate	...14g	Saturates	......2g

20 MINS   15 MINS

SERVES 4

INGREDIENTS

1 medium eating apple

1 medium ripe pear

2 tbsp lemon juice

2 oz low-fat spread

4 rectangular sheets of phyllo pastry, thawed if frozen

2 tbsp low-sugar apricot jam

1 tbsp unsweetened orange juice

1 tbsp finely chopped unsweetened pistachio nuts, shelled

2 tsp confectioners' sugar, for dusting

low-fat custard, to serve

1 Preheat the oven to 400°F. Core and thinly slice the apple and pear and toss them in the lemon juice.

2 Over a low heat, gently melt the low-fat spread.

3 Cut the sheets of pastry into 4 and cover with a clean, damp dish cloth. Brush 4 non-stick large muffin pans, measuring 4 inch across, with a little of the low-fat spread.

4 Working on each pie separately, brush 4 sheets of pastry with low-fat spread. Press a small sheet of pastry into the base of one pan. Arrange the other sheets of pastry on top at slightly different angles. Repeat with the other sheets of pastry to make another 3 pies.

5 Arrange the apple and pear slices alternately in the center of each pastry case and lightly crimp the edges of the pastry of each pie.

6 Mix the jam and orange juice together until smooth and brush over the fruit. Bake for 12–15 minutes. Sprinkle with the pistachio nuts, dust lightly with confectioners' sugar and serve hot with low-fat custard.

VARIATION

Other combinations of fruit are equally delicious. Try peach and apricot, raspberry and apple, or pineapple and mango.

Baked Pears with Cinnamon

This simple recipe is easy to prepare and cook but is deliciously warming. For a treat, serve hot on a pool of low-fat custard.

NUTRITIONAL INFORMATION

Calories 207   Sugars 35g
Protein . . . . .3g   Fat 6g
Carbohydrate . . .37g   Saturates 2g

10 MINS   25 MINS

SERVES 4

INGREDIENTS

4 ripe pears

2 tbsp lemon juice

4 tbsp light muscovado sugar

1 tsp ground cinnamon

2 oz low-fat spread

low-fat custard, to serve

lemon rind, finely grated, to decorate

1 Preheat the oven to 400°F. Core and peel the pears, then slice them in half lengthwise and brush all over with the lemon juice. Place the pears, cored side down, in a small non-stick roasting pan.

2 Place the sugar, cinnamon and low-fat spread in a small saucepan and heat gently, stirring, until the sugar has melted. Keep the heat low to stop too much water evaporating from the low-fat spread as it gets hot. Spoon the mixture over the pears.

3 Bake for 20–25 minutes or until the pears are tender and golden, occasionally spooning the sugar mixture over the fruit during the cooking time.

4 To serve, heat the custard until it is piping hot and spoon over the bases of 4 warm dessert plates. Arrange 2 pear halves on each plate.

5 Decorate with grated lemon rind and serve.

VARIATION

For alternative flavors, replace the cinnamon with ground ginger and serve the pears sprinkled with chopped stem ginger in syrup. Alternatively, use ground allspice and spoon over some warmed dark rum to serve.

Apricot & Orange Jellies

These bright fruity little desserts are easy to make and taste so much better than store-bought jellies. Serve them with low-fat ice cream.

NUTRITIONAL INFORMATION

Calories 206	Sugars 36g	
Protein 8g	Fat 5g	
Carbohydrate . . .36g	Saturates 3g	

4¹/₄ HOURS   25 MINS

SERVES 4

INGREDIENTS

8 oz no-need-to-soak dried apricots

1¼ cups unsweetened orange juice

2 tbsp lemon juice

2–3 tsp clear honey

1 tbsp powdered gelatine

4 tbsp boiling water

TO DECORATE

orange segments

sprigs of mint

CINNAMON 'CREAM'

4½ oz medium-fat ricotta cheese

4½ oz low-fat unsweetened fromage blanc

1 tsp ground cinnamon

1 tbsp clear honey

1 Place the apricots in a saucepan and pour in the orange juice. Bring to a boil, cover and simmer for 15–20 minutes until plump and soft. Leave to cool for 10 minutes.

2 Transfer the mixture to a blender or food processor and blend until smooth. Stir in the lemon juice and add the honey. Pour the mixture into a measuring pitcher and make up to 2¹/₂ cups with cold water.

3 Dissolve the gelatine in the boiling water and stir into the apricot mixture.

4 Pour the mixture into 4 individual molds, each ²/₃ cup, or 1 large mold, 2¹/₂ cups. Leave to chill until set.

5 Meanwhile, make the cinnamon 'cream'. Mix all the ingredients together and place in a small bowl. Cover

the mixture and leave to chill until set.

6 To turn out the jellies, dip the molds in hot water for a few seconds and invert on to serving plates.

7 Decorate with the orange segments and sprigs of mint. Serve with the cinnamon 'cream' dusted with extra cinnamon.

Strawberry Meringues

The combination of aromatic strawberries and rose water with crisp caramelized sugar meringues makes this a truly irresistible dessert.

NUTRITIONAL INFORMATION

Calories	145	Sugars	........35g
Protein	.........3g	Fat	..........0.3g
Carbohydrate	...35g	Saturates	.....0.1g

1 HOUR   3¹/₂ HOURS

SERVES 6

INGREDIENTS

3 egg whites, size 2

pinch of salt

1 cup light muscovado sugar, crushed to be free of lumps

1½ cups strawberries, hulled

2 tsp rose water

⅔ cup low-fat unsweetened fromage blanc

extra strawberries to serve (optional)

TO DECORATE

rose-scented geranium leaves

rose petals

1 In a large grease-free bowl, whisk the egg whites and salt until very stiff and dry. Gradually whisk in the sugar a spoonful at a time, until the mixture is stiff again.

2 Line a baking sheet with baking parchment and drop 12 spoonfuls of the meringue mixture on to the sheet. Bake in a preheated oven at 250°F for 3–3½ hours, until completely dried out and crisp. Allow to cool thoroughly.

3 Reserve ½ cup of the strawberries. Place the remaining strawberries in a blender or food processor and blend for a few seconds until smooth.

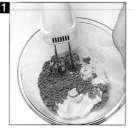

4 Alternatively, mash the strawberries with a fork and press through a strainer to form a purée paste. Stir in the rose water. Chill until required.

5 To serve, slice the reserved strawberries. Sandwich the meringues together with fromage blanc and sliced strawberries.

6 Spoon the strawberry rose purée paste on to 6 serving plates and top with a meringue.

7 Decorate with rose petals and rose-scented geranium leaves, and serve with extra strawberries (if using).

Pears with Maple Cream

These spicy cinammon pears are accompanied by a delicious melt-in-the-mouth maple and ricotta cream–you won't believe it's low in fat!

NUTRITIONAL INFORMATION

Calories	190	Sugars	.......28g
Protein	.........6g	Fat	..........7g
Carbohydrate	...28g	Saturates	......4g

10 MINS   25 MINS

SERVES 4

I N G R E D I E N T S

1 lemon

4 firm pears

1¼ cups hard cider or unsweetened apple juice

1 cinnamon stick, broken in half

mint leaves to decorate

M A P L E   R I C O T T A   C R E A M

½ cup low-fat ricotta cheese

½ cup low-fat unsweetened fromage blanc

½ tsp ground cinnamon

½ tsp grated lemon rind

1 tbsp maple syrup

lemon rind, to decorate

1 Using a vegetable peeler, remove the rind from the lemon and place in a non-stick skillet. Squeeze the lemon and pour into a shallow bowl.

2 Peel the pears, and halve and core them. Toss them in the lemon juice to prevent discoloration. Place in the skillet and pour over the remaining lemon juice.

3 Add the cider or apple juice and cinnamon stick halves. Gently bring to a boil, lower the heat so the liquid simmers and cook the pears for 10 minutes. Remove the pears using a draining spoon; reserve the cooking juice. Put the pears in a warm heatproof serving dish, cover with foil and put in a warming drawer or low oven to keep warm.

4 Return the pan to the heat, bring to a boil, then simmer for 8–10 minutes until reduced by half. Spoon over the pears.

5 To make the maple ricotta cream, mix together all the ingredients. Decorate the cream with lemon rind and the pears with mint leaves, and serve together.

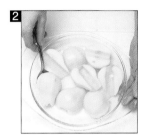

COOK'S TIP

Bartlett or Conference pears are suitable for this recipe. Pears ripen quickly and can bruise easily. It's best to buy them just before you plan to cook them.

Sticky Sesame Bananas

These tasty morsels are a real treat. Pieces of banana are dipped in caramel and then sprinkled with a few sesame seeds.

NUTRITIONAL INFORMATION

Calories 215   Sugars 38g
Protein . . . . .6g   Fat 3g
Carbohydrate . . .41g   Saturates 1g

10 MINS   20 MINS

SERVES 4

I N G R E D I E N T S

4 ripe medium bananas

3 tbsp lemon juice

4¹/₂ oz superfine sugar

4 tbsp cold water

2 tbsp sesame seeds

²/₃ cup low-fat unsweetened fromage blanc

1 tbsp confectioners' sugar

1 tsp vanilla extract

lemon and lime rind, shredded, to decorate

1 Peel the bananas and cut into 2 inch pieces. Place the banana pieces in a bowl, spoon over the lemon juice and stir well to coat–this will help prevent the bananas from discoloring.

2 Place the sugar and water in a small saucepan and heat gently, stirring, until the sugar dissolves. Bring to a boil and cook for 5–6 minutes until the mixture turns golden-brown.

3 Meanwhile, drain the bananas and blot with paper towels to dry. Line a baking sheet or board with baking parchment and arrange the bananas, well spaced out, on top.

4 When the caramel is ready, drizzle it over the bananas, working quickly because the caramel sets almost instantly. Sprinkle the sesame seeds over the bananas and cool for 10 minutes.

5 Mix the fromage blanc with the confectioner's sugar and vanilla extract.

6 Peel the bananas away from the paper and arrange on serving plates.

7 Serve the fromage blanc as a dip, decorated with the shredded lemon and lime rind.

Summer Fruit Salad

A mixture of soft summer fruits in an orange-flavored syrup with a dash of port. Serve with low-fat fromage blanc.

NUTRITIONAL INFORMATION

Calories . . . . .110 Sugars 26g
Protein . . . . .1g Fat 0.1g
Carbohydrate . . .26g Saturates 0g

 5 MINS   10 MINS

SERVES 6

INGREDIENTS

⅓ cup superfine sugar

⅓ cup water

grated rind and juice of 1 small orange

2 cups redcurrants, stripped from their stalks

2 tsp arrowroot

2 tbsp port

1 cup blackberries

1 cup blueberries

¾ cup strawberries

1½ cups raspberries

low-fat fromage blanc, to serve

1 Put the sugar, water, and grated orange rind into a pan and heat gently, stirring until the sugar has dissolved.

2 Add the redcurrants and orange juice, bring to a boil and simmer gently for 2–3 minutes.

3 Strain the fruit, reserving the syrup, and put into a bowl.

4 Blend the arrowroot with a little water. Return the syrup to the pan, add the arrowroot and bring to a boil, stirring until thickened.

5 Add the port and mix together well. Then pour over the redcurrants in the bowl.

6 Add the blackberries, blueberries, strawberries, and raspberries. Mix the fruit together and leave to cool until required. Serve in individual glass dishes with low-fat fromage blanc.

COOK'S TIP

Although this fruit salad is really best made with fresh fruits in season, you can achieve an acceptable result with frozen equivalents, with perhaps the exception of strawberries. You can buy frozen fruits of the forest, which would be ideal, in most supermarkets.

Chocolate Cheese Pots

These super-light desserts are just the thing if you have a craving for chocolate. Serve on their own or with a selection of fruits.

NUTRITIONAL INFORMATION

Calories 117   Sugars 17g
Protein . . . . .9g   Fat 1g
Carbohydrate . . .18g   Saturates 1g

 40 MINS   0 MINS

SERVES 4

INGREDIENTS

1¼ cups low-fat unsweetened fromage blanc

⅔ cup low-fat unsweetened yogurt

1 oz confectioners' sugar

4 tsp low-fat drinking chocolate powder

4 tsp cocoa powder

1 tsp vanilla extract

2 tbsp dark rum (optional)

2 medium egg whites

4 chocolate cake decorations

TO SERVE

pieces of kiwi fruit, orange, and banana

strawberries and raspberries

COOK'S TIP

This chocolate mixture would make an excellent filling for a cheesecake. Make the base out of crushed Amaretti di Saronno biscuits and egg white, and set the filling with 2 tsp powdered gelatine dissolved in 2 tbsp boiling water.

1 Mix the fromage blanc and low-fat yogurt in a bowl. Sift in the sugar, drinking chocolate and cocoa powder and mix well.

2 Add the vanilla extract and rum (if using).

3 In another bowl, whisk the egg whites until stiff. Using a metal spoon, fold the egg whites into the chocolate mixture.

4 Spoon the fromage blanc and chocolate mixture into 4 small china dessert pots and leave to chill for about 30 minutes.

5 Decorate each chocolate cheese pot with a chocolate cake decoration and serve with an assortment of fresh fruit, such as pieces of kiwi fruit, orange, and banana, and a few whole strawberries and raspberries.

Almond Trifles

Amaretti biscuits made with ground almonds, have a high fat content.
Use biscuits made from apricot kernels for a lower fat content.

NUTRITIONAL INFORMATION

Calories 241   Sugars 23g
Protein . . . . .9g   Fat 6g
Carbohydrate . . .35g   Saturates 2g

 1¼ HOURS   0 MINS

SERVES 4

INGREDIENTS

8 Amaretti di Saronno biscuits

4 tbsp brandy or Amaretti liqueur

8 oz raspberries

1¼ cups low-fat custard

1¼ cups low-fat unsweetened fromage
    blanc

1 tsp almond extract

½ oz slivered almonds,
    toasted

1 tsp cocoa powder

1 Place the biscuits in a mixing bowl
and using the end of a rolling pin,
carefully crush the biscuits into small
pieces.

2 Divide the crushed biscuits among 4
serving glasses. Sprinkle over the
brandy or liqueur and leave to stand for
about 30 minutes to allow the biscuits
to soften.

3 Top the layer of biscuits with a layer
of raspberries, reserving a few
raspberries for decoration, and spoon over
enough custard to just cover.

4 Mix the fromage blanc with the
almond extract and spoon over the
custard. Leave to chill in the refrigerator

for about 30 minutes.

5 Before serving, sprinkle with toasted
almonds and dust with cocoa powder.

6 Decorate the trifles with the reserved
raspberries and serve at once.

VARIATION

Try this trifle with assorted summer
fruits. If they are a frozen mix, use
them frozen and allow them to thaw
so that the juices soak into the biscuit
base—it will taste delicious.

Spun Sugar Pears

Whole pears are poached in a Madeira syrup in the microwave, then served with a delicate spun sugar surround.

NUTRITIONAL INFORMATION

Calories	166	Sugars	41g
Protein	0.3g	Fat	0g
Carbohydrate	41g	Saturates	0g

🍰 20 MINS 🕐 35 MINS

SERVES 4

INGREDIENTS

⅔ cup water

⅔ cup sweet Madeira wine

½ cup superfine sugar

2 tbsp lime juice

4 ripe pears, peeled, stalks left on

sprigs of fresh mint to decorate

SPUN SUGAR

½ cup superfine sugar

3 tbsp water

1 Mix the water, Madeira, sugar, and lime juice in a large bowl. Cover and cook on HIGH power for 3 minutes. Stir well until the sugar dissolves.

2 Peel the pears and cut a slice from the base of each one so they stand upright.

COOK'S TIP

Keep checking the caramel during the last few minutes of the cooking time, as it will change color quite quickly and conpanue to cook for several minutes after removing from the microwave oven.

3 Add the pears to the bowl, spooning the wine syrup over them. Cover and cook on HIGH power for about 10 minutes, turning the pears over every few minutes, until they are tender. The cooking time may vary slightly depending on the ripeness of the pears. Leave to cool, covered, in the syrup.

4 Remove the cooled pears from the syrup and set aside on serving plates. Cook the syrup, uncovered, on HIGH power for about 15 minutes until reduced by half and thickened slightly. Leave to stand for 5 minutes. Spoon over the pears.

5 To make the spun sugar, mix together the sugar and water in a bowl. Cook, uncovered, on HIGH power for 1½ minutes. Stir until the sugar has dissolved completely. Conpanue to cook on HIGH power for about 5–6 minutes more until the sugar has caramelized.

6 Wait for the caramel bubbles to subside and leave to stand for 2 minutes. Dip a teaspoon in the caramel and spin sugar around each pear in a circular motion. Serve immediately, decorated with sprigs of mint.

Tropical Fruit Fool

Fruit fools are always popular, and this light, tangy version will be no exception. Use your favorite fruits in this recipe if you prefer.

NUTRITIONAL INFORMATION

Calories 149   Sugars 25g
Protein ....6g   Fat 0.4g
Carbohydrate ...32g   Saturates 0.2g

35 MINS   0 MINS

SERVES 4

INGREDIENTS

1 medium ripe mango

2 kiwi fruit

1 medium banana

2 tbsp lime juice

½ tsp finely grated lime rind, plus extra to decorate

2 medium egg whites

15 oz can low-fat custard

½ tsp vanilla extract

2 passion fruit

1 To peel the mango, slice either side of the smooth, flat central stone. Roughly chop the flesh and blend the fruit in a food processor or blender until smooth. Alternatively, mash with a fork.

VARIATION

Other tropical fruits to try include papaya purée, with chopped pineapple and dates or pomegranate seeds to decorate. Or make a summer fruit fool by using strawberry purée, topped with raspberries and blackberries and cherries.

2 Peel the kiwi fruit, chop the flesh into small pieces and place in a bowl. Peel and chop the banana and add to the bowl. Toss all of the fruit in the lime juice and rind and mix well.

3 In a grease-free bowl, whisk the egg whites until stiff and then gently fold in the custard and vanilla extract until thoroughly mixed.

4 In 4 tall glasses, alternately layer the chopped fruit, mango purée, and custard mixture, finishing with the custard on top. Leave to chill in the refrigerator for 20 minutes.

5 Halve the passion fruits, scoop out the seeds, and spoon the passion fruit over the fruit fools. Decorate each serving with the extra lime rind and serve.

Cottage Cheese Hearts

These look very attractive when they are made in the French coeur à la crème china molds, but small ramekins could be used instead.

NUTRITIONAL INFORMATION

Calories 114	Sugars 19g
Protein 9g	Fat 1g
Carbohydrate . . .19g	Saturates 0.4g

1¹/₄ HOURS   0 MINS

SERVES 4

INGREDIENTS

5½ oz low-fat cottage cheese

⅔ cup low-fat unsweetened fromage blanc

1 medium egg white

2 tbsp superfine sugar

1–2 tsp vanilla extract

rose-scented geranium leaves, to decorate (optional)

SAUCE

8 oz strawberries

4 tbsp unsweetened orange juice

2–3 tsp confectioners' sugar

1 Line 4 heart-shaped molds with clean cheesecloth. Place a strainer over a mixing bowl and using the back of a metal spoon, press through the cottage cheese. Mix in the fromage blanc.

2 Whisk the egg white until stiff. Fold into the cheeses, with the superfine sugar and vanilla extract.

3 Spoon the cheese mixture into the molds and smooth over the tops. Place on a wire rack over a tray and leave to chill for 1 hour until firm and drained.

4 Meanwhile, make the sauce. Wash the strawberries under cold running water. Reserving a few strawberries for decoration, hull and chop the remainder.

5 Place the strawberries in a blender or food processor with the orange juice and process until smooth. Alternatively, push through a strainer to purée. Mix with the confectioners' sugar to taste. Cover and leave to chill in the refrigerator until required.

6 Remove the cheese hearts from the molds and transfer to serving plates.

7 Remove the cheesecloth, decorate with strawberries, and geranium leaves (if using) and serve with the sauce.

Orange Syllabub

A zesty, creamy whip made from yogurt and milk with a hint of orange, served with light and luscious sweet sponge cakes.

NUTRITIONAL INFORMATION

Calories 464   Sugars 74g
Protein ....22g   Fat 5g
Carbohydrate ...89g   Saturates 2g

1½ HOURS   10 MINS

SERVES 4

I N G R E D I E N T S

4 oranges

2½ cups low-fat unsweetened yogurt

6 tbsp low-fat skimmed milk powder

4 tbsp superfine sugar

1 tbsp grated orange rind

4 tbsp orange juice

2 egg whites

fresh orange zest to decorate

S P O N G E   H E A R T S

2 eggs, size 2

6 tbsp superfine sugar

6 tbsp flour

6 tbsp whole-wheat flour

1 tbsp hot water

1 tsp confectioners' sugar

1 Slice off the tops and bottoms of the oranges and the skin. Then cut out the segments, removing the zest and membranes between each one. Divide the orange segments between 4 dessert glasses, then chill.

2 In a mixing bowl, combine the yogurt, milk powder, sugar, orange rind, and juice. Cover and chill for 1 hour. Whisk the egg whites until stiff, then fold into the yogurt mixture. Pile on to the orange slices and chill for an hour. Decorate with fresh orange rind and sponge hearts.

3 To make the sponge hearts, line a 6 × 10 inch baking pan with baking parchment. Whisk the eggs and superfine sugar until thick and pale. Sieve, then fold in the flours using a large metal spoon, adding the hot water at the same time.

4 Pour into the pan and bake in a preheated oven at 425°F for 9–10 minutes until golden and firm to the touch.

5 Turn on to a sheet of baking parchment. Using a 2 inch heart-shaped cutter, stamp out hearts. Transfer to a wire rack to cool. Lightly dust with confectioners' sugar before serving with the syllabub.

Mixed Fruit Brûlées

Traditionally a rich mixture made with cream, this fruit-based version is just as tempting using unsweetened yogurt as a topping.

NUTRITIONAL INFORMATION

Calories 165	Sugars 21g	
Protein 5g	Fat 7g	
Carbohydrate ...21g	Saturates 5g	

 5 MINS   🕐 5 MINS

SERVES 4

I N G R E D I E N T S

1 lb prepared assorted summer
   fruits (such as strawberries, raspberries,
   blackcurrants, redcurrants, and
   cherries), thawed if frozen

¾ cup half-fat heavy cream alternative

¾ cup low-fat unsweetened fromage blanc

1 tsp vanilla extract

4 tbsp demerara sugar

1 Divide the prepared strawberries, raspberries, blackcurrants, redcurrants, and cherries evenly among 4 small heatproof ramekin dishes.

2 Mix together the half-fat cream alternative, fromage blanc and vanilla extract until well combined.

3 Generously spoon the mixture over the fruit in the ramekins, to cover the fruit completely.

4 Preheat the broiler to hot.

5 Top each serving with 1 tbsp demerara sugar and broil the desserts for 2–3 minutes, until the sugar melts and begins to caramelize. Leave to stand for a couple of minutes before serving.

COOK'S TIP

Look out for half-fat creams, in light and heavy varieties. They are good substitutes for occasional use. Alternatively, in this recipe, omit the cream and double the quantity of fromage blanc for a lower fat version.

Pavlova

This fruit meringue dish was created for Anna Pavlova, and it looks very impressive. Use fruits of your choice to make a colorful display.

NUTRITIONAL INFORMATION

Calories 321   Sugars 37g
Protein . . . . .3g   Fat 18g
Carbohydrate . . .37g   Saturates 11g

1¹/₂ HOURS   1¹/₂ HOURS

SERVES 8

I N G R E D I E N T S

6 egg whites

½ tsp cream of tartar

1 cup superfine sugar

1 tsp vanilla extract

1¼ cups whipping cream

2½ cups strawberries, hulled and halved

3 tbsp orange-flavored liqueur

fruit of your choice, to decorate

1 Line a baking sheet with baking parchment and mark out a circle to fit your serving plate. The recipe makes enough meringue for a 12 inch circle.

2 Whisk the egg whites and cream of tartar together until stiff. Gradually beat in the superfine sugar and vanilla extract. Whisk well until glossy and stiff.

3 Either spoon or pipe the meringue mixture into the marked circle, in an even layer, slightly raised at the edges, to form a dip in the center.

4 Baking the meringue depends on your preference. If you like a soft chewy meringue, bake at 275°F for about 1¹/₂ hours until dry but slightly soft in the center. If you prefer a drier meringue, bake in the oven at 225°F for 3 hours until dry.

5 Before serving, whip the cream to a piping consistency, and either spoon or pipe on to the meringue base, leaving a border of meringue all around the edge.

6 Stir the strawberries and liqueur together and spoon on to the cream. Decorate with fruit of your choice.

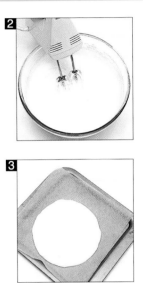

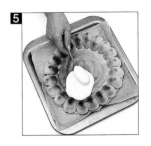

COOK'S TIP

If you like a dry meringue, you can leave it in the oven on the lowest setpang overnight. However, do not use this technique with a gas oven – but in an electric oven or solid fuel cooker it would be fine.

Almond Cheesecakes

These creamy cheese desserts are so delicious that it's hard to believe that they are low in fat.

NUTRITIONAL INFORMATION

Calories . . . . .361 Sugars 29g
Protein . . . . .16g Fat 15g
Carbohydrate . . .43g Saturates 4g

1¼ HOURS   10 MINS

SERVES 4

I N G R E D I E N T S

12 Amaretti di Saronno biscuits

1 medium egg white, lightly beaten

8 oz skimmed-milk soft cheese

½ tsp almond extract

½ tsp finely grated lime rind

1 oz ground almonds

1 oz superfine sugar

2 oz raisins

2 tsp powdered gelatine

2 tbsp boiling water

2 tbsp lime juice

TO DECORATE

1 oz slivered toasted almonds

strips of lime rind

1 Preheat the oven to 350° Place the biscuits in a clean plastic bag, seal the bag and using a rolling pin, crush them into small pieces.

2 Place the crumbs in a bowl and bind together with the egg white.

3 Arrange 4 non-stick pastry rings or poached egg rings, 3½ inches across,

on a baking sheet lined with baking parchment. Divide the biscuit mixture into 4 equal portions and spoon it into the rings, pressing down well. Bake for 10 minutes until crisp and leave to cool in the rings.

4 Beat together the soft cheese, almond extract, lime rind, ground almonds, sugar and golden raisins until well mixed.

5 Dissolve the gelapane in the boiling water and stir in the lime juice. Fold into the cheese mixture and spoon over the biscuit bases. Smooth over the tops and chill for 1 hour or until set.

6 Loosen the cheesecakes from the pans using a small spatula and transfer to serving plates. Decorate with slivered toasted almonds and strips of lime rind, and serve.

Mocha Swirl Mousse

A combination of feather-light yet rich chocolate and coffee mousses, whipped and attractively served in serving glasses.

NUTRITIONAL INFORMATION

Calories	 130	Sugars	.... 10g
Protein	.... 5g	Fat	.... 8g
Carbohydrate	.... 11g	Saturates	...... 5g

🖐 🖐

🍰 1¹/₄ HOURS   ⏰ 0 MINS

SERVES 4

INGREDIENTS

1 tbsp coffee and chicory extract

2 tsp cocoa powder, plus extra for dusting

1 tsp low-fat drinking chocolate powder

²/₃ cup low-fat crème fraîche, plus 4 tsp to serve

2 tsp powdered gelatine

2 tbsp boiling water

2 large egg whites

2 tbsp superfine sugar

4 chocolate coffee beans, to serve

 1 Place the coffee and chicory extract in one bowl, and 2 tsp cocoa powder and the drinking chocolate in another bowl. Divide the crème fraîche between the 2 bowls and mix both well.

2 Dissolve the gelapane in the boiling water and set aside. In a grease-free bowl, whisk the egg whites and sugar until stiff and divide this evenly between the two mixtures.

3 Divide the dissolved gelapane between the 2 mixtures and, using a large metal spoon, gently fold until well mixed.

4 Spoon small amounts of the 2 mousses alternately into 4 serving glasses and swirl together gently. Chill for 1 hour or until set.

5 To serve, top each mousse with a teaspoonful of crème fraîche, a

COOK'S TIP

Vegetarians should not be denied this delicious chocolate dessert. Instead of gelapane use the vegetarian equivalent, gelozone, available from health-food shops. However, be sure to read the directions on the packet first as it is prepared differently from gelapane.

Index

A

Almond Cheesecakes 252
Almond Trifles 245
Angler Fish with Coconut 164
Apricot and Orange Jellies 239
Autumn Fruit Bread Pudding 224

B

Bacon, Bean, and Garlic Soup 42
Baked Pears with Cinnamon 238
Baked Sea Bass 177
Baked Stuffed Onions 66
Balti Dhal 199
Balti Scallops 167
Banana and Lime Cake 233
Basil and Tomato Pasta 205
Beef and Orange Curry 89
Beef and Vegetable Soup 38
Beef Daube 96
Beef Goulash 92
Beef Teriyaki 97
Beet and Orange Salad 208
Beet and Potato Soup 25
Biryani with Onions 198
Boiled Beef and Carrots 93
Bruschetta 60
Butterfly Shrimp 163

C

Caribbean Shrimp165
Carrot and Cumin Soup 34
Carrot and Ginger Cake 232
Charred Tuna Steaks 172
Cheese and Chive Scones 62
Cheese, Herb, and Onion Rolls 61
Cheesy Ham Savory 85
Chicken and Almond Rissoles 81
Chicken and Cheese Jackets 79
Chicken and Coconut Soup 45
Chicken and Ginger Stir-Fry 140
Chicken and Leek Soup 44
Chicken in Spicy Yogurt 127
Chicken Tikka 130
Chicken Tikka Kabobs 131
Chicken with a Yogurt Crust 126
Chicken with Two Sauces 146
Chicken with Whisky Sauce 147
Chilled Cucumber Soup 24
Chilli con Carne 88
Chinese Vegetable Pancakes 196

Chocolate and Pineapple Cake 231
Chocolate Cheese Pots 244
Chunky Potato and Beef Soup 39
Citrus Duckling Skewers 156
Coconut and Crab Soup 47
Coleslaw 215
Consommé 37
Cool Cucumber Salad 213
Cottage Cheese Hearts 248
Crab-Stuffed Red Snapper 182
Cranberry Turkey Burgers 75
Crêpes with Curried Crab 70
Crispy Stuffed Chicken 137
Crispy-Topped Fruit Bake 226
Cucumber and Tomato Soup 23

D

Delicately Spiced Trout 176

E

Eggplant Cake 201

F

Festive Apple Chicken 154
Filipino Chicken 141
Fish and Crab Chowder 32

Fish-Flavored Pork 100
Fragrant Asparagus Risotto 192
Fruit and Nut Loaf 227
Fruit Loaf with Apple Spread 228
Fruity Muffins 236
Fruity Pork Skewers 104
Fruity Potato Cake 235

G

Ginger Beef with Chili 98
Ginger Chicken and Corn 135
Grapefruit and Coconut Salad 210
Green Bean and Carrot Salad 216
Green Fish Curry 187
Grilled Chicken 153

H

Harlequin Chicken 144
Herrings with Tarragon 180
Hot and Spicy Rice Salad 211

I

Indian Potato and Pea Soup 36
Indonesian-Style Spicy Cod 178
Italian Platter 84

J

Japanese Plaice 179
Jerk Chicken 150

K

Karahi Chicken 129
Kibbeh 116

L

Lamb and Barley Broth 43
Lamb and Potato Moussaka 119
Lamb and Tomato Koftas 83
Lamb Couscous 121
Lamb Dopiaza 122
Lamb Hotch Potch 112
Lamb Kabobs with Herbs 118
Lamb with Rosemary 110
Lemony Angler Fish Skewers 166
Lemony Spaghetti 204
Lentil and Ham Soup 41
Lentil Pâté 55
Lime Fricassée of Chicken 151

M

Mackerel with Lime 175
Masala Kabobs 120
Mediterranean Chicken 145
Mediterranean Fish Soup 46
Melon and Mango Salad 212
Mexican Chicken 152
Mexican Potato Salad 209
Mexican-Style Pizzas 193
Minted Fennel Salad 218
Minted Onion Bhajis 52
Minted Pea and Yogurt Soup 28
Minty Lamb Burgers 82
Minty Lamb Kabobs 117
Mixed Bean Soup 20
Mixed Bean Stir-Fry 203
Mixed Fruit Brûlées 250
Mocha Swirl Mousse 253

Moroccan Couscous Salad 214
Mushroom and Ginger Soup 33
Mushroom Cannelloni 207

N

New Age Spotted Dick 229

O

Oat-Crusted Chicken Pieces 78
Orange Syllabub 249
Oriental Shellfish Kabobs 160
Oriental Vegetable Noodles 197

P

Pan-Cooked Pork Medallions 107
Pan-Seared Halibut 183
Paper-Thin Fruit Pies 237
Parsley, Chicken, and Ham Pâté 76
Partan Bree 48
Pasta Provençale 64
Pavlova 251
Pear and Roquefort Salad 219
Pears with Maple Cream 241
Pesto Pasta 206
Poached Salmon 173
Pork and Apple Skewers 105
Pork Chops and Spicy Beans 109
Pork Stroganoff 102
Pork with Fennel and Aniseed 99

Pork with Plums 106
Pork with Ratatouille Sauce 103
Potato and Bean Pâté 56
Potato and Mushroom Hash 58
Potato and Tomato Calzone 194
Potato Hash 195
Potato Skins with Guacomole 57
Pot-Roast Orange Chicken 143
Poussin with Dried Fruits 142
Provençale-Style Mussels 169

R
Red Lentil Soup with Yogurt 29
Red Mullet and Coconut Loaf 73
Red Pepper Soup 21
Red Roast Pork in Soy Sauce 101
Rice and Tuna Peppers 72
Rich Fruit Cake 230
Risotto Verde 191
Roast Duck with Apple 155
Rogan Josh 90

S
Salmon with Caper Sauce 174
Salmon Yakitori 162
Savory Hotpot 115
Savory Pepper Bread 63
Scallop Skewers 161
Seafood Pizza 186
Seafood Stir-Fry 168

Shepherd's Pie 94
Shrimp Bhuna 171
Smoked Fish and Potato Pâté 69
Smoked Haddock Soup 49
Smoky Fish Pie 185
Sole Paupiettes 184
Soufflé Omelet 68
Spiced Apricot Chicken 132
Spiced Fruit Soup 26
Spicy Chicken Tortillas 80
Spicy Chickpea Snack 65
Spicy Dhal and Carrot Soup 35
Spicy Jacket Potatoes 59
Spicy Lentil Soup 30
Spicy Mexican Beans 202
Spicy Tomato Chicken 128
Spinach and Orange Salad 217
Spinach Cheese Moulds 54
Split Pea and Ham Soup 40
Spun Sugar Pears 246
Steak in a Wine Marinade 95
Steamed Chicken Parcels 136
Steamed Stuffed Snapper 181
Sticky Chicken Wings 149
Sticky Sesame Bananas 242
Stir-Fried Lamb with Orange 114
Strawberry Meringues 240
Strawberry Roulade 234
Stuffed Mushrooms 67
Stuffed Tomatoes 190
Summer Fruit Clafoutis 223
Summer Fruit Salad 243

Summer Pudding 222
Sweet and Sour Chicken 139
Sweet and Sour Drumsticks 77
Sweet Lamb Fillets 113
Sweet Potato and Onion Soup 31

T
Tamarind Beef Balti 91
Tangy Pork Fillet 108
Teppanyaki 138
Thai Potato Crab Cakes 71
Thai Red Chicken 133
Thai-Style Chicken Skewers 134
Tomato and Pepper Soup 22
Tropical Fruit Fool 247
Turkey and Vegetable Loaf 74
Turkey with Redcurrant 157
Turkish Lamb Stew 111
Two-in-One Chicken 148

V
Vegetable Curry 200
Vegetables with Tahini Dip 53
Venison and Garlic Mash 123

W
Winter Puddings 225

Y
Yogurt and Spinach Soup 27
Yucatan Fish 170